WOMAN AT THE WINDOW

WOMAN AT THE WINDOW

BIBLICAL TALES OF OPPRESSION AND ESCAPE

NEHAMA ASCHKENASY

WAYNE STATE UNIVERSITY PRESS
DETROIT

02 01 00 99 98   5 4 3 2 1

LIBRARY OF CONGRESS CATALOGING-IN-PUBLICATION DATA

ASCHKENASY, NEHAMA.

   WOMAN AT THE WINDOW : BIBLICAL TALES OF OPPRESSION AND ESCAPE /

NEHAMA ASCHKENASY.

      P. CM.

   INCLUDES BIBLIOGRAPHICAL REFERENCES AND INDEX.

   ISBN 0-8143-2626-9 (ALK. PAPER).—ISBN 0-8143-2627-7 (PBK. :

ALK. PAPER)

   1. WOMEN IN THE BIBLE.   2. BIBLE. O.T.—CRITICISM, INTERPRETATION,

ETC.   3. BIBLE. O.T.—FEMINIST CRITICISM.   I. TITLE.

BS575.A78   1998

221.9'22'082—DC21   98-14988

GRATEFUL ACKNOWLEDGMENT IS MADE TO THE MARY DICKEY MASTERTON FUND FOR

FINANCIAL ASSISTANCE IN THE PUBLICATION OF THIS VOLUME.

FOR MY BELOVED DAUGHTERS

JENNIFER (HAGIT)

SHE OPENS HER MOUTH WITH WISDOM

AND ON HER TONGUE THE LAW OF KINDNESS

פיה פתחה בחכמה

ותורת חסד על לשונה

(PROV. 31:26)

AND

SHIRA

GIFTED OF MIND, BEAUTIFUL OF FORM

טובת שכל ויפת תאר

(1 SAM. 25:3)

CONTENTS

PREFACE

The past two decades or so have witnessed a proliferation of studies of the literary art of the Bible as well as of female protagonists in biblical tales. This embarrassment of riches is both a bonus and a worry to a writer: a new work can easily turn into a discourse with other recent readings, burying the beauty and clarity of the tale itself under scholarly debate. Further, any new study that treads familiar grounds is inevitably required to justify itself and point out the new perspectives it has to offer.

As a reader and student of the Hebraic literary genius, with a special interest in the peregrinations of female characters in this tradition, I have found myself on the two extreme ends of a spectrum that ranges from little scholarly interest in biblical females to the popularity of the subject we are currently witnessing. When my earlier study, *Eve's Journey: Feminine Images in Hebraic Literary Tradition,* came out in 1986 it was greeted as breaking new ground. A woman-centered, literary reading of biblical tales was somewhat of a novelty, and a study of the odyssey of biblical prototypes within the tradition, their persistence and reincarnations in later periods, had never been attempted before. The latter endeavor has not been duplicated so far, but since the appearance of *Eve's Journey* several outstanding works, applying women's perspectives to the reading of biblical texts, have been published; these range from radical feminist readings to women-centered studies that combine feminist sensibilities with respect for the sacred text. Nevertheless, I have chosen to return to the biblical text in search of paradigmatic feminine situations, this time with an eye not on their migration within the tradition, but on their internal meanings within the biblical context and parameters.

Eve's Journey was interested in the evolution of feminine images from their original appearances in early Judaic sources to contemporary works. It posited the historical mode and tested the evolving historical texts against ancient prototypes. It concluded that while cultural attitudes and historical realities changed, those early female images remained constant and fixed, underlying texts produced by many writers: religious and secular, early and modern, mystically inclined and politically oriented. It further illustrated that while male protagonists progressed in accordance with new historical realities and ideas as well as evolving literary genres, female characters only changed their disguises but not their literary roles or existential essence. When it came to literary conceptions of gender primary structures remained unaltered. Female protagonists maintained predictable and known positions, repeating old formulas that assigned them to represent immutable cosmic or psychic forces in the male universe. In *Eve's Journey* my interest in biblical women was tied to their historical journey and mutations in post-biblical texts. I studied them as starting points in the evolutionary process that I charted. Thus Dinah was shown to be not only a biblical protagonist but the trigger of a whole narrative corpus that extended to contemporary works.

In the present study I have returned to the original storehouse of images to find why they have persisted by closely scrutinizing some of the biblical tales with an undeniable (though often hidden) female angle. Focusing on the artistic aspects of these tales, I have tried to approach them without a preconceived agenda. At the same time, one of my objectives was to uncover the cultural standards (and very often, double standards) that drive the tale within its linguistic, ethical, and dramatic fabric. In terms of methodology, my intention has been to apply the techniques of literary criticism to a series of isolated tales. Feminist critics, in their rush either to condemn the text or redeem it from its male-bent environment, often neglect nuances of style and other narrative strategies that make the biblical tale a classic artistic endeavor. Narrative aspects of the biblical tale have often been sacrificed by feminist scholars who approach the text with a given ideology that by definition condemns every male-authored text as sexist and hostile to women. Furthermore, together with losing sight of a tale's literary properties, some scholars have neglected to consider the original Hebrew in which the text was written. I have found some recent conclusions arrived at by feminist scholars to be completely alien to the text, stemming from a reading that relies exclusively on one translation or another. Any discussion of the Hebrew Bible, even if it is written in another language and aims at non-Hebrew readers, must take into account the original language and base its findings on a reading loyal to its characteristics and peculiarities.

One of the main reasons that propelled me to return to the biblical tale at this time is the joy that I, and many of my students, derive whenever we read the biblical tale for its drama, suspense, and sensitivity to the predicament of the individual. Every Bible course creates its own dynamics of interpretation, offering new nuances and angles during class discussions, especially when the students come from a diversity of backgrounds and professions. I have watched lawyers among my students taking special delight in Potiphar's wife astutely creating an alibi for herself and proving to be knowledgeable in current rules of evidence. I listened to a police chief in my class propose a conspiracy theory to illuminate the Judges tale of the concubine in Gibea. The eternal text has not been exhausted yet and it still enfolds mysteries that make the reading and studying of it forever exciting and pleasurable.

Of contemporary scholars who inspired my own interpretive reading of the biblical text I wish to mention Robert Alter and Meir Sternberg for their rigorous literary analyses, as well as Phyllis Trible, who combines scrupulous Bible scholarship with literary sensitivity and feminist awareness. Judith A. Kates and Gail Twersky Reimer should be commended for their successful efforts in two recent collections which helped create a receptive and respectful environment for a woman-centered reading of biblical texts. I also wish to thank David H. Hirsch of Brown University, an astute reader of literary texts, for his constant encouragement and readiness to lend creative advice and support. Warm thanks to another Brown professor, my brother David Gottlieb, for serving as an initial sounding board for my ideas. I owe a special debt of gratitude to Arthur Evans, director of Wayne State University Press, under whose aegis *Eve's Journey* was first published and later given a new life in paperback, for encouraging me to develop *Woman at the Window* from a mere concept to a book-length study.

*A note on the Bible translations in this volume: I have used my own translation and also consulted the translations offered in the respective Anchor Bible editions as well as the King James version and the Revised Standard Version.

THE ANCIENT IMAGE

The Texts
2 Kings 9:30–34
Judges 5:28
Joshua 2:15
1 Samuel 19:12
Judges 4:18

This book owes its title to an image prevalent in the arts, architecture, and literary texts of ancient Near Eastern civilization. This image, of a woman looking through the window, appears in a number of biblical narratives as well. In the ancient works of art, the image is that of a female head encased in a window and peering through it to the outside. The most famous is the Phoenician ivory relief of "Woman at the Window" from the eighth century BCE, the property of the British Museum in London, in which the window frame is triply recessed on the top and sides.[1] Plaques displaying a woman looking through the window decorated couches and other furniture in ancient Near Eastern houses, and were also used as ornaments in windows. A relief from Ninveh portrays the Assyrian king Ashurbanipal reposing on a couch, the legs of which are embellished with reliefs of two women looking out of twin windows.[2] The woman at the window appears, too, in religious artifacts connected with the cult of Ashtart and her counterparts. A stone relief from the Hauran represents the Great Mother holding her breasts and looking out of the window.[3] Invariably, the woman looking out of the window is linked to the cult of fertility, or may sometimes stand for the goddess of fertility herself.

The window appears also in connection with male figures in Egyptian and Near Eastern art. The image of Pharaoh at the Window of Appearances represented the monarch as the dispenser of gifts and bounty to his people, while the image of Ashtart at the window displayed the goddess' fecundity and the gift of fertility that she bestowed on her followers.[4] Spatial openings were linked to female sexuality and fertility. House-shaped incense burners found in Beth-Shean which feature a number of openings as well as doves, also symbols of fertility, are believed to come from a temple of the goddess that probably existed in that city. Literary texts of the region paralleled the art. Mesopotamian texts, for example, refer to a "goddess of the window," a form of Ishtar.[5] In the Hellenic culture, too, the representation of Aphrodite showing herself through the window carried the meaning of the woman offering herself.

By all accounts, the fenestrated woman in ancient art is linked to the cult of fertility and the practice of temple prostitution. The woman at the window exhibits the essence of her femininity, her sexual availability and her fecundity. Freud's interpretation of gates, doors, windows, and other openings as possessing sexual symbolism, indicating the entrance to the womb, is reinforced by these art works, which are saturated with powerful sexual connotations. The image is linked to female deities who possessed omnipotent power and often used that power to taunt or punish men, adding a sense of awe to the image of the woman-at-the-window (or doorstep) in both the artifacts and the literary texts. The opening, like that of "Mother Earth," may sometimes be the gate not to pleasure but to death and damnation.[6]

Nevertheless, if the suggestion of fertility and sexuality, in both their pleasurable and frightening aspects, were central to the image in ancient times, they are only part of the impact that the image has on the modern reader or observer. When viewed from the distance of generations, through lenses that are not committed to the ancient cultural symbolism, another interpretation of the "woman at the window" arises. The pictorial image of the woman at the window gives the impression of a person hemmed in, even locked in. In the visual and plastic arts, the female viewed as sitting by the window and staring into the open space is at least doubly encased; first, by the framed picture or relief, and second, by the window itself. The famous Phoenician relief that shows three recessed encasements, with the woman's head appearing from the depth of the plaque, heightens the sense of incarceration and confinement. Furthermore, the female figure in many of these art works, invariably presented with her back to the indoor space and her eyes fixed on the outdoors, transmits a feeling of longing for the unknown, of wishing to escape from her confining surroundings. It is very possible that just as these images are steeped in the ancient cult of the fertility goddess, they also represent an everyday reality: women usually stayed indoors, leaving the public domain to the man. Yet they probably spent much time at the window, joining public life vicariously, as spectators rather than active participants. The female figure in the ancient graphic and plastic representations seems fixed at the window, immobile, firmly secured by the window casing as well as by the frame of the art piece. Thus, the suggestion is of closed horizons which may be searched by the gazing eyes, but not explored freely by the mobile person.

Later art is more explicit in utilizing the window as an image of wished-for freedom, highlighting the confining nature of the indoors. In the works of Baroque painter Johannes Vermeer the dark room and its walled-in dwellers are usually in the foreground of the painting, often with their back or side to the window. The window, however, draws attention to the stifling enclosure of the interior space, offering the only means of escape.[7] It has been noticed that in modern art "the window expresses longings for worlds other than those confining, unhappy places of the present."[8]

The biblical tales that narrate a woman looking through the window, or standing at her doorway, are not many, but their pagan connection is undeniable. Jezebel, the daughter of the Phoenician king, Etbaal, marries King Ahab of Israel and induces him to build altars and sanctuaries to both Baal and Ashtart (1 Kings 16:31, 32). At the end of her life, widowed and having learned that her son, the king, was assassinated, she welcomes the usurper by appearing at the window, eyes painted and hair stylishly coiffed (2 Kings 9:30). It is hard to imagine that Jezebel means to flaunt her sexuality at this moment in her life. Rather, as the priestess of Ashtart, daughter of a king who was probably priest of Baal or even deemed half-god (Etbaal), Jezebel means to die in all her glory. By appearing at the window she recaptures for the last time her godlike splendor; and by painting herself she redefines her feminine and sexual powers. These powers, in connection with Jezebel and many other sexually powerful females in biblical narratives, are ultimately viewed as evil. As a woman who engaged in brutal killings of innocent civilians as well as God's prophets, Jezebel is the epitome of evil in the Bible. The image, however, underlines Jezebel's personal predicament as well. She is portrayed time and again as a woman who oversteps her feminine boundaries and takes political matters in her hands. Her exasperation with the weak Ahab, who is not "manly" or regal enough in her eyes, is dramatically presented in the tale of Nabot's vineyard (1 Kings 21). In this scene, Jezebel is the biblical precursor of Lady Macbeth. She is even more evil than her later incarnation since she carries out the murderous conspiracy herself, without her husband, and never expresses any regrets or pricks of conscience.

When Jezebel appears at the window for the last time, defeated but spiteful, she exudes not only the powers of her femininity but also her ultimate vulnerability, her inability to truly participate in political and history-making events. Jezebel's debacle is not only that of evil, but that of the female who chose to forget that the position "at the window" meant her removal from the male world of politics and history.

The image of Jezebel appearing at the window at the end of her life thus combines many of the elements of her existence. By reasserting her status as the goddess of fertility and birth in the very last moments of her life she reminds the biblical reader of her pagan origins, of her cultural and religious foreignness. The scene reinforces her inhuman depravity and her almost magic powers, as well as her defiance of death. Yet, strangely, Jezebel at the window becomes a paradigm of the female existence in general by suggesting man's fear of the woman's sexual powers, the association of these powers with evil, and the inevitable defeat of a woman who tries to step out of her fixed place "at the window" and participate in the male sphere.

Another woman who "looks through the lattice" is the mother of Sisera, the chieftain of the Canaanite army, and enemy of the Israelites during the times of Deborah the prophetess (Judg. 4,5). She is not linked directly to fertility but her language is blatantly sexual and graphic. As a high-class lady, depicted as surrounded by "wise women," she probably also serves as a priestess. Her violent language and the joy that she takes in the vision of her son molesting the Israelite women define her as evil and sexually depraved. While waiting at the window for her son to return from the battlefield, however, she also reinforces the conception of the female sphere as hemmed-in and sedentary, juxtaposed with that of the male as free and mobile.

The window may sometimes impart the sense of the woman's enterprising spirit, her ability to use precisely that which characterizes her cultural and social limitations as a means of helping a man, or men, in trouble. This is true of the Canaanite harlot Raḥab, who assists Joshua's spies to flee through the window (Josh. 2:15), as well as of the Israelite Michal, daughter of King Saul, who lowers David through the window, helping him escape Saul's wrath. The woman using her disadvantage as a form of power, then, is another idea connected with the image of the window. Yael the Kenite who appears at the entrance of her tent to lure Sisera, the enemy of the Israelites, is a variation of this image. She helps deliver the people of God from their enemy. Under the guise of domesticity and sexual vulnerability she is able to overpower the mighty man, thus revealing the more frightening elements associated with the image of the woman-at-her-doorway.[9]

I have chosen the image of the woman at the window as the title of this study because many of the elements suggested by the image apply to the Bible's conception of the female in general, in spite of the strong link of this image to pagan, non-Israelite practices and attitudes. The element of spatial constriction that this image suggests characterizes the existence of most biblical women. But spatial constriction implies temporal narrowness as well and highlights biblical women's marginality in time. "To escape the world or society," wrote Tom Driver, "is to escape history," since "time and space are coordinates."[10] If women were doomed to always look through the window, they were removed not only from geography but also from history. This argument also implies that Hebrew women's lives ran counter to the very essence of the Hebraic conception of Israelite destiny as a historical journey, anchored in past memories of events that occurred in time and place, and looking toward a redemptive future. The thesis of this study is that in its view of women, the Bible shuttles between its antipagan view of Israelite destiny and the nature-bound worldview of paganism. Driver's observations about the conception of time and space in Hellenic thought and art apply to Near Eastern paganism as well. Paganism was nature-oriented, viewing human time as a cycle of changeless recurrences and thus "enclosed within itself," with the future necessarily closed, not open to novelty and change.[11] In Hellenism, the oppressive sense of the endless repetition of time, viewed as a curse, resulted in a tendency to translate time into spatial terms.[12]

While the "Greeks thought only of space," the Hebrews thought "only of time."[13] The Bible's conversion of the pagan nature festivals into celebrations of historical events reflected its history-oriented theology. The Hebraic consciousness of history was founded on the assertion of man's freedom and of the future as potentially open. Further, as Erich Auerbach has suggested, the great male heroes in the Bible have distinct life histories during which their personalities change and develop. There is a dynamic quality to the lives of the biblical characters, in contrast with the static nature of the Homeric heroes.[14] Even the geographical journeys of the biblical heroes record their spiritual and mental evolution rather than physical adventures on an horizontal plane.

In its imaginings of the female sphere, however, the Bible often returns to the pagan view of humanity and its place in the cosmos, thus creating a further divide between the sexes, which was not only social and political but also theological. It was as if the Hebraic theology of a purposeful progress within history, imbued with past memories and filled with the promise of the new and changing, did not include the female destiny, or was found inadequate in explaining the feminine existence. The sexual and reproductive connotations in the image of the woman-at-the-window, the understanding of the woman as an instrument of fertility, characterize the biblical conception of the feminine. The Bible reflects the feminine mode of experience as removed from history and the realm of freedom and anchored in nature and its cycle of birth and death. The woman as a creature of nature, manifesting in her ability to give birth an identification with the earth and the cycle of seasons, and tyrannized by the rhythm of her biological nature, is opposed to the view of humanity as history-bound, with a capacity for choice and redemption within time.

The woman at the window as reflective of the prototypical female position postulates the subordination of the element of time to the element of space in the woman's existence. At the same time, the encasement within the window highlights not only the woman's removal from history, but her spatial constriction as well. The architectural style of the culture bespeaks its social and existential attitudes; the woman is placed at an entrance, but the opening suggests a prison rather than the open vistas. The woman is not about to come out of the entry, but will forever remain looking out from a point within. The spatial opening does not provide her with a means of exit. Rather, it is an opportunity for the male to enter and invade. As a pictorial correlative of the woman's sexuality, the image thus proclaimed the woman's position as an object to be penetrated and violated, rather than as a free agent moving in space.

Taking its cue from this ancient image, the present study focuses on biblical tales that interpret the woman's life through the medium of space. It further examines how in placing the woman within a spatial context the Hebraic perception of space is subverted. It opposes the Hebraic notion of space subordinated to time, and geography translated into history; it also reverses the Hebraic idea of movement on the horizontal plane as reflection of a spiritual, vertical energy as well. Rather, in many of these tales, the man is time and the woman is translated into a spatial element, an object with an opening, or a territory to be invaded. Man is history and woman is geography; he represents chronological progression, and she the subjection to the immutable rules of nature; he is the creator and mover of civilization, and she is the inanimate terrain, the silent and passive witness to the march of men through history.

Furthermore, within the framework of the biblical tale, men are given ample *lebensraum*. Male protagonists populate the arena, are constantly in motion, and monopolize the dialogues. Consequently, the feminine presence is frequently edged out and obliterated from the scene, reduced to a blank point. Even in tales that focus on the feminine predicament, men crowd the canvas so that the woman disappears from the space of the tale. Thus the imagery of place and location reduces the woman manifold: it creates an understanding of the female mode as geography, a land to be conquered and a terrain to be subdued. It further removes her from the progress of civilization and anchors her existence in the circular mode of nature rather than in the linear pattern of history, thus relegating the female to the pagan universe, an inferior state in the eyes of biblical man. Lastly, it often results in the complete dislodging of the female from the canvas.

This study examines instances where the female's assertion of spatial freedom and mobility is interpreted as violation of space and time, as intrusion into the male sphere and his claim on history. It further looks for those examples where the woman's intrusion is punished by her complete removal from time and space, as well as those where the woman succeeds in redefining her existence in the biblical-historical terms. Tales where the Bible's patrilocal and patrilineal practices are reinforced by the image of the woman-at-the-window will be juxtaposed with those where women find a way to circumvent their definition in geographical, nature-anchored terms and move to the chronological-historical mode. The woman's most successful avenue of flight is through the medium of language. Therefore, the final chapter discusses those narratives in which the woman's linguistic dexterity and ingenuity open for her vistas otherwise closed by her culture.

Finally, a few words about the interpretive methodology that underlies this study. More than any other text, the Bible is a feast to the literary critic because it is simultaneously a theological document, an ethical code, a historical chronicle, and an anthropological record, as well as an artistic endeavor consisting of poetry and fiction. This diversity of applications is further enriched by the fact that biblical literature originates from several authorial sources. Within each of the above categories Scriptures speak to us in a multiplicity of voices. Beyond the shared theological and moral doctrines, the biblical texts include a variety of ideological platforms and political preferences. It is precisely the heterogeneity of the authorial sources that validates our pursuit to uncover hidden agendas, muffled voices, and counterculture attitudes.

We may assume that all voices are united by their patriarchal tenor, coming as they are from male narrator(s) nurtured in a male-dominant culture and a largely father-oriented religion. But just as these men differed in their attitudes to the role or validity of the monarchy, for example, is it not possible that they displayed a variety of attitudes regarding society and gender? It is easy to adopt the assumption that all texts regarding women serve the men's manifest ideology of the supremacy of the male and betray his subconscious fears of the power of the female. Only the most narrow reading, however, will not admit that some men and women in the Bible transcend gender stereotypes and surprise us. We should not exclude the possibility of male authors who have opinions regarding gender roles that depart from the norm.

Furthermore, the number of narratives that unexpectedly shift gears and focus on a female character, when the historical and theological purposes of the text do not warrant it, suggest the hand of a literary genius, a scribe who must serve the culture but whose artistic intuition sees in the female figure and her tale an attractive avenue to pursue, in spite of the irrelevance of this pursuit to the overall historiosophic purpose. What about the artist who is ahead of his times, whose visions rise above the here and now to conceive of new social and moral orders? Would that talent not be inclined to give voice to an attitude to women that is alien to his own contemporaries? What about the realists who take a look at life and observe that real people, men and women, do not conform to cultural stereotypes? What about men like Hannah's husband, Elkanah, whose definition of love is surprisingly egalitarian, more in line with Erich Fromm's theories than with that of the dominant biblical voice? What about the sensitive artist who is pained to see any type of oppression, be it class- or gender-based; a writer who, while recording the rape of Dinah or of the concubine in Gibea in the deceptively "neutral" voice of the chronicler of events, still makes the men so offensively self-centered and self-serving, and the female victims so conspicuously absent from the canvas and the dialogues, that in fact we find that he is telling us a different story than the one he is supposed to? The theory forwarded here implies a certain tension between the narrator and the historical material handed to him by tradition. Although he is bound by the historical and theological significance of his story to anchor it in the patriarchal framework, his artistic sensibility may sometimes tell him that it is in the woman and her personal ordeal that the story should find its consummation. This theory also suggests that some of the Hebraic storytellers possessed a liberal-minded, forward-looking attitude that penetrated the gender-based narratives, if only in a suggestive, muffled manner.

Because most texts originated in an oral tradition, we have to look for the group that constituted the core of the storytelling practice, the female community, as the originator of some of the narrative materials in the Bible, especially those that are oriented toward women's issues or have been sidetracked into focusing on the female figures. As Edward F. Campbell suggests, women, especially the "wise women" who appear in a number of biblical narratives, were the locus of storytelling art in ancient Israel.[15] We may then look for the female voice behind some of these tales. When we sense defiance of the exclusively nature-oriented definition of the female, overt or covert, or hear an untypical nonsexist remark or a nonpatriarchal attitude, we may attribute these to the artistically gifted women who gave a nontraditional twist to some of the tales. Even if later redactors muted the counterculture voices, we are in a position to uncover them.

The question of whether the original author meant to alert us to all those hidden meanings and voices that we today find in the biblical text may be answered, then, by another question: which author? The plurality of voices allows for the plurality of hermeneutics. Whether we have the right to make gender issues in the Bible of central significance, just because they are important to our culture today, is another question that can be answered in the affirmative. Every generation has read the biblical text somewhat differently, applying to it its own perspectives and contemporary concerns. Our generation, especially, has reassessed and questioned traditional and inherited assumptions about the biblical text. The sheer dynamics of the history of ideas inevitably lead to tension between the sacred text, which has come to us intact and unaltered, and the changing attitudes of every generation.[16]

The Judaic tradition has sent us a twofold signal regarding the text and its interpretation. On the one hand, it forbade tampering with the sacred text itself, ruling out the possibility of editing a corrupt letter, word, or phrase, or of reconstructing an incomplete syntactic unit. On the other hand, it encouraged the creative interpretation of the text as soon as Scripture was canonized. The ancient sages urged us to read and reread the Bible and look for the hidden layers of meaning enfolded in them, implying, in effect, that each generation may read the holy text through its own lenses: "Turn it and turn it again, for everything is in it." The body of literature called Midrash, in both its halachic and aggadic applications, is the prototype of creative exegesis, employed by the rabbis as a tool not only to explicate and expand the terse biblical text, but to comment on and address issues and concerns that they shared with their contemporaries at that particular moment in time.

Thus the exegetical elasticity suggested by the Judaic hermeneutic tradition may allow us to penetrate beneath the surface to uncover an awareness that the biblical narrator was either not fully conscious of or took pains to hide, and which the particular sensitivity of our age may help detect. This endeavor is not a betrayal of the text nor an imposition on it of modes of thought and perceptions that are alien to biblical people. I subscribe to T. S. Eliot's opinion that the conscious present is an awareness of the past in a way and to an extent that the past's awareness of itself cannot show. Thus the question of what the original narrator meant should be changed to what his text betrays—intentionally or not. Deciphering the meaning of verbal lacunae or redundancies, codes that alerted the ancient commentators and produced the midrashic style of interpretation, would be a more relevant endeavor.

The main thrust of the interpretive approach offered here is a geometric adjustment: moving the female figure, usually at the background of the scene, or often edged out completely, to the center of the canvas. If she is not there, then her absence is a gaping hole in the middle point of the geometric circle; if her voice is not heard, then her silence is a soundless scream that saturates the male linguistic give-and-take. If she journeys through distances, the question is whether her trajectory is converted from the geographical to the historical. Thus we pursue not only those tales where the protagonist's femininity is defined strictly in terms of the tyranny of her biological cycle, but also those cases where her feminine faculties help her transcend the earth-bound existence of humanity and join the historical journey of the Israelite man.

CHAPTER 1

WOMAN AT THE WINDOW

1. THE TREACHEROUS MATRON LOOKS "THROUGH THE LATTICE"

The Text *See also Judges 4: 18–21*

From the window she looked out and moaned /
  The mother of Sisera (looked) through the lattice
Why is his chariot so late in coming /
  Why are the beats of his chariotry so tardy
Her wise ladies answered her / She even returned answer to herself
Have they not found and divided booty /
  A womb or two wombs to each man
A booty of many colors to Sisera /
  A plunder of many-colored needlework /
    Colored needlework for the necks of the spoilers
      (Judg. 5: 28–30) *Judges 5: 24–30*

Sisera's Mother

"Woman at the window" is by necessity a conformist, occupying the position of the spectator assigned to her by the male community. By acquiescing to her position at the window she helps uphold a system in which men run public life, engage in the affairs of the world, and make decisions that would inevitably affect her own life and fate. At the same time she is eagerly looking out, hoping to participate in the lives of men, if only vicariously. Her far-off gaze means that the center of her existence is not the room to which she turns her back, but the remote, unattainable, and exciting male arena.

Nevertheless, the woman's adulation of men results in treachery to her own sex, in the loss of sensitivity to the predicament of women. Being enclosed in the house results in the denigration of the feminine and identification with the man's values which inevitably lead to loss of compassion toward members of her sex. No other woman epitomizes better all these symptoms than the mother of the Canaanite chief Sisera (Judg. 4:28–30), who delights in the vision of her ruthless son and his soldiers molesting the Israelite women.

Sisera's mother appears in Deborah's victory hymn, and therefore we have to consider as well the woman-singer who filters the scene through her own particular lenses. Deborah is the epitome of the nontraditional woman, a prophetess and a military consultant, who exhibits poetic powers as well. When she imagines Sisera's mother, she does not claim to be actually watching the woman. The poetess uses poetic license to conjure up an invented scene for the sake of enriching her ode. Deborah places the Canaanite mother in a pagan pictorial context that she is most probably familiar with, "at the window." The Hebrew prophetess is making two statements, one about the nature of Canaanite women, the other about the dehumanization of all women, which results from the position "at the window."

Deborah attributes to Sisera's mother natural maternal feelings, describing the old lady as worried that her son is late and hoping that he has emerged victorious from the battle. When envisioning Sisera's success, and the booty that he will bring home, however, the mother and her female advisors reveal excessive cruelty which, surprisingly, is not aimed at the enemy soldiers but rather at the women captives who will be taken by him. The various English translations use language that is much less crude and graphic than the Hebrew, which reads: "One womb or two wombs / for each man" (4:30); instead of the noun "girl" she resorts to the synecdoche "womb." Deborah thus attributes to the Canaanite noble ladies the inclination to reduce the woman from a whole human being to a sexual organ. They delight not only in their army's assumed victory, which is understandable, but also in the way their sons and husbands will ravish and abuse other women.

The Canaanite matron could not be oblivious to the fact that rape is mainly a female experience, and that she and her daughters might be victims of sexual violation at any moment. If the gates to her palace were broken down by enemies and she was forced away from her comfortable, seemingly protected position at the window, the Canaanite grand lady and the females in her home might meet the same destinies that she now imagines for the Israelite women.

24

The positioning of women at spatial openings, the window and the lattice, is juxtaposed with the images associated with men. Sisera's mother asks not about her son but about his "chariot" and the "sound of his chariotry" (4:28). These images of mobility and boisterous action are the opposite of the encased window, which denotes a sedentary position as well as both imprisonment and vulnerability to invasion. Furthermore, Deborah attributes to Sisera's mother the tendency to convert human beings to objects. In the old lady's language, the essence of masculinity is represented by noisy, speeding vehicles, while femininity is merely a "womb." Men are promoted to powerful, larger-than-life instruments of war, while women are reduced to their sexual organs.

We have no way of knowing whether the historical woman, Sisera's mother, was really that cruel. Deborah may have based her portrait on rumors, or on her general knowledge of Canaanite women. These women may have been known for their lack of female solidarity. It would be expected of them to rejoice at the prospect of acquiring the Israelite women as slaves; but enjoying the scene of the molestation of women proves the lack of any feelings of sisterhood as well as denigration of their own femininity. The Canaanite women accept the fact that to be a woman means to be sexually abused. They may not realize that they are betraying their own womanhood and accept the male paradigm of women as sexual objects to be degraded and molested. Simone de Beauvoir's claim that patriarchy succeeded because of female compliance and cooperation is exemplified here.[1] Interestingly, Deborah attributes to the privileged ladies this cooperation in their own subjugation. One might have expected women of the lower classes to be more submissive and accepting of the male culture, which dictated the molestation of the enemy women. Because of their own experiences they could have been less sensitive toward other women's sufferings. In this case, however, even a woman who is relatively powerful has no respect for her own femininity and yields completely to the tenets of masculine conduct.

Furthermore, in positioning the women at the window Deborah may be saying something not only about the Canaanite women, but about all women of that culture and region who accepted the rules that constricted women's lives. The ladies looking through the lattice represent the experience of confinement within the four walls of the patriarchal home, the destiny of all women. These privileged women may feel safe in the palace of the mighty nobleman Sisera. Nevertheless, Deborah implies that being hemmed in, kept powerless and practically imprisoned, led to the women's denigration, or even hatred of their own sex. Deborah means to present more than just the cruelty of the Canaanite people, men and women; she intends to portray the dehumanizing impact of the position "at the window" on women.

We now understand why it is precisely Deborah who is able to reflect on women's unusual cruelty toward women. Deborah has known the life of a man of her generation, enjoying freedom and mobility, and gaining the respect of her people. Only a woman with Deborah's vantage point could understand the detrimental effects that the narrowing of women's parameters produced. By evoking the powerful images of spatial limitations, the window and the lattice, Deborah has shown how women enclosed and shut up may become desensitized to women's ordeals and programmed to put the male needs and pleasures ahead of their own. Due to Deborah's ode, the vicious ancient matron is forever frozen in our cultural memory as the mother who looks through "the lattice," and as a classic example of how the position "at the window" dehumanized women and made them a vehicle of male power, silent collaborators in the intimidation of women.

2. YAEL AT HER DOORSTEP

The Texts
Judges 4:1–24; 5:24–27
Proverbs 7:6–27; 5:3–5; 2:16–18

So that Sisera alighted from his chariot, and fled away by foot. . . . And Yael went out to meet Sisera, and said to him: "Turn in, turn in my lord, fear not." And when he had turned in to her tent, she covered him with a blanket. And he said: "Give me, I pray thee, a little water to drink, for I am thirsty." And she opened a bottle of milk, and gave him drink, and covered him. . . . Then Yael, Heber's wife, took a tent peg, and took a hammer in her hand, and went softly to him, and drove the tent peg into his temple, and fastened it to the ground, for he was fast asleep and weary. (Judg. 4:15,18,19, 21)

Between her legs he tumbled, he fell /
Where he tumbled, there he fell down, dead
(Judg. 5:27)

In Yael's tale the vision of the woman standing at the opening to her tent may transmit a sense of female vulnerability and exposure to danger, but it is quickly transformed into a frightening assertion of the woman's dangerous sexual powers. It is not possible to isolate Yael's encounter with the terrifying general Sisera, who controls "nine hundred chariots of iron" (Judg. 4:3), from the larger context of the tale of Deborah and the military triumph of the people of Israel over an awesome adversary. It is Deborah who encourages the Israelite chief of the army to confront Sisera who has plagued and oppressed her people for twenty years. Yael comes to the scene only in mid action, when the Israelites have already defeated Sisera and his army, and the mighty

Sisera disembarks his chariot and finds himself on foot, running for his life from the battlefield.

We observe Yael directly as a protagonist in a dramatic episode and then indirectly, when she is praised by Deborah in her victory ode. As the tale's highlight shifts from the wide vistas of Deborah's career to the narrow confines of Yael's tent, we are introduced to a woman who is much more typical of her culture and times than Deborah. Yael's people, the nomadic Kenites, have moved their encampment to a new location to avoid getting in the middle of the military activity and to maintain their neutrality. Unlike Deborah, Yael is first seen as a home-bound, domestic person; she ventures out of her tent only to invite Sisera in, and immediately returns inside with her guest. The tent figures prominently in Yael's tale as well as in Deborah's verses on Yael. Not only does Yael belong to a tribe of tent-dwellers, but the tent is emblematic of her existence; as wife of the head of the tribe she leads a sheltered life in the tent.

The text does not disclose to us whether Yael just happens to stand by her entrance when Sisera passes by, or that, having heard rumors of how things have turned out on the battlefield, she stands outside on purpose, out of curiosity and boredom. Yael may have been inside but heard the urgent footsteps of Sisera.[2] She seems to be waiting. No one else is around and there is an eerie quiet to the scene.

Yael's tactic is to assume the role of the homemaker and nurturer who is completely ignorant in political matters. Sisera does not imagine that the woman would have the courage to make a decision on the spot that would defy her tribe's neutrality in the present conflict. Sisera is no fool, however, and while he seems tired, he is wary, and Yael has to coax him in. She disarms him by her subservience, calling him "my lord" and twice inviting him to "turn in" and "turn in to me." When, apparently, he still hesitates, she encourages him some more: "fear not" (Judg. 4:18). Yael enhances her domestic, nurturing image by covering him with a blanket, and offering him milk, instead of the water he requested.

That the motif of "milk instead of water" is more than just a revelation of the woman's kindness is not lost on Deborah, who repeats this image in her ode.[3] In ancient mythological imaginings, as well as throughout the history of literature, woman, water, and milk have been tied together.[4] In Egyptian hieroglyphics, for example, the water jar is a symbol of femininity. Thus when Sisera asks Yael for water, he implies that he wants more than just a drink. When Yael responds by giving him milk, she more than hints at her readiness to satisfy him with the totality of her femininity.

The subtext of an erotic drama that underlies this tale is woven into the fabric of its imagery, while the narrative language itself remains innocuous, "clean" of any explicit sexual reference. But the dialogue between the man and the woman, which turns from formal to intimate, also intensifies the sense that more is going on than the text imparts directly. The man and the woman initially address each other in a formal and respectful manner. She calls him "my lord" and adheres to all the laws of hospitality; he adds to his request for water the word "*na'*," ("please," or "I pray thee"). Yet after the man has had his milk, and the woman covered him with a blanket (this latter act is mentioned twice), Sisera becomes bolder, and commands the woman in a familiar, even masterful tone: "Stand in the door of the tent" (4:20). The sexual act, implied in the symbols of water, milk, and blanket, is interpreted by the man as a sign of his domination of the woman and results in a new relationship, one in which the woman is seen as slave and the man as master.[5] Now he orders her to take once more the familiar female position, at the entrance to her tent, this time to protect him and deflect his pursuers.[6] Sisera's falling asleep is not only a sign of physical exhaustion; it signifies that the woman has succeeded in deceiving the man with her façade of docile, nurturing femininity, and has gained his complete trust.

The woman-at-her-doorway, however, only seems as harmless and powerless as the woman-at-the-window. The mere fact of Yael venturing outside and inviting Sisera in should have been ominous to the man. Sisera is wrong in assuming that the woman is now fully under his control. Although the sexual intimacy has given him the illusion of power, it has in fact placed him at her mercy.[7] Deborah, in her ode, reinforces the sexual nature of Yael's tactics: "Between her legs he tumbled, he fell / Where he tumbled, there he fell down, dead" (5:27). The various translations that read the Hebrew word *regel* as "foot" rather than "leg," and *bein* as "at" rather than "between," miss the sexual connotation and flatten the much more daring language in the Hebrew. Deborah's imaginative recreation of the scene brings to light the submerged sexual tension in the tale. Deborah also uses the "water instead of milk" motif with poetic exaggeration, thus heightening the atmosphere of sensuality in Yael's tent: "He asked water, she gave him milk / she served him cream in a lordly dish" (5:25).

Yael's homespun strategy is clear even when she steps out of her womanly docility and turns her home into a bloody scene of slaughter by using the readily available tent peg. Thus the irony of Sisera's life and destiny comes full circle: he terrorized his neighbors with his reputation as a man of war, "for he had nine hundred chariots of iron" (4:3), and ends his life in a woman's tent, covered by her blanket, and slain by a wooden tent peg.

Yael steps out of her tent one more time, to invite another man in; this time it is Barak, in hot pursuit of his enemy. Yael again talks cunningly, but with a view to surprise Barak pleasantly. There is, however, a slightly sarcastic edge in her address to Barak. She does not tell him what happened, only that she can show him the man he is looking for. When Barak enters the woman's tent, he finds his enemy dead. There is a tone of superiority and power in

Yael's words to Barak, born of her pride in having overpowered the great enemy of the Israelites. Yet, Yael then recedes from the scene, presumably spending the rest of her life in her enclosed tent. Where her husband has been all this time, we do not know. Have the men of her tribe abandoned the women and escaped to a safe place until the war between the Israelites and the Canaanites is resolved? If so, then the imperative of protecting the womenfolk is once again proven to be hollow, perhaps a noble sentiment which in reality is never practiced.

The tale of Yael is exceptional in that the woman is seen as helping change the course of history by the actual killing the enemy, a means usually taken by men. A closer look, however, tells us that Sisera is defeated and doomed even before he arrives at Yael's doorstep. The tale of his assassination is added as a dramatic twist that enhances the beauty of the tale, but not the essence of the historical narrative. It provides an inclusio structure to the narrative in Judges 4, which starts with a woman, Deborah, and ends with another woman, Yael. Yael makes a courageous political decision, but in view of Sisera's obvious defeat it merely reflects the woman's intelligence and her correct reading of what her husband would have done. Yael remains within the domestic, and her frame of reference is exclusively feminine and sexual, as shown by the tent, the milk, the blanket, and the euphemistic "legs."

Nevertheless, the picture of the maternal homemaker who rises to a historic occasion that brings a momentary mutation to her nature and then slips back to her feminine docility is misleading. Yael's sexual tactic of luring the man into her house and seducing him, only to overpower and kill him, is expunged from the outer layer of the tale, since the culture meant to put Yael on a pedestal as the heroine and savior of the people, rather than as the sexual seductress. Deborah's ode, too, puts Yael's action in the framework of divine justice, thus mitigating the horrifying aspect of the scene in which a woman kills a man who trusted her enough to fall asleep in her home. The result is a cleaned-up version that is nevertheless vitalized by a darker side which ties the heroine to the more dangerous women the Bible warns men about, who use their sexual favors to disarm and overpower men. If taken out of its historical and theological context and reduced to its primary core, the Yael-and-Sisera scene is patterned along the lines of the "strange woman" episodes in Proverbs, and contains all the elements of the archetypal male experience that results in the "fear of women." "at the window of my house..."

The longest and most elaborate of these episodes (Prov. 7:6–27) brings into high relief aspects that are muted and suppressed in the Yael narrative. The strange woman going against the culture is reflected in the reversal of the familiar images. The teacher, the neutral and wise observer of life and its pitfalls, looks through the window of his house and watches a foolish young man being lured into a woman's house: "For at the window of my house I looked through the lattice / And beheld among the simple ones / I discerned . . . a young man void of understanding." The woman, who should be safely ensconced at the window, is out on the street. The poet uses sarcasm and comedy to describe her movements: "She is noisy and ungovernable / her feet do not remain in the house. Now she is outside, now in the streets / and she lies in wait at every corner." Unlike Yael, the woman boldly claims that she stepped out of her house to look for the young man: "So I came out to meet thee / diligently to seek thy face, and I found thee." She then invites the young man to her house with the promise of sensual and sexual pleasures, which are only euphemistically and symbolically referred to in the Yael scene, but more directly spelled out here. The comforts and pleasures of the woman's lavish home and perfumed bed are the antithesis of the austerity of Yael's tent. Thus the plainness of the tent camouflages its threatening aspect. The basic "milk" and "blanket" in the Judges story become "myrrh, aloes, and cinnamon" and "the tapestry of the yarn of Egypt." The "strange woman" assures the young man that her husband has gone on a long journey. Yael makes no reference to her husband, but it is clear that all Kenite men are mysteriously absent from their camp. Yael reassures Sisera with simple language, "turn in" and "fear not." The strange woman, on the other hand, seduces the man with "her much fair speech" and "the smoothness of her lips" (7:21). In both cases, the sexual encounter ends in disaster for the man. The killing of Sisera is described in gory and graphic details: Yael drives the tent peg into the man's temple and fastens it to the ground. The young man of Proverbs is not actually murdered at the hands of the woman; the "dart" that "strikes through his liver" is metaphorical, a reference to the financial and social ruin the affair will cause him.

Furthermore, the Judges characters are named and are actors in history while the Proverbial figures are prototypes, the sexual seductress who is the evil influence and the agent of death and hell, and the gullible, inexperienced young man. The protagonists in Proverbs are not named, nor are they anchored in time and place, since they are meant to enact a recurrent, archetypal human drama. The teacher creates the scene as a cautionary example, a pedagogic device that dramatizes to the young man the inadvisability of yielding to a promiscuous woman. The comic tone that is mixed with the somber warning— as well as the fact that the "strange woman" in Proverbs is counterbalanced by the image of the Woman Wisdom—mitigates the terror in the scene. It may seem initially that the Proverbs scene is capable of releasing in man the primordial "fear of women," while the tale of Yael suppresses the danger of the woman and highlights her achievement, condoned by God and His people. Stripped of its historical veneer, the Judges tale is equally frightening, if not more so, since it lacks the hypothetical quality of Proverbs. As a concrete example of a universal human situation, with real people and a historical event, the Yael-and-Sisera scene reinforces feminine treachery. Once the woman steps out of her abode and invites the man to enter, opening herself and her home to the man, he is at her hands. The "dart" that pierces the young man's liver in Proverbs is only metaphorical, but Yael's wooden peg is more real and frightening since it illustrates how the most innocent domestic tool can turn deadly in the woman's hands.

The woman-at-her-door is a variation of the woman-at-the-window, but with a more hostile, negative edge to it. It locates the woman's power in her sexual availability, viewing the woman's "entrance" as a deadly trap, and serves as a warning to man to beware the woman who steps out of her domain. Behind the historical Yael who has done God's work and played a role in actual events, there is the universal deadly woman whose existential center is anchored not in time but in her internal empty space that can turn into the gaping grave and therefore has to be feared and controlled by man.

3. DEBORAH UNDER THE PALM TREE

The Text
Judges 4, 5

> And Deborah, a woman prophetess, wife of Lappidot [or: woman of fire], she judged Israel at that time. And she sat under the palm tree . . . and the children of Israel came up to her for judgment. And she sent and called Barak . . . and said to him: "Has not the Lord God of Israel commanded, saying, Go and gather your men to Mount Tabor . . . and I will draw out to thee Sisera, the Captain of Yabin's army, with his chariot and his multitude." . . . And Barak said to her: "If thou wilt go with me, then I will go, but if thou wilt not go with me, then I will not go." . . . And Deborah arose, and went with Barak. (Judg. 4:4–8)

The two images discussed previously, Sisera's mother looking through the window and Yael waiting at her doorstep, come to us from different perspectives. Sisera's mother is the exclusive creation of Deborah, and her position at the window is a poetic image presented in Deborah's victory ode. Thus, there is no historical verification of the scene of Sisera's mother dramatized by Deborah, or even of the fact that Sisera's mother was alive at the time, let alone that she was waiting for her son by the window. Yael is a figure in the historical narrative, and her actions are part of the chronicle of events, but she appears in Deborah's ode as well. These scenes in Deborah's ode belong to the very few in the Bible where the point of view is female. Therefore we can learn a few things about Deborah the woman, especially the meaning that she attributes to the woman-at-the-window and woman-at-her-doorstep.

The spatial image connected with Deborah is the open countryside, "under the palm tree," where she probably held court and received the litigants from all the tribes of Israel. This is rather unique, for even the women who are seen as journeying in the open road emerge from the house, while the prophetess is initially described as sitting under the eponymic tree "the Palm of Deborah."[8] The ease with which Deborah can move from one place to the other makes her an exception in the culture, because she herself places the two women whom she highlights in her poem within restrictive boundaries, one encased by the window, and the other sheltered in her tent.

Deborah is a woman aware of walking a tightrope. Not only has she been accepted as a prophetess and a judge, a religious, social and legal authority, but she seems to be the only person in her generation to have the stamina for military action. In one key statement, interpreted in different ways, she betrays her sense of the hazards of her unique position among her people: she warns Barak that if she joins him "thou shalt scarcely attain honor on the journey that thou goest, for the Lord will yield Sisera into the hands of a woman" (Judg. 4:9). Here she seems to express her conviction that her continued success depends on her ability to stay within the limits of her position as prophetess and judge. If she adds military victory to her laurels, she may incur the jealousy of the chief of the army, and therefore she suggests that he should gather the army by himself.

Deborah's statement has also been seen as a prediction that a woman will determine the outcome of the war, and thus as an allusion to Yael's future action. If this is the meaning of Deborah's words then she is a proud woman who does not hesitate to announce to the man that women, too, may take an active role in military affairs. Both interpretations originated in male readers and, while contradictory, both reveal Deborah's uneasy position in a society that promotes male supremacy.[9] The first shows Deborah as heedful of male sensitivities, the second as eager to promote female interests. I prefer not to read Deborah's words as prophecy, but to see in them a somewhat ambiguous statement regarding women's roles in military matters. She is afraid to offend Barak, but she must prepare him for an unexpected resolution of the military conflict that might take away the glory from him and give it to a woman, be it Deborah or someone else. So while Deborah acts as an equal in the male world, she is still first and foremost a woman who is somewhat uncomfortable in that role, since it is so unique and does not reflect the collective female destiny of her era.

Thus when Deborah places Sisera's mother at the window, she draws on a female representation prevalent in the culture of the whole region, as well as on a female pose known from everyday life. Deborah's commentary on the image is that this familiar feminine condition dehumanizes women and makes them traitors to their sex. On the face of it, Deborah is celebrating the Israelites' victory over their enemies, highlighting the cruelty of the pagans through the image of the old mother, from whom we might expect tenderness rather than the viciousness that she displays. But Deborah is making a statement about women in general, revealing her position as a successful woman who, from a more liberated vantage point, can see more clearly what is wrong with her culture. Deborah unequivocally condemns the woman's position at the window. As this pose characterizes the lives of the majority of women in her times, then the prophetess is making a bold comment about the state of women in her time. At the same time, Deborah does not engage in blaming the male community, implying in a sense that women can take themselves off the window, as she has done, and courageously join the life of action.

Deborah's mission to enhance women's status and increase their power is further established in her poetic rendering of Yael's act. To make sure that Yael is described as a typical woman, Deborah reminds us of Yael's tent and her husband Heber. She then uses parallelism to serve her purpose of enhancing women's power: "He asked for water, she gave him milk / She brought forth cream in a lordly dish" (Judg. 5:25). The first line describes the event as we have witnessed it unfolding, the second does not repeat the first but exaggerates it, using poetic hyperbole: the milk drawn from a jar in the original tale is here offered in "a lordly dish" (or "a huge cup") and turns into "cream" (or "butter"). In the next verse the "hand" of the first line becomes "the right hand," symbol of power and might. The next two lines, together, intensify the horror of the original description of the act of killing and mimic the ascending progression of the act: "And she hammered Sisera, she smote through his head" is followed by the graphic consequences of the hammering and smiting: "She crushed and pierced his temple" (5:26). The next verse, in ternary structure, brings to light the suppressed sexual innuendo of the prose description of the actual event. Deborah repeats "between her legs" twice, and then, when the message is clear, she adds sarcastically: "Where he bent, there he fell, dead" (5:27).

Does Deborah mean to accomplish what the prose narrator did earlier, that is, enhance the deadly impact of the treacherous woman-at-her-door? Does the prophetess therefore serve the male community by validating, and even fanning the fire of, the collective male phobia of the "fear of women"? On the contrary, Deborah does her best to dissociate Yael's action from its heinous archetypal meaning and couch it in the language of blessing, redemption, and holy mission. Helping the people of Israel means "helping God" (5:23), and therefore Yael is seen as a divine messenger. Furthermore, Deborah attributes the blessing of Yael to God's angel, who curses those who did not come to the aid of the oppressed tribes, and blesses Yael who has. As a prophetess, Deborah has the authority to quote the angel of God, and thus she twice encases the blessing of Yael in the sacred: embedded in the blessing attributed to the angel is the prophetess' own blessing of Yael. Deborah is astute enough, however, to know that physical strength is important in military matters. Therefore Yael's divine mission does not stay within the spiritual; it takes on the form of great bodily strength. Her domestic tool is therefore commuted to "a workman's hammer" (5:26).

The technique of parallelism is a poetic correlative of Deborah's balancing tactics.[10] Deborah condemns women's subordination, but refrains from driving a wedge between the male and female community; she accentuates female might, even proclaiming boldly the deadly potential of woman's sexuality, yet she insists on depicting Yael as a faithful woman on a holy mission, thus dissociating the person from the pernicious archetype and diffusing its terrifying impact. Although she pays homage to femininity as a powerful theological and political factor, Deborah does not spurn the traditional female roles; she therefore introduces herself as first and foremost "a mother in Israel" (5:7). This may not necessarily mean that Deborah is a mother, but that she has adopted a maternal role toward all the people of Israel; it is telling, however, that this exceptional woman chooses to accentuate her motherhood rather than, say, her prophetic and legislative abilities.

The careful balancing strategy adopted by both the narrator and Deborah is evident in the attribution of the victory ode, which Deborah chants with Barak. The verb *vatashar,* literally "and she sang," is in the third person feminine singular, and therefore refers to a female singer. Yet there are two syntactic subjects attached to this verb, Deborah and Barak. Although this grammatical structure is not unusual in biblical Hebrew, some of the traditional commentators note that the biblical narrator is trying to indicate that Deborah composed and delivered the ode.[11] We might see in this peculiar grammar, which wreaks havoc on the principle of gender differentiation in Hebrew, another confirmation of Deborah's method of defusing potentially incendiary situations. Although she alone produced the song, she lets Barak share in the credit so that the effect is one of unity and accord between the prophet and the soldier, the spiritual leader and the man of action, female and male. This method is further exhibited in Deborah's carefully structured verse: "Awake awake Deborah / awake awake utter a song; Arise Barak / and lead away your captive, thou son of Abinoam" (5:12).

Deborah uses the technique of poetic parallelism as an ideological and tactical tool, reflecting the prophetess' harmonious vision of the scheme of things, where the individual's creativity is enhanced by social involvement, the prophet can be a military leader as well, the Israelite nation is restored to the God that they have forsaken, and the woman becomes an integral part of the nation's life and its destiny. Thus, paradoxically, the Deborah material in Judges contains some of the most disturbing images of women in the Bible, the treacherous woman-at-the-window and the deadly woman-at-her-doorstep, as well as the most dramatic biblical presentation of a woman who has lifted herself, and her sex, out of her biological prison and into history and the progress of civilization.

4. MICHAL BY THE WINDOW

The Texts
1 Samuel 18:14–29; 19:11–17; 25:44
2 Samuel 3:12–16; 6:14–23

And Saul sent messengers to David's house, to watch him, and slay him in the morning. And Michal, David's wife told him, saying: "if thou not save thy life tonight, tomorrow thou shalt be slain." So Michal let David down through the window, and he went, and fled, and escaped. (1 Sam. 19:11–12)

And as the ark of the Lord came into the city of David, Michal, Saul's daughter, looked through the window and saw King David dancing and leaping before the Lord; and she despised him in her heart. (2 Sam. 6:16)

The tale of Michal, King Saul's daughter who became David's first wife, is wrapped by two window scenes that mark her transformation from power to powerlessness. The chronicle of Michal's unhappy life is buried under the exciting saga of David's rise to power and his amazing success as a king loved by both the people and God. Bits and pieces of her story are interspersed into the epic of David's adventures, but she is never the center of interest, the main figure on the canvas. Yet the dispersed episodes about Michal, strung together and read in unity, are a paradigm of the deterioration of a charismatic, independent-minded woman in an environment hostile to female autonomy.

The window appears twice in the narratives about Michal, punctuating her tragic journey and illuminating the narrator's veiled admiration of the woman. The first time the window is mentioned in connection with Michal, she lets David down through a window in their home, helping him escape from Saul (1 Sam. 19:12). She reminds us here of the prostitute of Jericho, Raḥab, who also saves men by letting them down through the window. The window appears, too, in the last episode in which Michal participates. Here the Bible uses the same verb (in Hebrew) as in the description of Sisera's mother as well as Jezebel: Michal "looks through the window" and watches David dancing in front of God's ark as it is brought into the city of Jerusalem. The differences in the symbolism of the window between its first and second appearance cover the many meanings that the image of the window has played in ancient art; they also become a correlative of our protagonist's decline.

When Michal is first introduced to us, we are given a very unusual piece of information, repeated twice: that Michal loves David. Biblical women never express love for a man other than a son. Rebecca loves Jacob, but we never know if she loves her husband; on the other hand, the Bible tells us that Isaac "loved Rebecca." It appears that in biblical culture it was unseemly for a woman to declare her love for a man, or to make her sexual preferences known. Furthermore, if the culture was aware that women, too, had erotic preferences, it did not deem them important enough to be mentioned, since women did not marry in accordance with their wishes. For Michal to love David was not unusual, given his popularity among all Israelites, men and especially women; but for her to make it public meant that she was fearless and unorthodox. Unwittingly, Michal also made herself available, open, and thus vulnerable. Furthermore, usually it is the man's feelings that are given expression, and the woman's that are left unpronounced, while in this case the reverse is true. Without elaborating on David's feelings, the storyteller makes it clear, through this obvious lapse, that Michal is doomed.

Within the historical narrative Michal's feelings are important only in terms of the political circumstances of the strife between Saul and David. Saul uses his daughters as commodities, either as payment for favors or as bait to entrap his enemy. Saul first offers David his elder daughter Merab on the condition that David fight the Philistines. Saul's inner motives are made very clear to the reader: he hopes that the young man will be killed on the battlefield. Publicly the giving of the daughter is an award to the mighty warrior, in line with prevalent custom; the princess as a prize for a suitor's brave action or for his victory in a contest of power is a familiar motif in folk literature. For Saul the courageous feat is not required as proof of the young man's suitability as a son-in-law or of his sexual maturity, but is a tactic to get rid of a competitor.[12] Saul does not solicit the girl's opinion, and in the midst of the negotiations, Merab is given to someone else. The withdrawal of the girl is proof of Saul's increasing instability, of his erratic machinations. David's silence is meaningful, indicating that he is not heartbroken or disappointed. When Saul hears that Michal is in love with his enemy, he seizes the opportunity and simply tells David that he will become his son-in-law through his second daughter. David's silence is again telling, and it leads Saul to urge his servants to talk the young man into the arrangement. David's reluctance is probably tactical. He does not wish to seem too eager to marry into the royal family, and he even indulges in a lengthy speech about his own worthlessness and the honor such a marriage will bestow on him.

What is clear is that while Michal is the person who initiates the union, she is not a factor in either Saul's or David's considerations, nor is she present during the negotiations. When Saul offers Michal to David, he does not spell out her name, but simply refers to his "second" daughter. He further describes the alliance as David marrying into the king's family (in Hebrew, "marry unto me"). In the conversations between David and the king's servants, both parties refer to the proposed marriage as marrying (into) the king. It is clear that all concerned, except for the bride Michal, consider the union as a matter of a political contract, not love.

Saul plans to get rid of David by demanding a bride price of one hundred foreskins of Philistines, hoping that David would be killed during his attempts. When David survives, Saul appoints his daughter to be a spy in his enemy's house. Just as Saul used his daughter for his own purposes, however, she has used him for her purposes, for she made the king get for her the man that she chose. She has been able to utilize her father's conspiratorial plans toward David to her own benefit. It is clear that Saul's children, as well as his servants, see through the king and read his hidden thoughts.

Two diametrically opposite forces are at work in Michal's life. She thinks that she has the freedom that is accorded only to men in her culture, and she acts accordingly for a while. The underlying social restrictions, which she ignores or does not recognize, assert themselves and finally defeat her. The window first exhibits Michal's free spirit as well as her great love and devotion for David. When Saul sends his people to wait for David all night to ambush him in the morning, Michal warns him and helps him flee. This is the only domestic scene between David and Michal. There is a sense of a life interrupted, if not for David then for Michal. It appears that Michal's enterprising mind concocts the plan for David to escape through the window.

The spatial opening here is used by Michal to save her man. It is not the "window of appearance," but probably a back window. David's leaving through the window is sexually symbolic, however, for it seems that David will never enter Michal's life again. For Michal, the window is proof of her courageous resistance to her father, the king. To the reader as well, the window, open and used as a means of exit, represents freedom from oppression, countering the sense of restriction linked to the image. Nevertheless, we realize that the open roads belong to the man, David, who embarks on a journey, geographical and historical, that leads him to the throne. Michal is left at home, looking through the window to watch David disappearing into the dark forever.

The association with Raḥab points to Michal's sexually uninhibited attitude; but the ancient prostitute was unattached, completely independent. For the king's daughter, still bound by custom and tradition, that openness was double-edged. It gave the young woman the daring to pursue her love, but it also made her vulnerable, open to be hurt. It turns out, as well, that Michal's sense of freedom was illusory. It is true that immediately after David's disappearance Michal still displays her cunning and quick wit. She puts a dummy in David's bed to mislead Saul's messengers that David lies sick in bed, thus allowing David time enough to reach safety. Then, when the ruse is revealed and her father asks for an explanation, Michal's quick response is a lie that seems to satisfy her father: she brazenly claims that she was forced to help David under the threat of death.

Michal's allegiances are clear and unequivocal, and the reader is now waiting for the young couple's next move and their eventual reunion. Nevertheless, the biblical text abandons Michal as soon as she makes sure that David is safe, returning again to David's career as a fugitive from the wrath of a paranoid king and the various adventures that befall him. The reader's curiosity with regard to the charismatic Michal is not answered; she becomes a blank point, a non-person, occupying no place in David's thoughts or in the text. The next time that we meet Michal she is a changed woman, behaving as the typical daughter in the male-dominated family. No longer speaking or acting freely, she has relinquished her subject-position and become an object, "given" to someone else in marriage. This is noted almost as an afterthought or a small footnote in a brief comment listing David's new wives.

Michal's silence and compliance as the matrimonial transaction involving her goes on stand in sharp contrast to the outspoken and enterprising spirit that she showed earlier regarding matters of the heart. The metamorphosis of a woman who defied her father the king and lied to him for the man that she loved is reflected in the grammar that relegates her from subject to object as well as in the visual angle, in which she does not appear anymore, even when she is getting married. We are only told of an arrangement between two men, the woman's father and her new bridegroom. The outspoken and verbal Michal has no comment to make now, either in opposition to the new match or in compliance to it. For Saul, marrying his daughter off to another man is a signal to David that he no longer belongs to the royal family, that his marital connection as well as other claims to be part of the center of power have been dissolved. The political gesture of Michal's second marriage is clear, but the personal subtext is also significant. The scene of a man's nocturnal escape through the window is prevalent in the genre of romantic adventures, thus casting the tale of David and Michal in a romantic light. Nevertheless, as the relationship evolves, it becomes an ironic reversal of a romantic tale, precisely because it starts with all the right ingredients. The dashing young soldier wins the hand of the king's daughter after proving himself and passing a test put before him by the girl's father. In the David saga, the biblical narrative, which mostly stays away from the heroic and romantic, comes very close to creating a larger-than-life hero in the epic tradition. Michal initially presents herself as the right female counterpart of the romantic hero. When David fled Saul's murderous fury, Michal must have waited for him to send a signal for her to join him. After all, David and Jonathan, the king's son, managed to meet clandestinely a number of times. We know that Michal was brave and daring enough to risk her life for the sake of reuniting with her beloved David. Instead, while she was languishing at home, Michal was probably hearing rumors about David's romantic and marital doings. The spirit of romance, so strong in the initial scenes between David and Michal, never materializes. If Michal offered herself as the female half of the romantic couple, David denies her that role. David's lack of genuine attachment toward Michal, coupled with the woman's excessive, unconditional love for David, leads to the silent and passive pose that Michal adopts in the aftermath of David's escape.

Michal's transformation from subject to object, as well as her physical removal from the center of the arena, is repeated many years later, when she next appears on the scene. Then, she acts like a typical woman in patriarchal society, allowing herself to be acted on and moved from man to man. The occasion is again political rather than personal. David has risen to the throne after the death of King Saul and is about to be recognized by the last holdout of Saul loyalists. He is strong enough to make demands and asks for Michal's return. His claim is couched in legal, not emotional language: he wants his wife back not because he loves or misses her, or because they were brutally torn apart from each other, but because he paid an immense bride price for her (2 Sam. 3:14). At this sensitive point in David's political life, the return of Michal marks the final surrender of the former royal family, and serves as a symbol of the consolidation of power in David's hands.

There follows a scene that takes place in the open road. Michal and her second husband journey together until at a place named Baḥurim, the man is ordered to leave, and he turns away and leaves. As he accompanies his wife to her destination he cries bitterly, while Michal his wife says nothing. To one man at least, her second husband, Michal was dear, beloved. Her silence, on the other hand, is open to multiple interpretations. Was she silent because she had been emotionally dead for a long time, and no change in her life really mattered to her any more? Or was she silent because she was not as heartbroken as her husband and was not sorry to leave him even though he loved her? The second husband is, after all, weak and powerless. Unlike the young David who performed heroic feats to win Michal, this man cannot even protest properly and only cries. It would not be far-fetched to suggest that while Michal knows that she is losing a loving man, there is still hidden in her the younger woman who loved David passionately. There must be some hope awakened in Michal, for in her younger life, too, she preferred to miss all signals that told her that David did not really love her and only needed her as symbol of his rising fortunes.

The open road where Michal and her husband travel does not end with the scene of reunion in David's home. Again it is the elision that speaks loudly.

We assume that Michal arrived safely in David's home, but we do not know if he met her, what words were said on that occasion, or if anything was said at all. There is no reception at the palace gates, and no falling into each other's arms in the intimacy of the shared bedroom. After the hapless husband departs, Michal, too, disappears, although technically she still has a way to go before arriving in David's home, and the narrative resumes its political and theological bent.

The window comes to the fore again as emblematic of Michal's situation; but the scene itself marks a climactic moment in David's career. God's ark is finally being brought into the "city of David," after David has been reassured that this is God's wish. The celebratory atmosphere is enhanced by the many musical instruments that accompany the dancing crowds. David's joy and festive mood are unmistakable: he dances and "leaps before God vigorously" (2 Sam. 6:16). It seems that the "multitudes of Israel" have all congregated on this occasion, and everyone, man and woman, is outdoors, honoring God's ark. Michal, however, is seen at her window, observing David dancing in ecstasy and "despising him in her heart."

The contrast between "Michal, Saul's daughter, loved David" and "Michal, Saul's daughter . . . despised David" has no impact on David, but tells the tragedy of Michal. On the first occasion, Michal was Saul's unmarried daughter, in love with David, but on the second she was David's wife, and yet recognized only as the dead king's daughter, implying her isolation at court. Then, although Michal offers a reason why she despises David, we may be suspicious of it. She ridicules David for dancing as one of the simple people, making a spectacle of himself and behaving unregally. Some commentators take Michal's bitter words at face value and see in them her nostalgia for the older regime that was less populist and more regal. But there is no indication in the Bible that Saul's court was more sumptuous than that of David, and we know that Michal betrays her father the king and ties her destiny with a young man who was out of favor at court. Michal's words are those of a woman scorned, and they show that in the last stage in her life she has turned from David's lover into the defeated king's daughter.

Michal looking through the window may be likened to that of Jezebel, who tries to appear in splendor at the moment of her ultimate defeat. Furthermore, to the people of Israel, Michal may be associated with the pagan simply because of her estrangement from David's court and the perception of David as the divinely approved king and Saul as estranged from God. When Michal steps out of the enclosed space and into the crowds it is only to make some acid remarks to David, and in turn, be denigrated by him.

The sexual element usually suggested by the window is also at play here. Michal's wrath is further kindled by David's dancing among the women and inadvertently exposing himself. Both Michal and David mention the "handmaids"; she sneers at him for dancing with them, and he disdainfully promises that it would be his honor to gain these women's affection.

That Michal's sexual jealousy may be suggested as the real reason for her bitter exchange with David is made even clearer at the end of the narrative, when the Bible makes the short, cryptic statement that "Michal, Saul's daughter, had no children to the day of her death" (2 Sam. 6:23). The connection between the preceding episode and Michal's barrenness does not have to be spelled out. Although David forced Michal's return from her second husband, he did not receive her as a wife but as symbol of his political triumph. Michal's angry words are the eruption of the pent-up fury and humiliation that she has long felt toward her neglectful husband who has withdrawn his sexual favors from her and thus doomed her to the additional heartbreak of childlessness.

Two window scenes envelop Michal's tale. The first marks her spirit of love and hope, while the second presents the same person shrunken in stature and depleted in spirit. In the first episode, Michal is verbal and expressive about, and for the sake of, her love. In the last, she is also outspoken, but there is acrimony and despair in her language. In the two middle episodes, there is complete silence and passivity. Furthermore, the images connected with David—the redeemer of God's ark, the conqueror of cities, the favorite of the women, and the ecstatic dancer and singer—imply vigor and triumph that are political, theological, and military as well as sexual. Michal's frame of reference, the window, implies isolation, vulnerability, transformation, but also sexual punishment. The man will go on to be remembered by history, while the woman will leave no trace behind, since she has not even fulfilled the fertility function assigned to her by the window imagery.

CHAPTER 2

WOMAN ON THE ROAD
THE HAZARDS OF OPEN SPACE

1. THE RAPE OF DINAH

The Texts
Genesis 30:19–21
Genesis 34
Genesis 49:1, 5–8

Now Dinah the daughter of Leah, whom she had borne to Jacob, went out to see the daughters of the land. And when Shekhem, the son of Hamor the Hivvite, prince of the country, saw her, he took her and lay with her, and humbled her. And his soul was drawn to Dinah the daughter of Jacob, and he loved the girl, and he spoke tenderly to her. And Shekhem spoke to his father Hamor saying, "Get me this girl for a wife." And Jacob heard that he had defiled Dinah his daughter. Now his sons were with his cattle in the field; and Jacob was silent until they were come.

And Hamor the father of Shekhem went out to Jacob to speak with him. And the sons of Jacob came from the field when they heard it; and they were grieved, and they were very angry, because he had done a disgraceful thing in Israel in lying with Jacob's daughter; which thing ought not to be done.

And Hamor spoke with them saying, "The soul of my son Shekhem desires your daughter; I pray you give her to him for wife. And make marriages with us; give your daughters to us, and take our daughters to you. And you shall dwell with us, and the land shall be before you; dwell and trade in it, and get property in it."

And Shekhem said to her father and to her brethren, "let me find favor in your eyes, and what you shall say to me I will give. Ask me never so much dowry and gift, and I will give according as you shall say to me; but give me the girl for wife." And the sons of Jacob answered Shekhem and Hamor in cunning, because he had defiled Dinah their sister. And they spoke, and they said to them, "We cannot do this thing, to give our sister to one that is uncircumcised, for that would be a disgrace to us. But in this we will consent to you: if you will be as we are, that every male of you be circumcised, then we will give our daughter to you, and we will take your daughters to us, and we will dwell with you, and we will become one people. But if you will not hearken to us, to be circumcised, then we will take our daughter, and we will be gone."

And their words pleased Hamor and Shekhem, Hamor's son. And the young man did not delay to do the thing, because he desired Jacob's daughter; and he was the most honored of all the house of his father. And Hamor and Shekhem his son came to the gate of their city, and spoke with the men of their city, saying, "These men are peaceable with us; therefore let them dwell in the land, and trade in it, for the land, behold, it is large enough for them; let us take their daughters to us for wives, and let us give them our daughters. Only on this condition will the men consent to us to dwell with us, to be one people, if every male among us be circumcised. Shall not their cattle and their substance and every beast of theirs be ours? Only let us consent to them, and they will dwell with us."

And to Hamor and to Shekhem his son all that went out of the gate of the city hearkened; and every male was circumcised, all that went out of the gate of the city. And it came to pass on the third day, when they were in pain, that two of the sons of Jacob, Simon and Levi, Dinah's brethren, took each men his sword, and came upon the city unresisted, and slew all the males. And they slew Hamor and Shekhem his son with the edge of the sword, and took Dinah out of Shekhem's house, and went out. The sons of Jacob came upon the slain, and plundered the city, because they had defiled their sister. They took their sheep, their oxen, and their asses, and that which was in the city, and that which was in the field, and all their wealth, and all their little ones, and their wives they took captive, and plundered all that was in the house.

And Jacob said to Simon and Levi, "You have brought trouble on me to make me odious among the inhabitants of the land, among the Canaanites and the Perizities; and I being few in number, they shall gather themselves against me, and slay me; and I shall be destroyed, I and my house."

But they said, "Shall he deal with our sister as with a harlot?" (Gen. 34)

Then Jacob called his sons, and said, "Gather yourselves together, that I may tell you what shall befall you in days to come:

. . . .

Simon and Levi are brothers / Instruments of violence are their
swords
To their council let my soul not be joined / To their assembly let my
honor not be united
For in their anger they slew men / And in their wantonness they
lamed oxen.
Cursed be their anger, for it was fierce / And their wrath, for it was
cruel!
I will divide them in Jacob / And scatter them in Israel
(Gen. 49:1, 5–8)

Rape

The Bible provides several examples of women who dare to break out of their position at the window of the patriarchal home and venture onto the open road. The woman's motivation may be the search for excitement or the need to escape from an oppressive situation, but very often this search ends in the loss of freedom or even of life. Rape becomes not a remote tale of terror, but a gruesome reality. The tale of the rape of Dinah, Jacob's daughter, tucked in and buried under the saga of Jacob and his sons in Genesis, is a little narrative masterpiece that enfolds many of the responses, symptoms, and biases regarding rape that have persisted in Western culture to this day. As such, it sheds light on some of our culture's deep-seated attitudes, uncovering their roots, and helping us understand the more puzzling aspects of these responses, such as the tendency to blame the victim. A close textual analysis of this ancient tale would illuminate those aspects of rape that go beyond sex and violence, and the symbolism that has been attached to the act among men.

At the same time, modern theories of rape would help us understand some of the elements of the story, especially since the biblical text is terse, elliptical, and minimalist in style, suggesting motivations and emotions rather than explicitly informing the reader about them. Contemporary findings could expand the tale's significance beyond its chronological confines, but they might also be challenged by it. The tale might both confirm and question some of the current theories of rape.

Moreover, this tale is one of the earliest male-authored literary texts representing rape, and as such its resemblance to other tales of rape that bear the masculine inscription is of special interest. Feminist scholars have identified the strategy of elision, of simultaneously representing as well as removing the act of molestation from the narrative, as common in many male-originated tales of rape.[1] The present tale is a variation of this strategy. The act of rape is not obscured but is actually named and spelled out as physical violence perpetrated on a woman. Yet its victim, and therefore the act itself as a dramatic focus as well as a traumatic experience for the woman, seems to disappear very early from the narrative and its main concerns. The author's ambivalence to his material, the vacuum that he leaves where the woman and her reaction should be featured—which becomes both a gap and a telling absence—is another characteristic common to male narrators of tales of rape. Rereading the tale both from within its canonical interpretation by male commentators, as well as from a woman-centered vantage point, is another building block in contemporary attempts to reclaim texts about women created from a male perspective.

Mother and Daughter

Space and language interact in our tale as markers defining a woman's journey toward diminution and obliteration. Dinah is first introduced to us through the spatial perspective: she "went out" of one place, her father's home, to another place, the territory of the native people of the land. Her mobility in space is expressed in a verse that gives her the subject-position: Dinah went out. By venturing out of her family compound to explore a foreign territory, Dinah asserts her right for geographical mobility. She is immediately kidnapped, forced into her abductor's home, and pinned down by him in the act of rape until the territorial expanse that she has just experienced is narrowed down to the small space that she occupies in her diminished status as a sedentary, immobile object of rape. After the attack the woman is forgotten, obliterated from the tale. To exist is to conquer space; but Dinah ends up completely disappearing from the tale's orbit, so that midway into the tale, the reader is not even sure where she is.

No descriptive language is used to characterize Dinah, but by spelling out Dinah's reasons for leaving home the text suggests Dinah's personality as gregarious and somewhat restless, a young woman who craves companionship and who ventures out to look for it. Given this initial impression of Dinah, her subsequent silence is somewhat puzzling. Dinah is violated in the most painful, humiliating way, yet her voice is completely muffled. If she screamed for help, cried in shame, or in any other vocal way articulated her feelings at being so brutally attacked, the storyteller does not bother to record it. Even supposing that the inexperienced young woman did not protest, that she was flattered by the attention she received from an important Canaanite prince, the first man in her life, where is her vocabulary of surrender to the newly found sensations of pleasure and love? Later, when she is rescued by her brothers, the girl does not voice any surprise or sense of relief at being released; nor, conversely, if she did cooperate with her kidnapper, does she express fury with the fierce, militant brothers who are forcing her out of her (supposed) love-nest and back to the home of her stern, forbidding father.

In a tale that deals with an exclusively female experience of rape, only the men are allowed to talk. They express grief and anger, plan revenge, negotiate a bride price, and exchange heated words. Every male takes part in the multiple dialogues that lace the story: the girl's father, her brothers, her rapist, the rapist's father, and even the community. Dinah, however, says nothing. No wonder that both the ancient commentators on the story, the Jewish sages, and modern readers of the text (like Sternberg and Sarna) follow the literary focus of the tale, which is the internal fighting within Jacob's own family, and the family's precarious geopolitical existence within the Canaanite community.[2] Although remarking on the suppression of the woman's voice as one of the "gaps" in the tale, male readers, even those who apply modern structural theories to it, cannot rid themselves of the patriarchal angle of the story and the sexist bias at its heart.[3] The literary and psychological analysis, the speculation about motivation and designs, the attention to speeches and their possible intonation are therefore focused on the males who participate in this drama.

The present reading attempts to re-focus the text, forcing on it a center of interest that structurally and theologically belongs outside its perimeters, the female dimension. We will recover the elements that were pushed to the margins of the text as it came down to us through the ages, namely, the woman's psychic responses, the female predicament, the position of the speechless female community, and, mainly, the universal meaning to women that the tale imparts.[4]

The tale begins with a voluntary, defiant action taken by a young woman. Dinah leaves her tribe's encampment and goes looking for female friends from among the daughters of the land. The time is around the seventeenth century BCE. Canaan is occupied by various pagan tribes, some established in the land for many generations, all unfamiliar with the biblical God and the religious and moral codes of the Israelites. Jacob, like his ancestors Abraham and Isaac, is a nomad, traveling through the land with his wives and children, trying to strike roots, acquire land, and live in peace with the longtime inhabitants of the land. Nevertheless, the Israelites are perceived as foreigners, as potential usurpers who have no claim to the land and who can be forced to pick up and leave at any time.

The familial and tribal context of the tale is of great significance. Dinah has twelve brothers but no sisters. Who are her friends? With whom does she associate? How and where will she find her mate? These questions are not given any consideration within the tale, but Dinah's act of going out to look for female companionship speaks of her loneliness, perhaps even unhappiness, in her present existence, as well as great daring. For a biblical tale to open with an action taken by a woman is unusual. Genesis abounds with male tales, commemorating and often celebrating the lives of the patriarchs who entered into a covenantal relationship with God and founded the monotheistic religion. Women's lives revolve around the men as wives and mothers, but other than in these functions, their existence produces no dramatic stories. A tale that starts with an individual woman taking action not on behalf of her husband or son, but out of her own needs, and, furthermore, an action that is incongruous with existing mores and codes of conduct, creates anticipation for a change in the biblical venue. If the first verb in the tale applies to a young woman, then the unfolding drama should follow the girl's adventures. Are we to expect a saga that parallels that of Joseph's, where we follow a young man's geographical and psychological journey, his transformation from a vain and foolishly arrogant lad, safely ensconced in his father's home in Canaan, to a mature and wise person, fit to become the pharaoh's chief counselor?

Adding to these expectations for a tale of youthful adventures, maturation, and ultimate triumph is the information offered about the identity of the girl's mother. For the narrator to tell us that Dinah is Leah's daughter is both unnecessary, for we already know that Leah bore a daughter to Jacob, and unusual, since only the father's name counts in establishing a person's lineage. The image of the unhappy Leah, Jacob's hated wife, thus comes briefly to the fore, reminding us of the tragic destiny of this woman and asking us to draw a hypothetical analogy between mother and daughter. This fleeting moment in which it is possible for the reader to connect mother and daughter is unusual in Scriptures. Although the Bible recounts a variety of family relationships—fathers and sons, husbands and wives, and even fathers and daughters—it offers no tale that highlights the mother-daughter relationship.[5] Both traditional and modern readers of the story (such as Sarna and Sternberg) remark on Jacob's cold reaction to his daughter's ordeal, but fail to attribute crucial relevance to the mother's role. This is not surprising, since the mother, Leah, plays no part in the dramatic events that ensue; she is simply not there. Yet, the first verse of the story mentions Leah and therefore we should pause to consider her.

One might argue that from the point of view of the tale's internal logic Leah's mention is insignificant, that only the modern reader is aware of the crucial role a mother plays in her daughter's life and of the complex dynamics between mother and daughter. If the Bible pays no attention to this kind of interaction, why should we attribute any particular significance to the passing mention of Leah as Dinah's mother?

This is another example where the concept of the reciprocal reading is of relevance. The text tells us much not only about ancient times but also about ourselves today; in turn, we read the tale with the added insights that modern theories have made available to us. So whether the Bible does indeed wish us to pause and consider Leah's role becomes immaterial. We today know that the mother's role in her daughter's life determines decisions and actions taken by the daughter; and therefore Leah's presence here is critical. What is suggested here is not that the ancient storyteller was unaware of the complexities of interpersonal dynamics, among them those between mother and daughter, but that in times where the status-quo was maintained and girls' lives followed familiar routes, the daughter's rebellious impulses were of less significance. But if patterns are broken, then the mother's personality and experience become crucial. We should therefore make the most of the only biblical instance where it is possible for us to view a mother-daughter situation, if not an actual give-and-take between them. The dynamic quality of the tale's opening, the verb first (which is the usual rule of biblical Hebrew grammar), followed by a noun, which here is the girl's name, is somewhat slowed down by our temptation, at this point, to look not forward, "what will Dinah do next?" but rather backward, "how did Leah's destiny shape Dinah's?"

The controlling element in Leah's life was her rejection by Jacob. She was Laban's unattractive daughter who tricked Jacob into marrying her by coming to what was supposed to be her sister's wedding with Jacob disguised as the beautiful bride and remained forever the hated wife. The unhappy Leah rejoiced in the birth of each of her six male sons, repeating every time her hope that the sons will bring Jacob to her bosom.[6] The birth of a daughter, however, created no occasion for a naming ceremony in which the woman's hopes regarding her husband were semantically enfolded in the newborn's name.

The brief mention of Leah in the tale invites speculation. Is Dinah aware of her father's rejection of her mother? She probably is, since Leah has made no secret of her misery, kneading it into her own sons' destinies by attaching their names to it. If names are destiny, then Leah's sons forever carried with them their mother's unhappy existence, her diminishing hopes to gain Jacob's affections. Thus, even before our tale begins, we are aware of a family predetermined to be unhappy. The sheer mention of Leah's name sets the background of a dysfunctional family with four sets of half siblings, a patriarch who prefers one wife over the rest, and a desperately unhappy wife and mother, who probably inculcated a sense of rejection in her children.

The hapless Leah could not sustain her restless daughter or impart to her a sense of self-worth. A woman whose whole existence is defined by her longings for the husband who hates her, and who sees in the birth of each son a possible salvation, is not a mother who can fill her daughter's life with happiness and meaning or affirm the joys of female life. Dinah must have grown up filled with a double sense of isolation: not only does she belong to a tribe which is viewed with suspicion by its neighbors, but within the patriarchal tribe itself she is the daughter of the rejected wife.[7]

Moreover, if a daughter's action is very often the mirror opposite of her mother's existence, then Dinah's forceful, determined appearance in the text as the initiator of a bold move makes sense. To this biblical daughter, the mother is only a negative role model, an example she should not follow. Leah did all the "right things" expected of a woman in patriarchy: she complied with her father Laban's plans to deceive Jacob, she secured a husband for herself, and provided the family with male children. Leah's geographical perimeters were also in compliance with patriarchal rules for women: she moved from her father's home to her husband's. If all that brought Leah misery rather than happiness, however, then her daughter Dinah would carve out a different destiny. The mother was confined to the patriarchal domicile, so the daughter would abandon the safety of the home and move to the open space, to explore a new territorial and cultural ambiance. Leah concurred with the family's preference for endogamy and wedded her cousin, so her daughter would exit the family compound to look for a social life outside it. The ancient Judaic sages condemned Dinah as an early assimilationist, a woman who went out to look for a gentile.[8] The sages' observation, while sexist and ideological in its origins, is correct in one respect: it insightfully detects the act of seeking out strangers as a defining moment in Dinah's life, an intentional attempt to reverse her mother's endogamous example.

Furthermore, Leah had to veil herself, as well as use the cover of nocturnal darkness, in order to get a man, so Dinah would go out in the open, in broad daylight, to see and be seen. Leah was used as a passive object by her father, who connived to get rid of his unmarriageable daughter, as well as by her cold husband, for whom she was only an instrument of procreation. Dinah, therefore, would be the subject, the initiator and mover of events. As the tale opens, Dinah has indeed made herself the subject both grammatically and dramatically. She not only rejects her mother's model, but her actions prove that she tries to emulate the men in her environment. Her brothers' lives were characterized by spatial mobility, exogamous practices, and the freedom to choose their mates. As the tale opens, Jacob's sons are in the field, away from home. When they decide to avenge their sister's honor, they journey to the city of Shekhem, break into it, and wreak havoc. In another tale (Gen. 38) Judah leaves the family compound and settles down elsewhere with a Canaanite woman. Men often experience same-gender bonding, as displayed in a number of instances in Genesis. They also challenge social norms and succeed, as evidenced in Jacob's refusal to accept Esau's status as the firstborn, and in his bypassing of Laban's older daughter and proposing to the younger daughter. Dinah claims the same privileges. Dinah intended to follow the male model and seek same-gender bonding and assume the subject-position, that of the seeker of opportunities, unhindered by geographical and cultural constraints.

Yet in one respect Dinah might be closer to her mother than she realizes. Although Leah seems to be the typical female in patriarchy, docile and cooperative, she also displays an untypical sexual aggression: first in her initial pursuit and sexual entrapment of Jacob; and later, when Jacob divides his time among his wives, Leah trades mandrakes with Rachel in exchange for an "extra" night with Jacob. Here again, the ancient commentators' observation surprisingly buttresses our reading. The rabbis, in their mission to condemn the woman, drew a semantic analogy between the tale of Leah and that of Dinah, contending that just as Leah "went out" to the field to tell Jacob that he must spend the night with her, so her daughter "went out" with the sexual intention of luring a man.[9] To complicate matters, the noun for prostitute in post-biblical Hebrew is "she who goes out." Thus, in looking back, the reader might attribute additional connotations of sexual promiscuity to Dinah's seemingly innocent act of "going out." For the rabbis, the innuendo of a sexual motivation is enough to lead them to conclude with an elision: the act was more of a seduction than a rape.[10] To be fair to Dinah and truthful to the biblical text, we have no way of knowing that Dinah went out to look for a sexual partner. But if we apply the simple laws of nature and, in this particular case, the genetic factors as well, then we may safely propose that natural sexual curiosity did play a role in Dinah's action.

The question is: Will Dinah avoid her mother's tragic life by reversing Leah's example, or will the sense of doom introduced by the image of Leah prevail? Will the daughter free herself of her genetic destiny, or is she inevitably bound to repeat her mother's fate even though she has taken precautions to foil it? Furthermore, will Dinah be able to step out of the female mold into complete personhood, defined here as the ability to conquer space, journey through regions and cultures, and make her own choices?

She Asked for It

Unfortunately, departing from the confines of her family's territory is the only voluntary action taken by Dinah in our tale. As soon as she asserts her control over her destiny, she is seized by the son of the prince of the land and raped. Her attempt to extricate herself from her mother's typically female predicament catapults her into a typical female experience, one that most clearly exemplifies women's vulnerability, circumscribed existence, and status as easy prey.

From this moment on Dinah is transformed from the independent subject to the object of men: first as Shekhem's victim, then as the object of his ardent love, and later as the family's bargaining chip in prolonged and tricky commercial and political negotiations. Finally, she becomes the cause of great bloodshed and of a rift between father and sons. Although pivotal in the tale, Dinah is not only speechless, but seems to be absent. She disappears from both the trajectory and the discourse in the tale. The questions the reader is teased into asking have to do with the men in the tale. Were her brothers really angry about the rape or about something else? Does the rapist agree to become circumcised so he can marry Dinah and heal her wounds, or is he motivated by other considerations? Is Jacob angry with the man who caused his daughter's ordeal, or is he angry with her for damaging the family's honor and threatening its relations with its neighbors?

Dinah's silence is a structural device that heightens our interest in the story, a "gap" that adds to the beauty and power of this ancient tale of crime and vengeance. A male-centered literary reading, however, remarks on the aesthetic value of the woman's silence, but ultimately abandons the wordless Dinah in favor of the feuding males. A re-focused reading that places Dinah in her rightful, central place within the tale, however, sees in Dinah's puzzling muteness a stylistic technique to stimulate our curiosity about the woman herself as well as the meaning of rape in the ancient culture.

A memorable female protagonist in a modern novel, Caddy in William Faulkner's *The Sound and the Fury* (another "defiled sister"), is also deprived of a voice, and comes to life for us only through the eyes of her brothers. The analogy is only partially meaningful, however; Faulkner's Caddy does indeed have a very strong presence in the novel because her brothers' internal monologues center exclusively on her. The absent Caddy seems to occupy her male siblings' waking hours and fill their hallucinatory moments. The biblical Dinah, by contrast, hardly has this kind of psychic and existential impact on her brothers. She is their pawn in political and economic negotiations with their neighbors, a symbol of the family honor and strength, but as a breathing, living individual she has no relevance in their lives. It is not possible to read Faulkner's novel and not become intimately acquainted with Caddy's appealing personality, but it is possible to read the biblical episode and be carried away by the power struggle among the males and completely forget Dinah. Only if we reread Dinah's wordless absence as a scream can we do her justice. Dinah's silence should be read not only as a nice stylistic touch; it should be explored for its psychological roots, and it should also be seen as a cultural message sent to the woman in the tale and to all anonymous women on the fringes of the biblical arena.

A psychological reading of Dinah's muteness might tie the ancient rape victim to young girls in later times, like Maya Angelou, who also lost their speech as a result of rape, but who grew up in a culture that eventually gave them the opportunity and the medium to become the eloquent recorders of a woman's feelings of shame and guilt. Dinah's case is thus an early example of the loss of speech that can result from sexual assault. While the marriage negotiations proceed, she is still in a state of psychic trauma and unable to communicate verbally. Dinah's later silence, after she had been released and returned home, conveys a sense of overpowering guilt: she has been the cause of a great massacre in which all the males of one city were decimated, their wealth looted, and wives and children taken captive. The sense of guilt has been recorded as a typical victim's reaction, especially when the perpetrator is brought to justice. Angelou tells of being consumed by guilt when she learned that her molester was found murdered.[11]

If Dinah was not traumatized beyond words, if the man's attention and tenderness following the rape mitigated her initial shock, then her silence may have been an age-old female tactic of survival. Protest and resistance could have further angered the perpetrator, while, conversely, any campaigning on his behalf could have further enraged her family and cast her in the disgraced status of the sexual collaborator.[12] No matter what the woman will say, she will bring more unwanted attention to herself; the resort to silence, "playing dumb," may be the best strategy for withstanding her ordeal.

The psychological angle alone still does not account for the narrator's failure to inform us that Dinah was left verbally incapacitated by the trauma of the rape, or to provide us with some other reason for her condition, if it is indeed a clinical one. Dinah's silence is a textual fact—no words are attributed to her—but it is not a textual element. Neither the protagonists or the recorder of the events observed or remarked on her silence within the text.

The full significance of Dinah's removal from the verbal fabric of the tale can be understood only if we move beyond the stylistic and psychological implications to consider the cultural context, both in terms of the culture's approach to rape and how it allows rape to be represented. Dinah's verbal absence may be best understood as a cultural comment, a message to women that rape will not be considered as a woman's ordeal but as an event significant to men, and that its repercussions are economic and political rather than emotional. The values and mores of a male-dominant civilization are created by men and thus they define the socio-cultural context of rape.[13]

Although Dinah's emotions are not deemed important enough to be recorded, the men's reactions are amply conveyed. Most disturbing is Jacob's attitude, which is that of a stern patriarch, not a loving father. He decides to keep silent when he hears that his daughter has been "defiled" and wait for his sons' return. For Jacob, Dinah becomes, within the cultic frame of thinking, defiled and impure. But Jacob has no reaction to his daughter's feminine and human predicament; the father does not acknowledge his daughter's suffering and personal humiliation, but reacts as the head of a religious community that has specific terms for the particular state in which Dinah now finds herself. Jacob further acts as the diplomatic and responsible head of the tribe, but not as the concerned father, when he decides to wait for his sons, who are away in the field, before he reacts.

Strategic caution might explain why Jacob makes no public comment, or why he does not challenge or reprimand the Hivvites, why he does not immediately confront them and ask for apologies and recompense. He needs the enforcement of his impressive adult sons. We have no evidence that Jacob is simply controlling his emotions. We know from other episodes that Jacob is a highly passionate man. He bursts out crying the first time he sees Rachel, and he is inconsolable when Joseph is lost. Therefore, Jacob's apparent lack of emotion and his sober, calculated reaction, while politically wise, seem to reveal a certain coldness and lack of fatherly affection for his daughter. The only time in the tale when he reveals emotions is at the end when he heatedly reprimands his sons for the massacre that they have perpetrated, which might jeopardize the Israelite's precarious political position. Jacob's reticence stands in contrast to his sons' emotional reaction and their genuine sorrow and concern for their sister. During the marriage negotiations with the Hivvites, Jacob remains silent and allows his sons to deal with Shekhem and his father. When Dinah finally returns home after a bloody rescue operation, Jacob does not find it necessary to talk to the girl herself. Instead, he criticizes his sons for acting recklessly and endangering the entire clan.

Significantly, Jacob's wrath is directed only at Simeon and Levi, two of Dinah's six full brothers, who broke into Shekhem's house to get to their sister, but who, unlike the other brothers, did not take part in the looting of the city. Jacob thus betrays his dislike for the sons of his unloved wife, as well as a lack of paternal affection toward the daughter born to him by this wife. Later, when Jacob is on his deathbed he also censures Simeon and Levi severely for the violence and cruelty that they supposedly committed: "Cursed be their anger for it was fierce / and their wrath, for it was cruel" (Gen. 49:5–7). Ironically, while Jacob singles out Simeon and Levi to condemn them, in the story itself they stand out as more sincere and devoted to their sister, and less greedy, than the other brothers.

Jacob's angry final words may give us a clue to his underlying emotion throughout the sequence of events: Jacob is furious, not with the Hivvites, but with his own daughter. The anger that should be directed at the perpetrator of the crime is conveniently directed at its victim. If the girl had not broken customary patterns, if she stayed at home, none of this would have happened: the rape, the bloody revenge, and the danger to the tribe's very future in the land of Canaan.

Unfortunately for Dinah, Jacob fails to realize that so much of his own personality and modes of conduct, especially in his youth, are mirrored in his daughter. Jacob, too, was a young person who defied accepted customs. Ancient traditions gave privileges to the firstborn in the family, but Jacob tricked his brother into selling him the birthright, and his father into giving him the blessing intended for his brother. Jacob further attempted to destroy old molds when it came to marital customs by proposing to Laban's younger daughter when he knew full well that the older daughter was still not spoken for. Jacob's life was characterized by great mobility and epic movements across large spaces. He left his home in Canaan to go north, to Padan Aram, then returned to Canaan, wandered through the land, and finally died in Egypt. Yet he disapproves of his daughter's wanderlust. If Jacob did see his youthful self replicated in Dinah, it is the mark of the patriarchal state of mind that what might be a source of pleasure to a modern father, seeing his own youthful self repeated in his daughter, is an experience not known to the ancient paterfamilias.

The father's disapproving, cold reticence is somewhat mitigated by the brothers' genuine sorrow and concern for their sister. In the final analysis, though, the brothers' treatment of their sister is somewhat impersonal and very possessive. They do not refer to Dinah by her name, but only as "our sister," implying that their concern for her is primarily motivated by the fact that whatever happens to their sister reflects on them. For Jacob's sons, who attempt to transform their status from that of foreign nomads to lawful residents and landowners, the violation of their sister by the prince of the land is a political warning. In a sense, if the daughter is molested, the whole tribe is seen as raped; the act implies that the woman and her tribe have no rights or status in this land. By courageously rescuing their sister, the brothers are making a political statement to the neighboring tribes, signaling to them that they will not tolerate any form of threat to their honor and to their claim to the land.

We notice, as well, that the male lexicon is filled with cultic-theological terms (the girl is "defiled," the Israelite's religion insists on circumcision), or commercial ones (if you marry into our tribe you will benefit economically and become proper residents of the land as well); but the girl's physical or emotional condition does not find its proper language. The speakers are men. Women, including the girl's mother, are absent, and the conversation centers on the "masculine" concerns of trade and land. The Hivvites, too, agree to the circumcision not for romantic reasons but out of utilitarian considerations.

The Hivvites attempt to effect a male bonding at the expense of Dinah and the women of both tribes. Claude Levi-Strauss suggests that "marriage is an archetype of exchange" and that women are objects whose exchange between a group of men is a means of binding men together.[14] Thus the Hivvites propose not only the exchange of Dinah for a large bride price, but also the exchange of the tribal women between the two groups.

The political message that the brothers read into the rape of their sister is substantiated by the underlying sexual discourse. The rape of the woman has rendered her male kin female; the latters' response is to desexualize the Hivvites, taking away their masculinity temporarily, as they recover from their circumcision. The Hivvites then become "female," sexually weakened, immobile by pain and, most importantly, unable to protect their own females.

Thus the culture has transformed what should have been a woman's story into a drama about a male struggle for dominance. Internally, the rape exemplifies the sibling tension and rivalry in Jacob's polygynous family; it also offers another occasion for Jacob to display his unequal treatment of his sons. In terms of the geopolitical aspect of the tale, the woman's wrecked honor stands for the clash of two cultures and is tied to larger questions regarding the future survival of the family and the ownership of the land.

The brief episode of the rape of Dinah, inserted within the larger saga of the early Israelites' struggle to strike roots in the Land of Canaan, is a correlative of the geopolitical tension in the region.[15] The age-old close identification of woman with land or earth is meaningful in this context. It converts the story of the woman to a parable about men's fight for territorial, economic, and sexual dominance. Within the dramatic representation the woman is objectified and deprived of her humanity and individuality. She is the object of violation by a man, a commodity in commercial negotiations between two male communities, a catalyst of cementing or ruining male bonding. Femaleness becomes a mere token employed by feuding men; those who are able to appropriate women and usurp their bodies are "male," while those who are incapable of protecting their women are rendered "female." Dinah loses her individuality and becomes a cipher denoting femaleness, which is considered an inferior state of being, an insult that the two feuding male groups hurl at each other. But, as is often the case in male-authored narratives, the real person is submerged, silenced, and forgotten.

The tale imparts a cultural message that makes it a classic example of the meaning of being a female in a "rape society," as well as of the biased attitudes regarding rape and its victim that have persisted through the ages.[16] To be female means to be rapable, to lose the ability to speak, and to occupy as little space as possible. Spatial mobility, voluntary, independent action, diplomatic and economic negotiations, and decisions that determine the fate of the total community, such as wars and peace treaties, are the arena of men. Furthermore, if a woman leaves the protection of the patriarchal roof, she can expect to be molested. Therefore, venturing out of the family protection is tantamount to "asking for it"; the woman should not be surprised at the violent consequences of her irresponsibility.

Furthermore, a woman has no business breaking long-standing social and familial traditions; she must follow known patterns even if they bring only heartbreak and misery. If she dares expose herself to danger she will bring disaster not only on herself and her violator, but also on the entire community that might become involved in a bloody vendetta. Within the patriarchal trajectory there is no female perspective to rape; only men should handle rape in all its aspects, dealing with the rapist as well as with the victim. Women should not be involved since they have nothing to offer. The more powerful a woman's tribe is, the more it is likely to use force to avenge the act of rape, causing the cruel victimization of many innocent people. Many acts of rape might result if the one act of rape becomes known. No matter how much the woman has suffered, her father, representing the voice of patriarchal society, will be angry with her, will not sympathize with her misery, and will consider her the cause of the scandal that has occurred.

Therefore, the avenged victim should feel responsible for transforming her own male kin to bloodthirsty savages. If a woman can at all help it, she must keep the rape a secret and not make it known to her family and community. If the rape becomes known, the woman's strategy for survival might be silence, disappearance from the scene, turning attention away from herself, as little assertion of her existence as possible.

The tale further exemplifies that most men did not condemn the act of rape for its moral wrong. The same men who were enraged at the rape of a woman from among their kin might be the brutal victimizers of the women of another clan. This stemmed from the approach that did not necessarily view a rapist as a sick, detestable person. The distance between sexual aggression and love was seen as small; the violent rapist could turn into a tender lover.[17] In rapid succession, the biblical narrator informs us that Shekhem rapes Dinah and then falls in love with her. Rape is not viewed as a serious offense against a woman's body and soul, but against her people as an ethnic, collective identity. A clan's protection of its women, and its fury at the molestation of its females, has not much to do with humanitarian compassion and collective loyalty. It is not the individual suffering woman who brings out the tribe's grief and sorrow. The woman, as the procreator and bearer of the future generation, stands for the land and the people that would own it. The molestation of a tribe's women signals the declining power of the tribe. It means that a stronger race has planted its seed in the tribe's females, and therefore, the next generation born on the land would belong to the new race. The woman's avengers are not motivated by compassion for her but by their concern for the tribal honor, as well as for their geopolitical survival and the preservation of their own seed on the land.

Throughout history soldiers of victorious armies engaged in mass rapes of the women of their defeated foes. The ultimate symbol of triumph was always the possession of the enemy's females. For the individual soldier, the act of rape meant probably a release of a heightened sense of violence and masculine potency, as well as the breaking of taboos, brought out on the battlefield. Collectively, though, rapes during war were motivated by one race's subconscious desire to completely dispossess and destroy the ethnic group or the people whom they had fought by impregnating their women, thus making them the carriers of the seed of the conquering race.

How can modern perspectives shed more light on this powerful ancient tale? Several current theories share the belief that rape is the ultimate expression of male violence toward women, but they differ in their interpretations of the role of rape in the history of civilization. Those who claim that women's subordination has its historical roots in the economic dependence of women on men in early societies see in all forms of aggression toward women a reflection of female subordination. A variety of studies conducted in this country, especially since the 1970s, have confirmed the theory that the impetus behind rape is not sexual desire but rather anger and hostility that result in many forms of antisocial behavior, one of which is rape. A male might take out his antisocial fury on women because women, like other disenfranchised groups throughout history, have been unable to reciprocate with violence. Shekhem, however, has no reason to enact antisocial fury. He is the son of the prince of the land, and as soon as his father hears of his son's wish to marry Dinah, he acts on his behalf. A materialistic interpretation of Shekhem's action might still be valid here. We have seen that economic considerations play a major part in the negotiations process. We understand that the Hivvites, though rulers of the land, have viewed the thriving Israelite nomads with suspicion and perhaps fear of their economic expansion. Shekhem may have chosen to send a political message to the Israelites through the woman because he figured that this was the easiest and safest thing to do. The materialistic theory, then, sheds light on the economic fear that might have subconsciously motivated Shekhem, and explains his rape of the defenseless Dinah as a gesture of hostility and defiance toward the economically ambitious Israelites.

A different theory of rape has been forwarded by modern feminists such as Susan Brownmiller and her followers, who claim that violence against women, especially rape, has been the main instrument with which men established and perpetuated their dominance over women.[18] Though committed by few men through the ages, rape benefited all men; it was a crime carried out by few men on behalf of many. The fact that crimes of violence against women still have low conviction rates, that blaming the victim of sexual violence is pervasive, and that sexual violence is not taken seriously may point to a tacit solidarity among men to use the violence perpetrated by some individuals, and publicly condemned by most men, as symbolic of the power of all men against women, a threat that would induce women to seek male protection and comply with male authority. The many statistics that prove that unattached women are more likely to be raped or robbed than married women again may imply a subtle hint from male society to women to look for male protection as a means of survival, thus sustaining the supremacy of the male and the submission of women. Furthermore, intimidation of women through sexual molestation and harassment has always served as a constant reminder to women of their vulnerability, and has serious consequences regarding the quality of women's lives. Women have developed fear of men, resulting in self-imposed constrictions, reluctance to open up to new opportunities, and in the tendency to toe the line and not overstep the boundaries of timid female behavior as defined by men.

The theory of the subconscious bonding of all men against women through the act of rape may on the face of it be challenged by the biblical tale. Our story shows quite the contrary, that rape has caused a serious and major rift between the Israelites and their neighbors; it also opened up family wounds and bared tensions between father and sons, and disagreement among the sons themselves. Nevertheless, a male bonding of some sort does occur. All men, whether Israelites or Hivvites, act the same: they are violent and they victimize women. Thus the message to women from both sides is the same, namely, that in the feuds between men it is women who will suffer most, that their suffering has a particular feminine slant to it, and that sexual victimization is the woman's fate. If Jacob's sons are furious with the Hivvite for molesting their sister, at the subconscious level they may be grateful to him for bringing home the point that women ought to stay under the protection of their men and not challenge male authority. Shekhem has made sure that Dinah will give no more grief to her father and brothers. The tale transmits the sense of the female fear of men, not only of the enemy, but also of her own kin, thus reinforcing Brownmiller's school of thought.

At the same time, Brownmiller's theory, that rape of one woman is a violent message from all men to all women, has to be somewhat modified in the light of our tale. Let us not forget that the biblical text is male authored, and therefore its male message should not be doubted. The men in this tale see in the rape of a woman a message from the men of one clan to the men of another clan. The universal message to all women is secondary in the tale, not its main purpose.

Where Is Dinah?

Our tale opens with Dinah leaving home, claiming the right to spatial mobility for herself and freedom from paternal supervision. It ends with Dinah's father complaining that the events that she triggered have further jeopardized the already precarious status of his clan. We know that Dinah's time in the open spaces is short-lived since she is immediately forced into Shekhem's house. But during the many sensational events that follow, Dinah is absent not only semantically; she seems to have disappeared from the spatial boundaries of the tale as well. The question is twofold: where is Dinah during the crucial events of the tale, and where does she want to be?

The answer to the first question is withheld from the reader until almost the very end of the narrative. During the marriage negotiations the brothers suggest that if the Hivvites are not interested in being circumcised then they, Jacob and his sons, will just take their sister and leave. Yet it comes as somewhat of a surprise that Dinah's brothers have to rescue her by force. If Shekhem indeed loved her as he claimed and wanted to change her status from a disgraced girl to a respectable woman, why did he not send her back to her father, to await the outcome of the negotiations? If Dinah became his lawful bride, she could then be brought to his home directly from her father's abode, following the route of every respectable virgin bride, from father to husband. If Dinah is still held in Shekhem's home after the initial act of rape, however, then she is virtually a hostage. No matter what conditions are being set during the seemingly civilized negotiations, Shekhem will always have the upper hand because he holds the woman. If the brothers do not agree to his proposal, he will have the woman anyway. The massacre that ensues is easier to explain. It converts the brothers from bloodthirsty, greedy savages to an army responding to hostage-takers with a show of force. If the premise is that Dinah must be returned home, then the only way to bring her home is by force, since Shekhem would not release her otherwise.

Did Dinah want to return home? Let us consider her situation, and reconstruct what actually happened to her. Dinah, of course, did not plan to be raped nor did she in any way lure Shekhem and cause him to rape her. Once she loses her virginity, however, it will probably be very difficult for her to find a respectable husband. Before her stretches a whole lifetime as a "defiled," unmarried woman at the mercy of her strict, unloving father, and, later, as a poor relative shuttling among her brothers' busy households. We know that women in captivity sometimes believe they have fallen in love with their captors. The crucial element is that Shekhem professes to love her, and he speaks "tenderly" to her. We never hear Dinah's father or brothers talking tenderly to her, not even when she is back and is probably looking for the father's loving embrace and comforting words. Given all this, it is not far-fetched to assume that Dinah, the nonconformist, decided to cooperate with her violator once she assessed the gravity of her social situation. Staying with the man who claimed to love her was certainly better than returning to an unhappy mother, a neglectful father, and hotheaded brothers.

Jacob's anger with his sons Simeon and Levi might imply that he did not view Shekhem as the only culprit. We may assume that Shekhem intimated to the family that he had Dinah's consent and was not keeping her by force. The absence of a reunion scene between daughter and parents thus makes more sense. The ancient rabbis, reading the text closely, but also building on oral traditions that were probably woven around the written tale, condemned the girl for resisting being freed from Shekhem's home. The sages said bluntly that Dinah refused to leave Shekhem's home and had to be dragged out of his house, explaining that "when a woman is intimate with an uncircumcised person she finds it hard to tear herself away."[19] The rabbis' commentary may have been propelled by their fierce campaign against those who attempted to marry outside the faith. Yet their reading, with all the sexist bias inherent in it, displays insight. They attribute Dinah's wish to stay with her attacker to base sexual motivation. But we may concur with their opinion that Dinah wanted to stay in Shekhem's home and become his wife, because that was the best option for her.[20]

As for Shekhem's claim that he loved Dinah and that his heart was tied to her: we may view this kind of "love" with suspicion and suggest that a man who is capable of raping a woman is not truly capable of loving.[21] Love, as Erich Fromm explains in *The Art of Loving,* is an act of giving, and it can happen only between equals.[22] Shekhem's initial act is taking by force someone who is inferior to him physically and socially. Nevertheless, given the customs of ancient times, where the lords of the land had total control over all aspects of their subjects' lives, and given Jacob's nomadic status, Shekhem's act was not out of the ordinary. He partially redeems himself in our eyes when he makes a sacrifice and agrees to the ordeal of circumcision. But even if we view Shekhem's conversion from a tormentor to a loving, considerate man as naïve, and male-engendered, the fact remains that to the inexperienced Dinah, who saw only rejection and coldness at home, Shekhem's protestations of love may have sounded sincere and, in return, elicited her own love. It is clear that Dinah was thus doubly victimized in the tale: first by Shekhem and then by her brothers.

We began our study of the Dinah episode by going backward in time to recall the sad life of Dinah's mother. We realized that Dinah's action, surprisingly refreshing and unexpected in a chain of tales devoted to men's doings, was "fraught with background," to use Erich Auerbach's description of biblical narrative, so we were justified in digging into Dinah's familial, and especially maternal, heritage.[23] The tale, however, has no closure as far as

61

Dinah is concerned—there is no "welcome home" scene, no warm embrace by any family member.

We cannot open the story up into the future, or move forward in time and space to envision Dinah's remaining years. We hear that Dinah was among those who immigrated with Jacob to Egypt many years later. We cannot rejoice in the fact that Dinah's cravings for new places and people were satisfied, if we consider that within the constraints of ancient times, for a woman who was no longer a virgin to be attached to her father meant a fate worse than death. We never hear from Dinah again, but we can safely say that the woman who ventured into the open spaces early in her life, to broaden the perimeters of her existence, spent the rest of her years under the most constricted, hemmed-in social and spatial circumstances.

2. THE HAPLESS CONCUBINE

The Text
Judges 19; 20:3–10

And it came to pass in those days . . . that there was a certain Levite sojourning on the far side of Mount Efraim, who took to him a concubine of Bethlehem Judah. And his concubine played the harlot (was faithless to him) and left him to her father's house in Bethlehem . . . And her husband arose, and went after her, to speak to her heart and bring her back. (Judg. 19:1–3)

And the man seized his concubine, and brought her out to them; and they raped her, and abused her all the night until the morning, and at dawn they let her go. Then came the woman in early morning, and fell down at the door of the man's house where her lord was, until it was light. And her lord rose up in the morning, and opened the doors of the house, and went to go his way; and, behold, the woman his concubine was fallen down at the entrance of the house, and her hands were upon the threshold. And he said to her: "Up, and let us be going." But there was no answer. . . . And when he was come to his house, he took a knife, and laid hold of his concubine, and divided her . . . into twelve pieces. (Judg. 19:25–29)

The "Official" Version: She Brought It On Herself

The tale of the concubine chronicles travels that embrace considerable distances. The traveling protagonists spend time in different patriarchal homes, and their adventures are punctuated by dialogues and verbal negotiations. At the dramatic heart of the tale is a scandalous event, the gang rape of a woman.

Although this woman is the one who travels, and the one on whose behalf the male protagonist travels, and on whose body a great crime is perpetrated, her presence, both physical and verbal, is an elision, a gap in the tale. The tale of the Levite and the concubine reads like a good detective story: there is a crime at its center, the obvious culprit(s), and the hidden criminal. The surface layer of the tale, providing us with the sequence of events, the conversations, and the geographical settings, is told in an undeniably male voice and identifies immediately the guilty parties. Yet, if we follow the tale through the blank spot at its heart, the unnamed, silent, and eventually mutilated woman, the subtext that comes to the fore offers a different version of the events and the personalities involved.

This is the account offered to us by a narrator representing the tenets of a male-dominant culture and committed, on the face of it, to chronicling an event with political and historical repercussions: A Levite takes a concubine for himself. The woman, an unfaithful sort, suddenly picks up and leaves her husband, returning to her father's home in Bethlehem, at the far end of the country. The Levite is left alone at home, in a desolate northern part of ancient Israel, a remote, hilly terrain, where one is bound to feel lonely even under happier circumstances. The woman's father lives in Bethlehem, an urban area, a much busier part of the land, more densely populated and accessible than the mountainous terrain of Efraim where her husband resides.

After four months the Levite realizes that his wife will not return to him on her own and sets out to Bethlehem, with an impressive entourage, to reconcile with his concubine. As he arrives, the young woman sees him first and lets him into the house, where her father welcomes him with great delight. The Levite spends several days with his concubine's father, eating, drinking, and making merry. On the fifth day he wants to leave early, but is persuaded to sit down for another feast with his father-in-law; when the party finally leaves it is rather late in the day. At sundown, the Levite decides to enter the Benjaminite city of Gibea, to spend the night there. The Levite and his entourage are taken in by a hospitable old man, but as they eat supper, a group of local thugs surrounds the house and demand that the old man deliver his guest to them. The old man offers his own virgin daughter and the Levite's concubine, and after back-and-forth negotiations the concubine is handed over to the noisy crowd outside. They torture and rape her all night, and in the morning her husband finds her dead at the doorstep. Outraged, he cuts her corpse into twelve parts and disseminates them all over Israel. The people of Israel are appalled, and a civil war ensues between the tribes of Israel and the tribe of Benjamin. The Israelites ultimately triumph but the war takes a costly toll on both sides. Finally, the tribes are reconciled and the people of Israel are reunited in peace. We must conclude that once again, as in the tale of Dinah, a woman's unwarranted act has resulted in a bloody war and loss of human lives.

The tale bears all the marks of a familiar situation in which women could find themselves not only in biblical times, but in more progressive times as well. A woman runs away from her husband's home; the natural place to go is back to her hometown, to father's home. She stays there, but not for long. No matter what her reasons are for leaving her husband, once he comes to fetch her, she will have to leave with him. The way back home is long and dangerous; the Levite talks to his male servant, but never addresses his wife. His silence is condemning, menacing. If she had not started it, if she had not left home, he would not have had to go to all the expenses and bother of traveling from one end of the country to the other, and they would not have found themselves in a desolate, dangerous place at nightfall. When the danger becomes imminent and the threat to their lives real, the woman will pay with her life. After all, she is the one responsible for this unfortunate situation in the first place; she put herself and her master in jeopardy, so she will suffer the consequences.

The gang rape that seems to be the dramatic climax of the suspenseful plot becomes secondary to the reader interested in the unnamed female protagonist. The rape and torture of the woman figure within the larger historical fabric of Judges as a prelude to and trigger of the civil war that followed. Because our mission is to recover and reconstruct the life of this ancient woman, however, this tale has a different focus altogether. It is a tale about the treachery of several patriarchal figures and their homes; consequently, it is about the evils of patriarchy, the illusory nature of its benign rule, and the dangers of making women dependent on men for their respectability, food, and sheer survival.

Father and Daughter

Three men, all older than the unnamed female protagonist, figure in this tale in major roles: her father, her husband, and the old man, her host. All three appear as possible protectors and benefactors of the woman, since all provide her with shelter. The three patriarchal homes are located in three different places in the country—the father lives in the south, the Levite in the far north, and the old man somewhere in between, though much closer to the father's home—so several journeys are being taken from one location to the other. These homes are not just three geographical points, however, for each becomes an emotional and dramatic center in the heroine's downward spiral to psychological and then physical ruin.

Our protagonist first travels from her father's home in Bethlehem to her husband's home in Efraim, presumably with her husband-master, the Levite. This trip is not narrated in detail for nothing out of the ordinary happens. She then takes to the road again, when she leaves her husband and returns home to her father in Bethlehem. We have to assume that the woman is unescorted, since she practically runs away from her husband. This trip, too, is uneventful. Although the woman travels the long way alone, nothing happens to her. She takes the same route again in the opposite direction, from Bethlehem to Mount Efraim, this time accompanied by both the Levite and a male servant. On this journey, the same route that seemed safe for the woman when she was on her own, proves to be deadly when she is escorted by two men. She is seized by a group of hooligans in Gibea, brutally raped and left for dead.

The three patriarchs and their homes prove to be incapable of protecting the woman. Of the three homes, the father's seems to be the safest; it is in the territory of the tribe of Judah, and we are to understand that the father is of this tribe. A man residing lawfully within the territory of his own tribe is, in the context of the tumultuous tribal relations chronicled in Judges, in an advantageous position. What is more, not only does this father own a home, but the town where his home is located is called Bethlehem, "the house of bread." There is a double sense of security, comfort, and plenty in these patriarchal quarters, ensconced in the midst of the extended family and tribe, in a town whose name alone suggests a large, embracing home-haven, well supplied with food and other physical comforts.

One day the heroine is torn away from the security of father's home in Bethlehem to become the concubine of a Levite who resides in the remote hilly part of the northern region of Israel. The change in life's circumstances and status for this young woman is dramatic and her new position in life stands in stark contrast to her previous existence. First, her master's home is not a house but a tent (19:9). Second, he belongs to a tribe that was allocated no land, but was dispersed among all the children of Israel. Therefore, while he resides in the region of Efraim, he is not an Eframite but a resident alien who owns no land or permanent home. Third, the young woman arrives in her new dwelling place not as its reigning mistress, but as the man's concubine, a servant-wife.

The first question the storyteller leaves unanswered is why the woman is taken as a concubine and not as a primary wife.[24] The Levite may already have a wife, or he may wish to wait until he has enough bride price to get a more desirable wife, either more beautiful or of a more distinguished family. Whatever the Levite's reasons are, he is not willing to bestow the status of a full-fledged wife on this woman.

But what about the father? Why did he agree to give his daughter away as a concubine? A concubine is virtually a servant; she lacks the social status, as well as the financial guarantees, enjoyed by a man's primary wife. We know that Leah and Rachel gave their handmaids to Jacob for the purpose of bearing children to him. A man could take a foreign woman captured in war as a concubine, or he could buy for himself a free Israelite girl from her father and make her his concubine.[25] So the father virtually sold his daughter to the Levite as a concubine. We know that this father is not a poor man, as is amply illustrated later. He may have been desperate to rid himself of his daughter because no other suitor presented himself. Greed may have played a part in the father's decision. The Levite may have offered him a better bride price than did others, but with the stipulation that the girl become a concubine only. The father could have, perhaps, married his daughter off as a primary wife if he offered a dowry; but he either was unwilling to part with the money, or he had other daughters to think of, or this daughter herself was a concubine's child and therefore less important among his daughters and not worthy enough for her father to spend money over.

It is even possible that the father did not get any bride price for his daughter since the Levite was not an affluent person. Levites lived off donations from the community in the midst of which they resided, and this Levite's congregation, "in the remote hills of Efraim," was probably impoverished and not in a position to afford a lavish lifestyle for their Levite. The Levite's mere willingness to take the Bethlehemite's daughter off her father's hands was temptation enough for the latter to agree to this arrangement. Only the Levite's social status sheds a more positive light on the father's compliance with the Levite's offer of an inferior marital arrangement. A Levite was a teacher and mediator between God and the community; he tended to the people's spiritual and cultic needs, and, as such, even a poor Levite was not an undesirable match for a daughter of an affluent, status-conscious father. If the father did have some doubts or reservations, then his future son-in-law's prestigious tribal affiliation may have allayed them.

Nevertheless, it is clear at the very opening of the tale that this young woman has been betrayed, that her father wanted her to leave home, and that he did not mind that she was leaving the patriarchal home as a daughter and moving to another home as a servant.[26] The father's attitude, coupled with the Levite's unwillingness to take her as a full-fledged wife, must have been a blow to the girl's self-esteem. Her silence, therefore, has a twofold origin: the narrator, like the father himself, does not deem it important to consider or record the girl's opinion, but he may also be transmitting to us the girl's shocked, speechless reaction to the sudden change in her life. She is treated like chattel, which is reflected grammatically as well: she is the object and the Levite the subject: he "takes" her.

She is not happy in her new home. Standards of living are certainly lower than those she has known in Bethlehem. Nor does she seem to have a man who loves her, for in the next verse this silent, acted-upon woman, a person timid enough not to protest vehemently at being reduced from daughter to servant, boldly takes action; she leaves her master-husband and takes to the road, on a long journey south to her father's home.

The storyteller does not openly explain why she leaves her husband. Nevertheless, two elements in the tale that come later help us understand, in retrospect, the possible reasons for the woman's departure. The Levite's action four months later, his decision to "speak to her heart," implies a sense of guilt. He understands that he must appease her, to ask forgiveness, while she is the wronged party that has to be dealt with kindly and tenderly and be gently persuaded to return.[27] When the Levite arrives in Bethlehem he does not register any grievance with the father, nor does he reproach him for letting his daughter stay away from her husband for so long. Surely had he felt that he was the wronged party, that he had a serious complaint against his concubine, the Levite would have talked to the father harshly.

For his part, the father, who was anxious to sell his daughter away for a life as an inferior wife, now allows her to stay home for four months (or, a year and four months, according to some readings). In a way, the girl is no longer under her father's control, and by not urging her to leave, the father is holding onto a property not his anymore. Nevertheless, the father never scolds his daughter for making such a daring, unusual move, never urges her to return to her lawful master. No conversation between father and daughter is given, but either the woman gave her father a report so convincing that he was moved to let her stay, or his daughter's unhappy appearance, perhaps even some evidence of physical abuse, makes the father relent and allow her in his house indefinitely. Although the reactions of both husband and father to the woman's unorthodox move is rather timid, the community's opinion is clearly against the woman. "She acted unfaithfully" (or "she played the harlot") is society's voice, its way of explaining the woman's abandonment of her husband. More than anything else, this phrase gives us a clear idea of the cultural attitudes and mores of the times. A woman who leaves her husband's home is by definition unfaithful, therefore deserving to have her action labeled "harlotry." If the woman was indeed a harlot, she would have been ashamed and afraid to run away to her father; her respectable, well-to-do father would not have opened his doors to her, and the Levite would not have come to talk "to her heart." It is clear that the phrase "acted unfaithfully" is not a description of facts, but a harsh moral judgment that the community has passed on an innocent woman who has acted in a manner highly irregular in this culture, one that might serve as a bad example to women. When the plot unfolds, the woman emerges not at all a harlot, but as a blameless, silent victim.[28]

At this point we may ask about the whereabouts of the girl's mother. Like Leah, this mother is not given a voice in a story that narrates her daughter's brutal victimization. We have no way of knowing whether the mother is dead, and therefore not there to sway her husband from giving their daughter away as a concubine, or whether she is still alive, but not in a position to intervene in her husband's decisions, or whether she herself is a concubine and therefore acquiescing to her daughter's fate as a repetition of her own.[29]

Other women, such as aunts or older sisters, are not there to offer the girl support. We know from the Book of Ruth that during the same period that our tale takes place Bethlehem had an active civic and communal life. The tradition of "justice at the gate" was practiced there, as were other biblical laws regarding contributions to the poor, levirate marriage, and various forms of collective and familial obligations. We also know from Ruth that the women of Bethlehem have their own active social life, and that they are curious about the lives of other women, especially those who have been away and returned home. The women of Bethlehem welcome Naomi when she comes home after a long stay abroad, wondering aloud about the change in her appearance and fortunes; later, they rejoice when Ruth gives birth to a son, and even name the child themselves. Where are they here? We have established that the Eframite community, loyal to their Levite, has branded the concubine a "harlot" for leaving her husband. What do the women of Bethlehem have to say? Where are they, or, indeed, where is the family and extended family?

The absence of the Bethlehem community highlights the young woman's isolation and adds to the stark effect of the tale. It also means that the girl's fate is completely in her father's hands, and he has decided that his daughter's future is with the Levite. It seems that no woman's interference will change his mind, or that no woman in his household or in the community at large dares, or cares to, speak on the girl's behalf. Culturally, the community's silence might mean a condemnation of the young woman. If her townspeople do not explicitly concur with the Eframites in calling the woman "unfaithful," they are nonetheless disapproving of a girl who took her fate in her own hands and abandoned her husband. The absence of dialogue among women, central in Ruth, may also point to the retiring personality of the protagonist. Unlike the articulate, vociferous Naomi, the heroine is shy, passive, and reticent. This further illuminates the concubine's personality and reinforces her innocence vis-à-vis the Levite: she ran away only when things got so bad that she was propelled to take action contradictory to her character.

Attention shifts to the impoverished Levite who puts the best face on embarrassing circumstances and decides to travel in style. He comes with a pair of donkeys and a male servant, trying to appear affluent to his father-in-law and attractive to his concubine.[30] These attempts on the part of the Levite are proof again that he is aware of the girl's grievances against him and that he intends to counter them. If she complained to her father about the harsh living conditions on the hillside of Efraim and that she had been treated like a handmaid rather than a wife, the Levite seeks to display that he can afford not one donkey but two, as well as a male servant, to the father and the whole community. If the girl reported emotional or physical abuse, he is prepared to affect a conciliatory, tender demeanor, to appear as a kindly, peace-loving, forgiving individual. We are anxious to witness the reunion between the husband and his young wife. How will the Levite mend fences, what words will he use that would speak directly to the girl's "heart," soften her resistance, and bring her back to him? Perhaps in the reunion scene some past misunderstandings will be cleared, apologies will be made, and we will be better able to understand the woman's reasons for her unusual act.

The expectations for an emotional meeting between husband and wife are not answered. The girl seems to see him first, as he approaches her father's house; apparently she has been spending time outdoors. We also know from Ruth that the women of Bethlehem are used to moving freely within the town. The girl's reaction is not given, for as soon as she sees her master she brings him into her father's house. She does not give the Levite a chance to talk to her, or the Levite is too tired and first has to go indoors and rest. The laws of hospitality demand that the guest's physical needs be attended to first. The girl's lack of reaction, however, stands in marked contrast to that of her father who is "delighted" to see the Levite whereas his daughter most probably is not.

The men engage in a prolonged feast of hearty food, good cheer, and merry company. But something strange has happened: the Levite no longer feels it necessary to apologize, talk tenderly to the girl, and court his way back into her heart. The father's joyous reception of him makes it clear to his guest that there is no need for apologies, that his coming all the way from the north to fetch his daughter is for the father enough of a gesture of making amends. If it is sufficient for the father, then the girl's feelings no longer count; her father will make her go back with her lawful husband.

Here is a typical feminine predicament: in a male-dominant society a wife has to be truly desperate, feel that life is unbearable, to leave her husband. Yet very often it is her own family who would urge her to go back, who would turn a deaf ear to her rightful complaint. The respectability of the whole extended family hinges on the actions of one woman. The father of the concubine is delighted because the cloud of gossip and shame is removed; his daughter will resume her married life, and all will be forgotten. The lack of a reunion scene between husband and wife, for which the narrator has prepared us, may be viewed as another stylistic technique of ellipsis, resulting in a multi-layered, ambiguous text. The gap may also be a representation of fact, namely that there indeed was no intimate moment between the Levite and his concubine worth mentioning. In other words, the elision is not a narrative strategy but a factual reality. The narrator's strategy lies in arousing the reader's expectations for something that never happens, rather than in withholding information, and so tease the reader into more speculation.

As the men indulge in five days of continuous fun, however, two dramatic undercurrents flow through the story. First, the young woman has been forgotten. The father, in his eagerness to please his son-in-law, has made a grave diplomatic mistake. Instead of insisting on a reconciliation between husband and wife, thus proving to the Levite that his daughter's happiness is important to him, the father has unwittingly communicated to the Levite that his real concern was with saving face, putting forward a façade of family harmony. The five days of male bonding, when the woman is probably preparing the meals and then serving them, but is never asked to sit with the men and give the Levite the opportunity to speak to her, teach the Levite that the girl's state of mind will not be a factor in her father's decision. From the woman's point of view nothing has changed. Since the Levite did not talk to her or even make any promises of changing his ways, the concubine has no reason to believe that her future life with him would be any different from her previous experience. She has probably not changed her mind about returning with the Levite since nothing of significance has transpired between the two. Her husband came to fetch her, but communicated nothing to her, making his trip an act of reclaiming a possession, not the gesture of a lover coming to court his beloved.

Second, it seems that while the father acts unwisely in his transparent eagerness to please the Levite, he does seem to be genuinely worried. If the father's goal was merely to get rid of his daughter, he would have allowed the Levite to leave when the latter was ready, on the fourth day or even before. Instead, the father keeps him three days and then another day and night and another full day. The only reason for the father's reluctance to let the couple leave is that he does have a bad conscience, that serious doubts are gnawing at him, that he feels that something is terribly wrong with this couple. But the father is either awed by the Levite's status or afraid to antagonize him, and thus he fails to confront his son-in-law about the causes of his daughter's flight. Instead, the father makes every effort to ingratiate himself with the Levite, to the point where the Levite has to be rude to his host and insist on leaving at sundown, the most dangerous time of day to be on the open road. The father's attempts at winning the Levite's heart are well-meaning but pathetic and ineffective.[31] Coaxing the Levite to "strengthen" his heart, when it is clear that it is the girl's heart that is broken, will only backfire. The more the father cajoles and pleads the stronger the Levite becomes as his fear of and respect for his father-in-law quickly diminish.

A hasty, irresponsible decision is made for which two men are accountable, yet for which only the young girl will pay the price. The Levite, after having been reluctantly detained by his father-in-law for yet another day insists on departing in spite of the late hour. He will not listen to the father's offer of another night of hospitality. The friendly, jovial atmosphere between the two men gives way to almost visible tension, finding its expression in the father's remark that implies that the Levite should not be so eager to return home because it is only a "tent." Either the Levite indeed owns a tent only, or the father is being sarcastic, alluding to the rundown condition of the Levite's house, as probably reported to him by his daughter.

Thus, the failure of the father's five days of diplomacy on behalf of his daughter is fully displayed. When the Levite finally leaves Bethlehem, he seems almost to escape an unwanted hospitality, and to defy openly the father's wishes. The spirit of conviviality and accommodation the father tried so hard to maintain becomes one of spitefulness, bitterness, and sarcasm.

The Doomed Journey "Home"

If there was a hidden masculine contest between father and husband during the five days of feasting, the Levite has gained the upper hand by leaving when he did. But the man's irrational insistence on taking to the road close to sundown is puzzling, for surely he has no intention of meeting with danger. One must conclude that the Levite's motivation has a streak of sadism in it. Scaring his concubine, as well as making light of her father's foreboding, must give him pleasure.

The young girl knows what she can expect at her husband's home. At this point we should reconstruct the Levite's personality, based on previous as well as unfolding events, so that we, too, can be fully aware of the girl's state of mind. The Levite is a pauper who nevertheless wishes to appear affluent. He is shallow, hungry for publicity and social recognition, and lies for the sake of enhancing his public stature. He is capable of emotional abuse toward his concubine, maintaining long, menacing silences, and treating her like a non-person. He is not averse to physical roughness and cruelty; soon he will forcefully throw her outdoors into danger, and later he will coldly and methodically dismember her body. Looking back, we can say that the moment when the young girl saw her tormentor approaching her father's home was a bitter one. She let him in with a sinking heart and was filled with terror when she saw her father's fawning, exuberant welcome.

With the silent girl at his side, a sense of doom and dread descends on the Levite and his party. The girl is on the road again. Her courageous flight has not resulted in the improvement of her marital situation. Her father has failed to turn the Levite's heart back to her in kindness and renewed tenderness. Instead, the Levite now knows that she is completely at his mercy. The young woman must feel dispirited, beaten, hopeless. She has lost her struggle for a measure of decent treatment in her master's house. She knows that the only option once open to her, fleeing to her father's house, is no longer possible. The paternal home was a temporary, fleeting respite from a bitter fate, but could not provide shelter and safety forever. The young girl will never act as an independent agent again and she becomes a passive, dejected, lifeless object, dead before she actually breathes her last.

The events that follow are horrible not only because of the evil actions of the people of Gibea, but because the Levite is unmasked and his ugly nature is revealed. The girl takes no part in the discussions about where to spend the night; only the men, the master and his servant, talk. The man's blatant ignoring of the woman's opinion is a promise of things to come, a message that he values the servant's views more than hers. She is less important than before, when he at least intended to "speak to her heart."

Geography again becomes meaningful. The servant, most probably a non-Israelite, suggests the city of the Jebusites. This town is also known as Jerusalem, which later will become the home of God's ark, a holy place for all Israelites. But this city will be the beloved Jerusalem, protected by God, only in the future. It is still a foreign city, and its inhabitants are not to be trusted. Ironically, the Benjaminite town of Gibea, to which the travelers finally turn, is a disappointment. The Levite and his entourage find themselves in the open town square, with no offer of a roof over their heads for the night. An old man appears, an Eframite residing in Benjaminite territory, and shows an interest in the travelers.

The Levite is in a position of needing help and has to color the truth and even lie to make himself a more attractive guest. Once he was the honored guest, lavishly courted by his father-in-law and then haughtily defying his host, now he has become an ordinary traveler who has to pander to his potential host. Therefore, he elaborates on the plentiful food and provisions he has with him and refers to his concubine, another possession at his disposal, as the old man's "maidservant." Furthermore, he establishes his own status in geographical terms; he is on his way from the prestigious town of Bethlehem to the "house of the Lord." His use of "the house of the Lord," rather than "my house" is a reflection of this man. Going to the "house of the Lord" endows his journey with respectability, while retrieving his runaway concubine is not an event the Levite cares to report. The lie and exaggerations work, and the company is invited to the old man's home.

The young woman comes under the protection of another patriarchal figure, and is inside his home. The men are again "gladdening their hearts" when a group of rowdy local thugs knock at the door. They demand to see the guest with the vague threat that they intend to challenge the stranger in some kind of rough masculine contest. In spite of the sexual connotations of the verb "to know" it is hard to pinpoint what the men of Gibea really want. They certainly intend to expose the old man's vulnerability. He, too, is an alien resident, and by offering hospitality when nobody else did, he showed up the local population's lack of manners. This act of implicit criticism of local customs demands revenge, in the form of dragging the guest from out the protection of his host, and "roughing him up," thus proving both his and his host's masculine incompetence. The sexual meaning looms large too, but this is a male contest, a conflict that belongs to the men's domain, where women are initially not mentioned. For these "macho" hooligans, tackling a defenseless woman is not thrilling. The old man, on the other hand, tries to bait them with two women, his virgin daughter and the sexually experienced concubine.[32]

The old man shifts the tenor of the negotiations from threats of physical, and perhaps sexual, violence to a clearly sexual meaning.[33] At first, the hooligans are not interested in either woman, which again proves that their immediate intent is not necessarily sexual. They may have not even figured out for themselves what they wished to do with the Levite. Once again, as Levi-Strauss has suggested, bonding between men will be accomplished by using the woman as a commodity to be traded. It seems that the old man understands that gang rape can be a catalyst for male bonding; he offers the women under his care to the hooligans as overtures of camaraderie.[34] By trying to bond with the perpetrators and defuse their animosity, the old man and his male guest become participants in the gang rape.

The turning point comes when the Levite takes action by forcefully seizing his concubine and throwing her outside. Contrary to the medieval laws of chivalry where a man is honor-bound to rescue a damsel in distress, our ancient biblical protagonist would sacrifice a woman, and one with whom he has shared a bed, to save his skin. The selfishness and ruthlessness of the act are the Levite's ultimate betrayal of the young woman in his care, revealing, too, his fury against her. What is more, while the woman is being raped and tortured all night, the old man and his guest feel safe enough to go to sleep. A third patriarchal home has proven dangerous for the young protagonist.

The ancient laws of hospitality protect only the men. The old man, the father of a daughter himself, has no sense of obligation toward the young women under his roof, only toward the male guest. He offers the concubine although she is not his. A man is in danger, his masculinity challenged, but it is the woman who will suffer. She will be violated, entered, so that the house sheltering the men will remain closed, intact. The door opens for a second so that the woman can be expelled, and then it closes shut to protect the men; it will reopen only the next morning, in broad daylight, when the danger is over. Behind the old man's conduct, as well as that of the Levite, is a great concern for appearances, for conforming to the laws of propriety as defined in that culture. The men's seemingly civilized conduct of kindness and hospitality is not motivated by humanitarian concerns but by their conformity to etiquette and custom, as well as by sheer selfishness.

The concubine collapses at the doorway of the house at dawn, her hands spread in a gesture of supplication and servility. The Levite, undisturbed about his concubine, and with not even simple curiosity about her fate, has resigned

73

himself to her loss and now prepares to leave his host's house, invigorated by an uneventful, comfortable sleep. When he opens the door on his way out he practically steps over the woman lying at the doorstep. He is unperturbed, addressing her coldly and briefly, "get up and let's go." This speech sounds even more heartless and cutting in Hebrew because of its brevity, only two words. The man does not stop to look at her injuries, to see whether she needs help, indeed to verify whether she is alive or dead. With chilling deliberateness, the Levite picks her up, puts her on his donkey, and goes home, expressing no grief, sorrow, or sympathy for the victim. Some of the traditional commentators are so sensitive to the gap regarding the woman's condition, that they find it necessary to explain that the woman did not answer because she was dead.[35] Although we will never know whether she was dead or exhausted, badly injured, and unconscious, it is clear that when the Levite first sees her he does not conclude that she is dead, since he talks to her, expecting her to get up and follow him home.

Three narrative gaps are noticeable here. The first is the removal of the rape scene from the foreground of the tale. This is a variation of the technique of rendering the act of rape invisible, detected by feminist critics in a number of literary texts, both ancient and modern.[36] The second is the failure of the narrator to report when the woman died, and the third is omitting when the Levite realizes the woman is dead. The first elision is rather subtle since the rape itself is not obscured, and its violence is clearly expressed (19:28). It is not presented from the point of view of the victim, nor from that of the perpetrators, nor from that of an observer of the scene, but rather from that of the man who threw her out and closes the door after her to save himself. The reader is thus made to follow the Levite, safe indoors, instead of the woman. We know that the Levite knows that the woman is being raped, but what the woman endures during the night remains a narrative gap. The rape happens "out there," while the Levite, and the reader with him, is "in here." The foreground of the tale is occupied by the Levite and the other people, now safely ensconced in the house. At the far background an atrocity is committed, though where exactly it happens, in someone's home or in one of the town's dark alleys, we are not informed.

The second elision, the moment of death, results from the first. Interestingly, the storyteller gives us a minute description of the gradual breaking of dawn as the woman gropes her way back to her host's house, but we are never told when she breathes her last. We know that she was tortured all night until the morning, that her tormentors finally let her go at dawn, and that the woman walked on her own, arriving at her host's doorstep at daybreak, where she and fell down and lay until light (19:25). The woman dies some time between the moment she falls at her host's doorstep and the moment her body is cut into twelve pieces, but this is all the text tells us.[37]

The more important elision is the Levite's failure to find out why the woman does not answer him. Did he establish that the woman is dead, and the storyteller just fails to inform us, or does the Levite not bother to find out the woman's condition? That the woman does not answer her husband is not an indication of her lifelessness; rather, it is consistent with the woman's mute demeanor throughout the tale. The Levite does not expect the woman to answer him, but to obey his command to get up and take to the road with him. Commentators have discussed all the possibilities behind the woman's failure to respond, without noticing that she is not expected to respond in language, only in action. Various conversations are conducted in this tale, but none involves the woman. On the road, the man converses with his servant, and not with her. The woman's voice, whether spoken or internal, never finds expression in this tale, thus adding to her status as a non-person. Thus, when the Levite does not hear her voice, he, more than the reader, cannot assume that she is dead, for she is characterized by her lack of language. He can learn more from her inability to raise herself from the ground, but this in itself does not mean that the woman is dead, only very weak. Furthermore, the story is so committed to the Levite's centrality and to the suppression of the woman that it does not say "and she did not answer," which would put her in a subject position. The text says, literally, "and no one answered," or, closer to the meaning of the Hebrew original, "and there was no response." By obscuring the moment of death and the Levite's definite knowledge of it, the storyteller accomplishes two contradictory goals. On the face of it, he camouflages and obfuscates the Levite's criminality. Yet the gap is so glaring that rather than conceal the man's depravity it actually draws our attention to it and puts the Levite's despicable action later, of cutting the woman's body to pieces, in the worst possible light.

That the man's failure to establish his wife's death is not only a literary ellipsis but an accurate chronicling of events becomes clear once we realize, together with the Levite, that the woman is worth more to him dead than alive. The publicity-hungry, opportunistic Levite seizes the moment; he is at the center of a cause célèbre. To get the most from the event, he cuts the woman's corpse into twelve pieces and spreads them in the twelve tribal territories. The "official" motive attributed to the man is that he wants to make a point about an outrageous event in the most shocking, grisly way possible. But to be able to dismember a person, or a corpse, one must be sadistic and vindictive. By cutting and scattering the young woman's remains, her husband has reduced her from a dead person to pieces of flesh. She has become a non-person and will never even get a proper burial.

The Levite's despicable nature is fully revealed in the self-serving public recounting of the events he later offers. Readers can put themselves in the place of both the ancient listeners, who may have heard only the Levite's version, and the later readers who can compare the Levite's version with the events as they were narrated and conclude that the Levite lied. The ancient storyteller has thus made future readers his confidants, while at the same time not offending his own culture by an outright condemnation of the Levite. In public, the Levite claims that the people of Gibea intended to kill him, which was not clearly indicated. He also omits several damning pieces of information: that he threw the young woman outside, that the men surrounding the house never demanded the woman, and that they first refused her when she was offered to them. Then he claims that the Gibean thugs killed the woman, while, again, we know that he never established definitely that she was dead in the morning, and that she had been alive and able to walk to the house after the rape.

The rest of the story chronicles a civil war between all the tribes of Israel and the tribe of Benjamin. In the aftermath of the war, the Israelites allow the Benjaminite men who have now lost their women to attack the people of a town that did not join the war, kill all of its males and married women, and seize its virgins. They further allow the Benjaminites to kidnap the daughters of Shiloh for brides. In other words, as a result of the murder of one woman, more women are victimized, widowed, killed, and raped, but the true culprits, the gang of Gibea and the Levite himself, are never punished.

As we try to make sense of this tale of atrocity we must distinguish between the purpose of the tale within the biblical canon and its meaning to us. The brutal treatment of the woman, culminating in her death, is only a prologue to an important event, the civil war between Israelite tribes. One might read here an attempt to paint the tribe of Judah (King David's people) in a favorable light, and the tribe of Benjamin (King Saul's people) in a bad light. The protagonists' proper names are not given, but their tribal affiliations are clearly pronounced. It is obvious that the tale was not narrated for the purpose of highlighting a woman's fate.

The storyteller, however, speaks to us in two voices. The laconic recording of the sequence of events, where only actions and speeches are given, provides the "official" version of the outrageous events. In this version, the collective voice is very clear regarding the identity of the criminals and the victims. The community's simplistic, black-and-white assessment marks the "good guys" as the friendly, anxious-to-please father, the bereaved Levite, whose wife had been brutally murdered, and the old man of Gibea, the epitome of hospitality and kindness to strangers. The "bad guys" are the Gibean thugs who surround the old man's house, cause a disturbance, and later gang-rape the concubine, as well as the Benjaminites who refuse to turn the criminals over. The woman is in between. She did not act criminally, but, like Dinah, her initial action, leaving the patriarchal home, started the trouble. Just as Dinah was considered loose because she "went out," so the concubine is considered a "harlot" because she left her husband.

Another picture emerges when we look more closely at each character's action, and deduce inner motivation and internal thoughts so that we can fill the gaps of this very terse tale, especially when we match actions as they occurred with public speeches that attempt to describe and interpret these actions. This reading exonerates the woman and puts the blame on the men in the tale and forces us to listen to the women's silent scream. The storyteller was sensitive to the woman's predicament, but the more "important" political and historical matters took precedence. The villainy of the Levite was probably not recognized by his contemporaries, but is fully appreciated by us, because the storyteller has subtly and masterfully laid the groundwork for a woman-centered reading of the tale, and made sure that the reader sees the Levite in his true light. The girl's domestic troubles and their causes are not depicted, but there are enough hints and suggestions regarding their nature and extent. Not surprisingly, even traditional Jewish commentators (like Ralbag) have remarked on the Levite's guilty conscience, on his abuse of the woman as the reason for her leaving, and on the innocent meaning of her desertion of her husband.

The storyteller has offered two tales enfolded in one: he has told a "man's tale," complete with male politics, civil war, and crisis management. Yet, he has skillfully presented a "woman's tale" as well, exposing the treachery of the patriarchal home in an unbalanced system where men are favored. The language of location (to dwell, to live, to come from) and the variations on the noun "house" (or home, tent, dwelling place, door, doorstep) that lace the narrative sound ironic. The concubine, who only looks to be in a safe place, finds herself forcefully thrown outdoors. Even the virgin daughter of the old man cannot expect to be protected in her father's house.

Furthermore, the modern reader is more sensitive to the marital abuse that is implied in the tale, and to the blind eye that the community at large, and even the woman's family, prefers to turn. This is coupled with the disparity between the public and the private man. The Levite is respected, he is granted hospitality by both his wife's family and a total stranger, and his voice is heard by all the people of Israel. Yet his private villainy toward the woman also comes through in the story. As such, this ancient tale is prototypical of the many cases in our own culture where a man's domestic violence collides with his public image.

It seems that the phenomenon of spouse abuse perpetrated by honorable citizens was known in ancient times too, and was noted by cultural commentators like our own storyteller. It is a secondary element within the fabric of our tale because of the social denial with which such observations were met. Both then and now we would like to believe that the home is the place of the ultimate safety for the woman. Our tale proves that there is not much difference between the patriarchal home and the open road; that danger is not a spatial matter, a question of where the woman is, but a human and social matter, whether the culture accepts the abuse of women. A tale that points out the danger of the open spaces for women, and that warns them not to steer away from the male-ruled home, ends up sending women a different message: that they should not wait for men to grant them physical safety and a sense of human worth.

CHAPTER 3

WOMAN VENTURES OUT
MOBILITY AND ITS BENEFITS

1. TAMAR AT THE CROSSROADS

The Text
Genesis 38

And it came to pass about three months after, that it was told Judah, saying, "Tamar thy daughter-in-law has played the harlot; and also, behold, she is with child by harlotry." And Judah said: "Bring her out and let her be burnt." As she was being brought out, she sent to her father in law, saying: "By the man, whose these are, am I with child." And she said: "Discern, I pray thee, whose are these, the signet, and the cord, and the staff." And Judah acknowledged them and said: "She is more righteous than I; because I gave her not Shelah my son." (Gen. 38: 24–26)

Women and Disguise

Several biblical women resort to wearing disguises and impersonating others. Leah doubles for Rachel, the "wise woman" comes before David pretending to be a widow, and Tamar plays the harlot at the crossroads. Nevertheless, such deception is not limited to women. Although Rebecca induces her son Jacob to don the sheepskin and lie to his father, it is Jacob who actually assumes his brother's identity. David, captured by the Philistines, feigns madness to save his life. In Israelite culture, these occasions are never theatrical in nature. They have no diversional purposes, and are not designed for entertainment or alleviation of boredom. Both men and women always have a clear, utilitarian goal in mind. The women dissemble mostly to fool male authority and outwit the existing system.

Role-playing, impersonating, and pretending are play-activities, necessary for the health of the culture as well as the individual.[1] Yet very little in biblical society is devoted to theatrical arts. The words for play in the Bible (of the root *shq* or *shq*) may sometimes have either a sexual connotation (Gen. 21:9, 26:8) or the grim, cynical meaning of fighting (2 Sam. 2:14). The closest the Bible gets to representing Israelite people engaged in recreational performances is the spontaneous dancing and singing of women to celebrate a national victory. But *ludic* activity as an end in itself seems alien to the biblical spirit. When Jacob plays Esau it is not for the sake of mimicry in the theatrical sense, but for a purpose that for him is serious and necessary. The modes of fiction and make-believe, essential in the Homeric epic and Hellenic literature, and part of Greek culture and its poetics of representation, are absent in biblical narratives, which are committed to the historical, rather than fictional, mode.

If impersonation is not a matter of *ludic* indulgence it is often a necessary measure taken by women who venture out of the patriarchal shelter and need a mask, a changed identity, as protection. Women who dare leave the patriarchal abode in order to accomplish an important goal adjust their personalities to accommodate the needs of the men involved. The transformation of the familiar personality is either radical, as in the case of Tamar playing the harlot, or a confirmation of the real person, as in the case of Abigail who acts as the moderate force to the variety of radical positions taken by the men around her. Or it may be a professional skill, as in the case of the two wise women who appear in two separate episodes in 2 Samuel.

Tamar Is Banished from Judah's Home

Within the biblical canon, the tale of the clever Tamar who outwits her father-in-law is not a tale of a woman, but of a man, Judah. It reinforces the patrilineal tradition by explaining how Jacob's fourth son, Judah, begot two sons late in life, after he had lost two of the three sons born to him by his first wife.[2] Nevertheless, it is also a woman's tale, in which the woman's interests clash with the man's, and her constricted existence and spatial disadvantages are juxtaposed with his sphere of multiple options and freedom of movement.

Judah, Jacob's fourth son, is establishing himself as a patriarch in his own right by separating himself from his clan and settling in a place called

Adulam. He marries the daughter of a Canaanite, and this union is fruitful, producing three sons. Judah is now a true paterfamilias, and the geographical distance from his own father offers him independence and authority.[3] Judah is soon exercising his power as head of the family by "taking" a wife, named Tamar, for his older son. The focus of interest shifts to Judah's home, where the sons turn out to be weak and impotent, the diametrical opposites of their vigorous and masculine father. Judah's firstborn, Er, dies before he manages to prove his virility by impregnating his wife. Tamar, the childless widow, becomes eligible for "redemption," that is, taken in marriage under levirate law by her brother-in-law for the purpose of bearing a son to carry the dead man's name.

Levirate law had its roots in two purposes. It guaranteed that a man who died childless would still acquire an offspring perceived by the community to be the dead man's heir and his perpetuity in time. It also took care of widows left with no form of security. If the woman had no male sons, her late husband's property went to his brother.[4] By marrying her brother-in-law and staying in her dead husband's family, the childless widow was saved from destitution.

The patriarch Judah, who navigates his sons' destinies, orders his second son, Onan, to redeem Tamar. Onan, however, refuses to impregnate the widow who has become his wife for the sole purpose of producing an offspring for his dead brother. The roots of the apparent lack of brotherly loyalty on Onan's part are not explained, but he may be displaying antagonism toward his father who had ordered him to marry his dead brother's widow and produce an heir. Onan's refusal to accommodate his father indicates resentment of the patriarch's ambition and despotism. There is tension and dissension in Judah's household, with the woman functioning as the emblem of the men's conflict. By making his sons' matrimonial decisions for them, Judah reinforces his authority over the grown men in his home, signaling that he sees in them his own lifeline to immortality, his genetic recreation, but not independent adults.[5] But Onan is punished by the ultimate Father, God, and he dies prematurely.

The center of the dramatic action then shifts from the father and his sons to the father-in-law and the young widow. Identifying Tamar, the young widow, as the cause of his sons' deaths, Judah decides to remove the woman from his home and protect his third son from the fate of his two older brothers.[6] Thus, Tamar comes to the fore for the first time and is addressed directly by Judah, who orders her to return to her father's home and remain there in the status of a childless widow, until his third son grows up and is ready to marry her. Tamar complies with her father-in-law's order. Her thoughts and reactions are unknown, but she must feel banished from her legitimate home. She is no longer her father's responsibility, and would have no claim to an affiliation with her father's clan. As part of Judah's extended family Tamar could expect to remain under the patriarch's supervision and protection.

Up to this point, Tamar is seen by us as a young woman taken by an influential patriarch and brought to his home as a daughter-in-law, and then returned to the status of a daughter when she is forced to reside once again in her father's home, this time as a childless widow. Tamar's maiden home and her father's name and family origins are deemed so unimportant that they are not mentioned earlier. Tamar is not "given" in marriage by her father, but is "taken" by Judah as a bride for his son, as if the woman has no father or family to negotiate for her. Tamar's father is referred to only when it befits Judah, and when his home becomes an attractive solution to Judah's problem. Judah thus accomplishes two goals: by sending Tamar away to a paternal home that never represented strong authority, Judah still has a tight grip over the woman. At the same time, the looser structure of Tamar's original family might lead the young woman astray and thus eventually offer Judah an alternative course of action, more desirable to him than giving Tamar as wife to Shelah.

The cruelty of Judah's action is made clearer when compared with Naomi's genuine concern for her widowed daughters-in-law (Ruth 1:6–17). Naomi's wish that the young women return home is not selfish; it is based on the absence of those elements that might make their journey to Bethlehem worthwhile: a living *levir,* an affluent, protective family, and a welcoming community. All these elements exist in the case of Tamar—her *levir* is alive and her father-in-law is affluent and powerful—and therefore she should not have been banished from Judah's home. Furthermore, Naomi actually prays that her dead sons' wives find husbands (Ruth 1:9). By urging each of her daughters-in-law to return to her "mother's home," Naomi evokes the location where female-centered activities, such as matchmaking and marriage negotiations, are conducted.[7] Judah, on the other hand, sends Tamar to the patriarchal home, where the interest in the young woman will not go beyond making sure that she does not disgrace the family.

The interesting dynamics that develop between the strong man and his daughter-in-law make us pause and look deeper into the relationship. Tamar is the passive, voiceless participant in a one-way dialogue between herself and Judah. He commands her to return to her father's home and gives her the reason: his third son Shelah is still too young to marry her. Judah softens the blow of banishment with the promise that it is only temporary, that she will have to "sit" in her father's home as a widow only until his youngest son Shelah grows up. Nevertheless, Judah is vague and does not promise Tamar that she will return to his home as Shelah's bride. His speech seems truncated, more like a stammer than a coherent proclamation. It is divided into three brief statements that are shorter in the Hebrew than in the translation: "Sit [as] a widow," "[in your] father's house," "until Shelah grows [up]." The dubious nature of his intentions is thus implied even before the narrator fully explains them. Instead of giving us Tamar's reply, or her inner thoughts in reaction to Judah's cruel decree, the narrator goes into Judah's mind and gives us his internal discourse: "for he said: Lest perchance he die also, as his brothers did" (38:11).

Thus we understand that under the civilized encounter between Judah and Tamar a different dramatic plot is evolving. Judah's intentions to avoid at all costs a marriage between Tamar and his younger son must be obvious to the young widow. Judah may have expressed his fears to those close to him, or he may have kept his plans to himself, but the fact that the storyteller quotes Judah's internal thoughts means that his intentions are transparent to others, especially Tamar. The verbal dialogue between Judah and Tamar seems one-sided, Judah commanding and Tamar wordlessly obeying; but behind it a different dialogue is taking place. Judah promises Tamar that she will return to his home when Shelah is fully grown, while Tamar is saying, internally, "I know that in your heart you have decided never to let me marry Shelah."

Even before Tamar actually entraps her father-in-law we have evidence that Tamar is the smarter of the two. Judah's devious plan, to remove Tamar from his home forever, is transparent (and therefore his internal speech is quoted), while Tamar manages to keep her own scheme concealed and unknown. Thus her inner thoughts remain a gap in the fabric of the tale. In this case, the gap is both a matter of the cultural attitude that neglects to take account of women's responses and a stylistic technique that draws our attention to Tamar's cleverness. The linguistic elision reflects a pliable, reticent, non-resisting demeanor that masks an active mind.

Although Judah speaks and Tamar listens and complies, there is a hidden, unarticulated exchange that goes on between the powerful patriarch and the widow who is both powerless and yet feared. This is a contest of wits and cunning. In this mental jousting Judah is the winner of the first round, for Tamar must pretend that she believes Judah's promises since she cannot challenge him on the basis of her suspicions alone. She has no recourse but to submit to her father-in-law's will and leave his home. In many ways, Tamar is now in limbo, tied to Judah's family and not free to marry someone outside it, yet barred from marrying Shelah, the sole surviving son.

Nevertheless, Tamar possesses knowledge about Judah, while Judah is ignorant about her. One piece of information that Tamar acquires by herself is Judah's inner thoughts concerning her, and his intention to keep her forever removed from his clan's orbit. If knowledge is power, then the twice-widowed, childless Tamar is more powerful than she seems to be, because she understands her adversary's innermost thoughts and has no illusions about his intentions.

Judah, who has practically condemned Tamar to loneliness and childlessness, shows no interest in the young woman after she has left his home, but

Tamar makes it her business to be informed about his every move. She knows both what is in her adversary's heart and what transpires in his home on a daily basis: that his wife has died, that Judah has recovered from his grief, and that he is going to participate in the sheep-shearing ceremony in Timnah. We do not know how she is able to gather all this information, but the narrator tells us that "Tamar has been told." The clever Tamar seems to have had spies in her father-in-law's house, people who keep her accurately apprised of Judah's life. For Judah, Tamar seems not to exist anymore, but he is very much part of her life; in fact, his life becomes her life. Judah is under the impression that his home is now safe from the deadly Tamar, since the woman is in effect doubly imprisoned: in her father's home, as well as in her status as a childless widow waiting to be redeemed. Tamar has to watch her every action. Any negative rumor about her conduct, any false step on her part, would be used by Judah against her.

Tamar deems it important to know Judah's movements and plans because she is devising a strategy to defeat him at his own game. He deceived her, so she is looking for ways to outwit him and reestablish herself in his home. Her reasons for planning to outmaneuver Judah go beyond the obvious wish to reclaim what is regarded by this culture as justifiably hers, that is, a place in Judah's family. A closer look at the family Judah has created yields a disturbing portrait and a new understanding of Tamar's position. In a way, Judah is the first man in Tamar's life. Of the men in Tamar's matrimonial home, Judah is the one whom she probably saw first. There is no romantic scene between Tamar and Er, her first husband, in which the man sees the woman, wants her, and asks his father to get her for him, as did Samson, or asks her father for her hand, as did Jacob. The sentence denoting Tamar's marriage to her first husband, Er, reads initially as if Judah has taken Tamar for himself: "And Judah took a wife / for Er, his firstborn." Judah sees Tamar and makes the decision to acquire her; in fact, he imposes her on his son, the latter having apparently no say in the matter. Tamar comes to Judah's household as a young bride and what she probably witnesses is a power play between a virile, authoritative patriarch and passive, weak sons. Both Er and Onan seem sexually inadequate. We are not sure if Er ever consummated his marriage with Tamar, but we know that he failed to impregnate his young bride. And we know that Onan is preoccupied with making sure that he does not impregnate her. Neither of Judah's two elder sons has the freedom to choose his sexual partner. In both cases their father arranges for them to marry Tamar. They both die young without leaving male heirs. Judah then prevents Shelah, his only surviving son, from maturing sexually by delaying his marriage to Tamar.

If the sons' deaths are explained by the pious storyteller as a sentence from God, and by the superstitious community as well as Judah as related to the "killer wife" Tamar, to us it may mean that the weakling sons could not survive under the glare of the forceful father who supervised their sexuality and curbed their masculinity.[8] Furthermore, Tamar seems to know that while Judah has controlled, and intervened in, his sons' sex life, he has strong sexual appetites himself. We know as well that unlike his sons, Judah was strong-minded enough to remove himself from his own father's domicile before proving his own sexual prowess and creating his own family. Judah did not wait for his father to find a bride for him, but chose his own wife. Of the four men that Tamar comes in contact with after she leaves her father's house, there is no doubt who is more appealing and exciting to the young woman.

Tamar is intimately familiar with more than just Judah's daily itinerary. She senses correctly when he will be ready to resume his sex life, and calculates almost the exact moment when he will be looking for a sexual partner. For these insights she needs more than the local gossips or the "spies" in Judah's home who sympathize with her and make sure that she is kept informed about Judah's activities. She has to possess a deeper understanding of the man, which comes from close observation and a strong emotional tie. Perhaps even unbeknownst to Judah, Tamar, during the time she spent in his home, learned to read his moods and needs, so that she could interpret them accurately even when she was removed from his orbit.

To attribute to Tamar a desire for Judah, at least an attraction to the vigorous older man, is not to take away from the purposefulness and the justice of her actions. It is to say that while she had to act like a harlot, who sleeps with a stranger for whom she does not care, Tamar slept with a man whom she knew very well and may have lusted after, or at least admired.

Judah's attitude toward Tamar is also more complicated than meets the eye. He acts as if he is furious with her even before he hears of her supposed infidelity. Sending her to her father's house is a gesture of disapproval and alienation, a punishment. Perhaps the patriarch himself is visited by incestuous sensations, by an unwanted attraction to the young widow in his house, coupled by his ambition to prove himself successful where his sons have failed. Nevertheless, Judah is a respectable citizen, abiding by law and custom and fearful of public scandal (38:23). Therefore, removing Tamar from his trajectory seems to solve the danger that she poses for him, too.

There is also a certain recklessness and lack of responsibility about Judah in contrast to Tamar's methodical, careful planning of her future. Surely Judah cannot delay action regarding Shelah and Tamar indefinitely. He cannot deprive Shelah of a sexual life forever, nor imprison Tamar by making her adhere to the custom of levirate, which prohibits her to remarry as long as there is a living *levir* who can redeem her, while at the same time not letting her enjoy the benefits of this custom, which are marriage and possible motherhood. While Judah procrastinates, Tamar is determined to break the deadlock.

Tamar Plays the Harlot

Tamar's strategy is a dialectic of opposites. On the one hand she puts herself in grave danger by leaving her father's home, taking off her widow's garments, and planting herself by the open road, as if waiting for customers. Sitting in a public place, the "entrance to Einayim," she is inviting a man to enter her, indicating that she is receptive, available, exposed in plain view. But if geographically she has opened herself to great risk, she has protected herself by covering her face with a veil, and more importantly, by transforming herself into what she is not. The donning of the veil and the altering of her image from that of a respected, home-bound widow to a loose, seductive woman are Tamar's disguises.

Thus, Tamar turns from the passive victim to the active arbiter of her own fate. Judah, a man who owns sheep and employs laborers, who is under the impression that he can manipulate his family and that his secret plans regarding Tamar are not obvious to the woman, is now the comic dupe. From the powerful ruler of the family, the patriarch who thinks that all the cards are in his hands, he turns into the fool who knows nothing and is blindly led by the cunning woman. Tamar is veiled but she can see, and the name, or rather the description, of the place where she has chosen to solicit Judah, "Einayim," "eyes" in Hebrew, is significant. She has a clear vision of what she is doing, in spite of the veil that impedes her ability to gain full view. "Petach Einayim" has been interpreted and translated to mean "crossroads" or "open road," but one cannot escape the literal meaning of the Hebrew: the opening, or gate, of eyes. The name of the place combines the twin aspects of Tamar's strategy. The first is making herself available for sexual intercourse and thus literally "opening" herself, or turning herself into a gate (and here again we are reminded of the age-old identification of women with spatial openings such as doors, gates, or windows). That the woman turns herself into an object with an opening is reinforced by the language that three times describes the sexual act as the man "going in to the woman": first in Judah's crude and graphic address to Tamar, then in Tamar's repetition of his offer, and then in the storyteller's narration of the act (38:16, 18). Again the vocabulary names the man as the "knower" and the female as the territory to be explored and "known." It is not clear if Tamar is fully aware that she is dehumanized in the process of turning herself from a living person who occupies space to an inanimate object, a territory that is entered and invaded, but the element of degradation is intensified by the crude language, thus adding to the sympathy the storyteller arouses for his heroine.

The second element in Tamar's successful strategy is her clear sight, her "eyes" that are constantly open and alert. The ancient sages were also intrigued by the name of the place, pointing out that "Petach Einayim" is nowhere to be found in the Bible as a name of a place. They therefore related the word to seeing, suggesting that Tamar lifted her eyes to the gates of heaven, pleading with God to make her mission a success; or, that Tamar, in her actions, opened Judah's eyes.[9] The ancient rabbis identified the heart of the dynamics between Tamar and Judah correctly: they attributed sight to Tamar, and lack of it to Judah. Judah, who thinks that he "sees" the woman, does not know what he sees. He thinks that he sees a prostitute and that he discusses a business deal with her, but he fails to recognize his wronged daughter-in-law and realize that she is making him correct a moral wrong. Tamar is "blind" to her surroundings since she wears a veil, yet she can see. Judah's vision is not obstructed by anything, but he does not see rightly; the irony is that his eyes do not serve him well while her eyes are not needed. Tamar's sight has more depth, it is the insight of strategy and wisdom. She combines the information that she gets from her "spies" with a clear and penetrating understanding of Judah's habits and needs.

The text further reinforces the theme of sight by using the word "to see" in key points and employing the literal meaning of seeing with regard to Judah, but the mental and psychological aspect of seeing, realizing, with regard to Tamar. In the opening of the tale (38:2) Judah "sees" a woman and takes her for a wife. Later, Judah "sees" Tamar, and he thinks she is a prostitute. Both times Judah's object is a woman, and the woman is in plain view, easy to be noticed. Tamar, on the other hand, "sees" that Shelah has grown and yet she has not been given to him (38:14). Tamar's "seeing" is not a matter of sight but of insight, a mental realization that Judah has no intention of ever allowing her to be his son's wife.

Tamar's knowledge of Judah extends to an understanding of the superficiality of his sight. When she sends him the pledges, she does not rely on his sight and requests that he not only look at the pledges, but "discern" them (38:25). Tamar asks him to recognize and understand the full implication of the pledges, not only that they belong to him, but the moral and human implications of her deception that they symbolize. Judah "discerns" the pledges (38:26), with the text in Hebrew repeating the verb Tamar has used. Thus, for the first time, Judah not only sees the surface of things, but comprehends their meaning. Therefore, his immediate reaction to the pledges is not merely a confirmation that the pledges shown to him are his. Instead, his words reflect a moral recognition: "she has been more righteous than I" (38:26). If, within the larger Genesis context, this is a tale about Judah's moral growth, then this moment is another step in that direction. Tamar teaches Judah to look at things for their ethical significance, just as later Joseph will be the catalyst of Judah's moral growth.

If we perceive as well that Judah sent Tamar away in order to escape the temptation of incest, then this ancient patriarch now becomes a comic

Oedipus, a man who does all he can to foil his predetermined incestuous fate, only to fulfill the exact terms of the foretold events. Judah's great illusion, that he is the one who "sees" life clearly, is analogous to that of Oedipus who in his hubris also believes that he can bring the truth to light. Like Oedipus, Judah trusts that physical distance will keep him from misfortune, and, like Oedipus, is mistaken. In the context of this analogy, Tamar is in the position of the blind prophet Tireses, who does not need his eyes to be able to see into the heart of things.

The physical risk that Tamar takes, dangerously displaying herself in full view, is not accompanied by any emotional revelation. She acts in secrecy and does not confide in anyone about her plans. We remember that Ruth, too, takes a great risk when she leaves home for the night and lies down at the feet of a man. Ruth, however, has the backing of an older, wiser woman, who could always testify to the good character and benign intentions of her widowed daughter-in-law, as well as take the responsibility for her unorthodox conduct. Tamar's secrecy, hiding both her mental decisions and physical movements, is contrasted with Judah's careless openness. Both his inner motives as well as external actions are known. In the negotiations between Tamar and Judah, the latter is too open, direct, and gullible, not suspecting anything where he should have guessed something. Tamar operates at both the literal level, obtaining concrete evidence that might later be useful, but also at the metaphorical level. For Judah, the pledges that he leaves with the woman, the seal-and-cord and the staff, are a collateral in a business deal, but for Tamar, they are the man's social as well as masculine identity. Not only does Judah leave with her his identification, but also his manhood (symbolized especially by his staff), and his seed that will thrive in Tamar's womb. The exchange between Judah and Tamar is reminiscent of the dialogue between Esau and Jacob that culminates in the former selling his birthright to the latter. Like Esau, Judah is impetuous, hungry, eager for instant gratification, and ultimately comical, while Tamar, like Jacob, is composed, calculating, and businesslike.

The text offers us only a glimpse of the technique of impersonation employed by Tamar. In order to play the harlot, Tamar, who has lived a sheltered life and moved only from her father's house to Judah's, has to use the language of one. Tamar repeats Judah's graphic offer to "go in to her" both to arouse him even more and to give authenticity to her impersonation of a prostitute. Tamar uses the language of a loose woman and bargains like a hardened prostitute who has been robbed and cheated by men in the past and therefore demands a pledge. Nevertheless, Tamar's language is not just literal but metaphorical. Her superiority lies in the knowledge that she alone possesses: Judah's "kid from the flock" is literal, Tamar's metaphorical.

Although she is not a prostitute with a history of abuse by men, Tamar knows what it is to be cheated out of what is rightfully hers, so her careful, deliberate negotiations may sound authentic. Nevertheless, attempting to imitate the language of an experienced, promiscuous woman would not be enough for Tamar to create a credible new persona for herself. Even if her face is veiled and her language uncharacteristic, Tamar is still a person whose physique and movements are known to Judah. Before mimicking a prostitute, Tamar has to de-emphasize those gestures that would be recognizable by others as hers. To deceive Judah successfully, as she does, Tamar must have a strong understanding of how she is perceived by others, since only then can she skillfully conceal her true identity. As experts in theatrical acting remind us, successful mimetic behavior is inextricably tied to one's sense of self.[10] Therefore, Tamar must be a person in tune with herself, knowing herself as well as the persona she cuts to those around her. Since Judah is familiar with her, Tamar's first concern is not how to impersonate a woman of another class, but how to suppress her own deportment and personal characteristics.

As much as Tamar's triumph depends on her total control of her being and therefore the ability to hide it, however, it also stems from Judah's flawed nature. We fault Oedipus for not being more cautious after learning of the prophecy that he would kill his father and marry his mother. To truly avoid the fulfillment of the prophecy, perhaps he should have refrained from killing any man and marrying any woman, especially one older than he. Similarly, we can fault Judah for not being more careful before having sex with a younger woman. Is the storyteller making fun of men's erotic discrimination as he did earlier with regard to Jacob, who happily slept with the unwanted Leah thinking she was his desired Rachel? Or did Judah feel a strong attraction to the young prostitute but dismissed it as meaningless? It seems that the experience was satisfying to both and therefore instantly bearing fruit. Tamar conceives after one sexual contact, while the unsuspecting Judah, in gratitude, hastens to send the promised payment, a kid from the flock.

Tamar returns safely to hide under the double cover of her father's roof and her widow's garments. She no longer needs the open road to obtain her ends since her feminine biological cycle is in control, with the embryo safely lodged in her womb. After she ventures onto the open road to accomplish her goal, she is immersed in her inner space. Cleverly, but dangerously, she waits for her pregnancy to show. Again she is taking risks: she might be punished severely by her father or brothers before word even gets to Judah. Furthermore, when Judah passes the cruel judgment on her, Tamar waits until she is literally taken to the stake before confronting him via messengers. Tamar could have let Judah know much earlier that she was pregnant by him, and thus avoid the horrible experience of being led to be burnt, but she means to have Judah exercise the utmost injustice and cruelty. Not only did he prevent her from becoming a mother, but when he hears that she is pregnant he does not stop to understand or to sympathize with her, but in two brief, cutting words (in Hebrew) he condemns her to be burned. Beyond the cruelty toward the woman and the double standard that Judah shares with his culture, one cannot but hear the sense of relief in Judah's voice as he pronounces his daughter-in-law's verdict. With Tamar's demise, his son will be saved from death, and Judah himself from incest.

The recognition scene is again a combination of the public and the private. Tamar is "taken out" of her home and led to death, with her pregnancy now serving as proof to the community witnessing the event that indeed Judah has passed the right judgment. But the moment that should reveal how right Judah was, and how he and his family have been wronged by the woman, is the moment when the opposite is established. Judah recognizes his injustice toward the woman. He connects his withholding of his son from Tamar to the latter's action. What for Judah has been a series of disconnected, meaningless events—an accidental sexual encounter, the disappearance of the harlot from the roadside, and the failure to deliver the pledges—becomes a moral journey toward a better understanding of his own selfishness.

Tamar, though, will never have a husband and Judah will not "know" her again. Nevertheless, God rewards her with two sons in place of those who died while married to her, and thus she becomes a legitimate member of Judah's clan. Mieke Bal sees in the ending of the tale a defeat for the woman, for Tamar gets neither Shelah nor his father, while the patriarchal drive to maintain the line and "restore" the "broken chronology" is successful.[11] Bal is right in assessing Tamar's role within the context of biblical history. Like the charismatic Hannah, mother of Samuel, Tamar briefly occupies center stage in the tale only to recede into the background when she has fulfilled her procreative function. Then the limelight once again shifts to the men. Yet within the perimeters of the dramatic narrative itself, it seems that Tamar's victory is undeniable. Her purpose has been to become a mother and establish herself within Judah's family, and this she has accomplished against all odds. Although Tamar exits the tale without a husband, one might argue that she has had enough weak males in her life. Judah, the only powerful, attractive man, is also ruthless and deceitful. The sons will provide her with the joys of motherhood and secure her an important position within the family as the mother of Judah's twins. Furthermore, Tamar is also vindicated by history by becoming the ancestor of King David, for Judah's union with her, rather than with his lawful wife, begins the line leading to David.

Tamar's strategy consists of spatial daring (positioning herself at the roadside) combined with the mental strength to reflect and focus intently on her goal, and come up with a risky scheme. As in the tale of the concubine, the paternal home is proven untrustworthy to the woman. Tamar is expelled from one, that of Judah, and then is practically imprisoned in her father's home. The latter offers her no protection from Judah's wrath; for while Judah banished her from his home, he still has full authority over her. At his command, she is seized from her father's home and taken out to be burnt. The young widow understands that to succeed in this culture she has to turn inwardly, toward her mind and body. Tamar triumphs through her clever thinking and planning, as well as through her body's ability to conceive almost on command. She is self-reliant, having been betrayed by her environment. We do not hear her father pleading on her behalf either when she is denied Shelah, or when she is sentenced to die. Tamar does not confide in women friends. They cannot be trusted because they are so powerless, although it is likely women were responsible for informing her about Judah's plans to participate in the sheep-shearing festivities.

The tale juxtaposes the man's powers with those of the woman's. Judah's power is first physical: he survives while his sons die prematurely. Judah obviously enjoys all the prerogatives of the patriarch, including legal authority over members of his family, even to the point of condemning one of them to death. Lastly, Judah's power is his virility, his ability to impregnate the young woman during a single encounter. Tamar's powers are different. To men, her powers are mysterious and evil: she is a husband killer. Yet her triumph is due to her vigilance, her focused attention on Judah, her insight into his nature, her total control and thorough knowledge of herself, her ability to pretend and use clever, incisive language, and lastly, her fertility.

As the tale moves toward its resolution, the storyteller informs us that Judah "knew her again no more," that he was never again intimate with her. The irony is that while sexually "knowing" her Judah at the same time was ignorant of her identity as well as her crafty plan. Judah never fully knew his young daughter-in-law or else he would have been more careful. The true "knower" is not the man but the woman. Tamar knew Judah well and she knew there was a difference between the public and the private man. In public Judah promised to give her Shelah when he grew, but Tamar knew that in his heart he never intended to do so. In public, Judah was an honorable man and a stern judge, demanding complete adherence to the law of his sons and of their widow, but Tamar knew that in private he would be carried away by the spirit of the sheep-shearing festivities and looking for sexual adventure. In the end, Judah, who believed himself discreet, is exposed publicly and put to shame. We can assume that Tamar will never have to seat herself at the roadside again, that her place in the patriarchal home is safe, that she will always be defiant, fearless, and amuse herself and her female friends with the tale of how she outwitted the mighty lion, Judah.

Tamar's tale provides a link in the string of tales that revolve around the sexual entrapment of a man by a woman, or women, beginning with the daughters of Lot conceiving from their father, to Tamar making Judah impregnate her, and culminating in Ruth "uncovering" Boaz's "legs" at the threshing floor.[12] Ruth's actions and lexicon are by far more dignified than those of Tamar's, but the latter is more daring, given the early times in which her tale is set. The narrative might seem to anchor the woman's strength in her sexual attraction and procreative powers. As we have seen, however, Tamar's psychological and mental maturity play a far greater role in her triumph than her biological functions. She allows herself to be used as inanimate territory to be invaded by a man, but her success is measured by the fact that she has firmly planted herself within the historical memory and consciousness of her people, and moved from a nameless instrument of procreation to the enterprising creator of the Davidic line.

2. ABIGAIL TAKES TO THE ROAD

The Text
1 Samuel 25

And when Abigail saw David, she hastened, and descended from the ass, and fell before David on her face . . . and said: "Upon me, my lord, upon me let this iniquity be." (1 Sam. 25:23–24)

"And it shall come to pass, when the Lord shall have done to my lord according to all the good that he has spoken concerning thee, and shall have appointed thee ruler over Israel; that this shall not be a cause of stumbling to thee . . . that thou hast shed blood causelessly. . . . And David said to Abigail: 'Blessed be the Lord God of Israel, who sent thee this day to meet me.' " (1 Sam. 25:30, 31, 32)

The tale of Abigail is framed by information about the woman's marital status; she is introduced to us as Nabal's wife, and she exits the tale as David's wife. As Nabal's wife, Abigail is mistress of a wealthy estate. As David's wife she is one of several wives of a man who leads a nomadic life as a fugitive sought by King Saul. Nabal provides her with a regal home where lavish parties are given into the early hours of the morning (25:36), while David and his group of outlaws hide "by the covert of the hill" (25:20). Although the Abigail episode may be regarded as a comic relief in the saga of David's tribulations before he ascends the throne, as the tale takes shape the charismatic David recedes to a supporting role and gives way to an even more fascinating person, the wise woman Abigail.

Nabal and Abigail are introduced to us as a study in opposites: he is coarse and ill-behaved, she is intelligent and beautiful. Nabal's surname, "Calebite," might affiliate him with the powerful Caleb clan, but it may also be a character or physical description—"doglike."[13] These stereotypical characterizations are soon animated in a dramatic example: Nabal acts in a mean-spirited way that is also foolish, and Abigail is called on to correct her boorish husband's mistake. Nabal rebuffs David's demand for compensation for protecting his shepherds when they camped in Carmel, claiming that David is no more than a worthless hooligan. The incident is a reflection of David's precarious position. Nabal represents affluent Israelites loyal to Saul who wish to maintain the status quo. From Nabal's point of view, David is asking for "protection money"—a form of extortion—for work he was not asked to perform.

Although Abigail is first seen as home-bound and unacquainted with her husband's dealings, she is made a participant in his affairs by one of the servants. It seems that the people around the couple are used to turning to Abigail when their master acts against his own interests. That they respect Abigail's intelligence becomes clear when the servant not only complains about the master's ill-tempered response to David, but explains in great detail why David's request was justified. In other words, although Abigail knows her husband's weaknesses, she would want to know exactly why his action in this case was ill-advised. She also learns that David has rounded up his warriors, intent on taking revenge of Nabal and his property.

Nabal and Abigail exemplify a variation on the "detestable father–admirable daughter" pattern, with the forbidding patriarchal figure of the husband taking the traditional place of the father.[14] David is the "other," the young man of an outside group, who will ultimately save the beautiful young woman from the ugly patriarch. The typology transcends the love theme and as well as gender. The two men—Nabal, older, affluent, and self-confident, and David, young, ambitious, and hotheaded—serve as foils to each other. Both are too extreme and irrational in their reaction, and their conduct could lead to disaster. These two figures exemplify Northrop Frye's formula of the polarized comic pair consisting of *eîron*, the self-deprecator, and *alâzon,* the boaster or impostor.[15] David is less than he really is, or will become, and therefore plays the *eîron,* using fawning language in his first message to Nabal and calling himself Nabal's "son" (25:8). The arrogant Nabal, in his social status and wealth, is more than his character warrants, and therefore is the *alâzon.* The moderate type between these two extremes is the *alêthes,* the truthful person, a role assumed by Abigail, who offers balance. Furthermore, if the *eîron* and *alâzon* are two extreme types with regard to truth, another pair of comic figures consists of two extreme types: the buffoon-churl (or the clown-boor), with the *eutrapelos,* the witty person, representing the middle way. Frye's comic formula applies to the three actors in this small drama. The two men assume the roles of the comic extremes: David is as ludicrous in his audacity and saber-rattling impetuosity as is Nabal in his crude, drunken boorishness. David shuttles between one comic extreme and the other, since he is both the *eîron,* the self-deprecator, and the *alâzon,* the boaster, especially when he becomes intent on revenge. The woman represents the golden mean between these two antithetical forms of distortion of reality and comic conduct.

Abigail is a variation on the "wise woman" figure. Although she is not labeled as such, she is presented as possessing "good intelligence" and has a moderating, calming effect on the reckless David. She may, indeed, be a particular example of the abstract, disembodied "Woman Wisdom" of Proverbs.[16] Abigail is thus an auxiliary character, an educational tool assisting David in his journey toward maturity and self-knowledge. Within the saga of David's tumultuous career, the Abigail episode serves as a step in David's education and his evolution from brashness and impulsiveness to moderation and restraint, qualities that he would later need as a leader.

Nevertheless, Abigail, not David, is the center of this episode, with the two men not only the opposites of each other but of her as well. Whatever position they take, she is the opposite, not as an extreme, but as the middle way, the golden mean. If Nabal is ugly, she is good-looking; if he is boorish, she is delicate and smart. If David is homeless, with no connection or roots, Abigail is mistress of a large and rich home, member of the Israelite elite. If David is too quickly offended and too ready to wave his sword, Abigail illuminates to him the virtue of patience and self-control. If David's view is limited only to the moment and the healing of the present injury, Abigail opens up to him the vision of the future and redemption in time.

Thus on the axis of comic types, Nabal occupies one comic pole and David the other, while Abigail provides the middle way and therefore the center. On the temporal axis, Nabal represents blindness to the march of fate by clinging to a failed king and not recognizing David's inevitable rise. David represents the young man's sense of urgency and impatience with the normal progression of time, his unreasonable attempts to speed up the pace of history. Abigail possesses a correct vision of the future, but also understands that destiny cannot be hastened. In this tale, David's situation is analogous to that of the youthful Prince Hal (in Shakespeare's Henry IV, Part One), who has to go through a period of training before he is ready to assume the responsibility of the throne. Comic excesses are seen by both the biblical narrator and Shakespeare as part of the young man's folly of which he has to be rid. David, in his brashness and impatience with time, is analogous to the saber-rattling Hotspur, who asks, "O, let the hours be short" (act 1, scene 3). Nabal, in his refusal to recognize the progress of time and history, is a villainous Falstaff, whose sphere is outside the clock and the calendar (act 1, scene 2).[17] Abigail teaches David to do what Prince Hal learns to do, namely, bide his time and join history at the appropriate moment. In terms of comic types, David's impetuosity is childishly comical, as is Hotspur's (act 1, scene 3). Nabal, getting drunk and making merry all night long, is Falstaffian when intoxicated as well as when he sobers up and has to come to terms with reality.

Abigail, again, teaches David to shed his waggish image and adopt a sober, realistic state of mind. The following table offers a view of the two systems of opposites presented here, regarding comic types as well as history, and the woman's position as the golden mean between two extreme forms of conduct:

Nabal—Abigail—David: Excesses and the Golden Man

		Axis of Comedy:		
		Nabal: Boorish, drunk (Falstaff)		
Axis of History:	Nabal: Defects from it (like Falstaff)	Abigail: The middle way regarding history and comedy	David: Wishes to speed it up (like Hotspur)	
		David: Saber-rattling, childish (Hotspur)		

Abigail steps out of her feminine role and, at the heart of the narrative, becomes an ungendered, cerebral presence with the power to reason and persuade. Yet her logically structured argument, which employs the right words that exhort without offending, is again framed by strong gender-based connotations. Abigail's strategy is a combination of sexual daring and sexual appeasement. By taking to the road, and apparently having to depart from the main road in order to meet David in his hiding place, Abigail acts in a way more typical of a man than of a woman. We remember that Jonathan, Saul's son, met with David under such circumstances, but the spunky Michal never did. By sending food as well as wine ahead of her, Abigail resorts to the feminine role of a nurturer, with the wine promising more than just the basic nourishment.

Between the moment Abigail sights David, and when she meets him, the text inserts David's additional bragging that he is going to decimate Nabal's entire household. Whether or not Abigail overhears these words she acts as if the matter is urgent. When she sees David she recognizes him immediately even though it is hard to imagine she saw David before. Most probably, she catches David in the midst of delivering the long tirade of boasts and threats (25:21–22), and thus she guesses that this is David. Although they have not been formally introduced, Abigail's intuition leads her directly to David. She quickly descends from her higher position on the animal, not to David's level, but to his feet, pleading with him to listen to her, and flattering him by calling herself his "handmaid" (25:24). Before David has a chance to give her permission to talk, Abigail embarks on a lengthy, thoughtful monologue. First she denigrates her husband, referring to him several times as "ignoble" or "uncouth," thus dissociating herself from him. She also claims not to have met David's messengers when they came to see her husband, implying that she usually participates in making decisions, giving credibility to the role of mediator she has taken. She then blesses David in God's name for having restrained himself from bloodshed. Rather than concluding that this is a later insertion, I see this as Abigail's tactic. She acts as if David has already had a chance to wreak revenge and has chosen not to. She calls the gifts that she has brought a "blessing," repeating David's euphemistic request for material reward.

Appearing to assume that an amiable rapport now exists between herself and David, Abigail boldly continues to tie her faith in David's glorious future with the warning to him not to engage in an impetuous act that would tarnish his image later. She does not remain within the exigency of the moment, but lays out her vision of David's future. Nabal called David a "servant" who broke away from his "master," thus alluding to David's homelessness. Abigail, on the other hand, talks about the "house" that God will build for David, implying more than a residence, but a continuous dynasty. She reiterates her vision of David's future as the "prince" or "master" of Israel, trying to lift him out of his present misery and fury to see the coming years stretching before him and expand his responsibility to the time God fulfills his promise.

Abigail takes a view of David opposite that of her husband. She seems acquainted with David's ambition and his special bond with God. Her lexicon of piety resembles many of David's speeches. She points out the moral reason why David should avoid bloodshed (the people who would be harmed, including her, are innocent), but also adds a pragmatic reason—the shedding of innocent blood will sully David's name. Abigail uses the tactic of flattery and appeasement, then appeals to his morality and, finally, to his good sense and ambition. She is mediator, teacher, and advisor combined.

Yet other dynamics develop while Abigail speaks passionately and David listens, culminating in Abigail offering herself to David, under the veiled language of "thou shalt remember thy handmaid" (25:31). In the last phrase Abigail retreats to her femininity, thus softening the audacity of her warning to David not to create an unnecessary obstacle to his rise and ultimate victory.

Abigail has thus averted potential carnage, steered David in the direction of self-control, and, in the process, has probably fallen in love with David. She springs out of her wifely anonymity and occupies the limelight momentarily, only to recede to the background when she becomes one of David's several wives (25:22–23). David's reasons for marrying Abigail are seen as politically motivated. Abigail's are not easily deciphered, and may be a combination of the political—tying her life to the future king's—and the personal—the exciting David is the very opposite of her uncouth first husband.

By taking to the open road Abigail has proven the breadth of her vision, her ability to look into the future clearly and correctly. At the end she is taken off the road and cut down to size by a narrator who has gone too far in his admiration of the woman, and now has to re-focus his narrative on David, the maker and carrier of the covenantal history. Abigail's reward is the conventional feminine good fortune: she has children with David. Nevertheless, for one brief moment she has occupied center stage, taking the limelight, as well as the narrative space, from the charismatic David.

3. WOMAN ON THE WALL

The Text
2 Samuel 20:13–22

And all the people that were with Joab battered the wall to throw it down. Then cried a wise woman out of the city: "Hear, hear, say," to Joab, "I pray you, come near here." . . . Then she spoke saying: "Surely in early times they would have spoken saying, Let them ask Abel to yield, and so they would have ended the matter. I am of the peaceable and faithful in Israel; thou seekest to destroy a city and a mother in Israel." And Joab said: "Sheba . . . has lifted up his hand against the king . . . deliver him only." And the woman said to Joab: "Behold, his head shall be thrown to thee over the wall." (2 Sam. 20: 16, 18, 19, 21)

The Wise Woman on the Wall

The scene of the wise woman appearing on the wall of her city during a military siege and saving her people from annihilation at the hands of the ruthless Joab has interesting parallels to an earlier incident narrated in Judges (9:50–56). In the earlier tale a woman drops a millstone on Abimelech, who has conquered the city of Tebets and is now surrounding a tower, the last stronghold, where the city's residents have taken refuge. Abimelech and his followers are known to be ferocious with their civilian victims. On a previous occasion, in the city of Shekhem, Abimelech burned down a tower where one thousand men and women found refuge. The same cruel fate is expected to befall the city of Tebets, when an enterprising woman appears on top of the tower and drops a millstone on Abimelech's head. Mortally wounded, Abimelech asks his arms-bearer to kill him, so that people will not say "a woman slew him" (9:54). The siege of Tebets thus ends without a massacre because of the courage and resourcefulness of an anonymous woman. The woman's domestic tool, the millstone, is reminiscent of Yael's wooden peg, proving that at the hands of a courageous woman, even a harmless household tool can turn into an instrument of war.

97

The drama of the unnamed woman who saves her besieged city by killing the leader of the pursuing army is tied to the tale of the wise woman talking Joab out of destroying her city more than structurally. Joab, David's military chief, mentions the event narrated in Judges on a different occasion, before his encounter with the "wise woman," and thus, his awareness of the historical precedent and those elements in it that he highlights are significant.

The story of the woman of Tebets causing the downfall of a powerful man is recalled by Joab when he becomes involved in David's plot to destroy Uriah, Bathsheba's husband. Joab ignored David's instructions to conspire with Uriah's men to abandon Uriah in the heat of the battle, and thus expose him to the enemy. Instead, Joab devised a plan that in his eyes was better, since it did not require sharing the conspiracy with other soldiers, but it resulted in the death not only of Uriah but of a large number of the best soldiers. In his instructions to the messenger who will bring the news to David, Joab is careful not to arouse the messenger's suspicion, and therefore he speaks circuitously, in a way that will be understood by David but which may confuse the messenger. Joab anticipates not only David's anger at the heavy price that was paid for the elimination of Uriah, but also the words that David would say to the messenger. In Joab's imagined conversation between David and the messenger, David would question Joab's tactics of sending a whole unit so close to the walls of the besieged city and recall a similar mistake made by Abimelech, which resulted in a woman dropping a millstone on Abimelech and killing him (2 Sam. 11:21). The event that happened many years before became an example of what should be avoided by an army besieging a walled city. It illustrated a tactical guideline mandating that an army should not come too close to a city's wall without proper precautions, which apparently is known to Joab as well as to David and to any military commander of the times. Although Joab makes the anticipated dialogue between his messenger and David quite vivid, when the actual conversation between king and messenger occurs David does not mention the historical precedent. Evidently, the tale of Abimelech and its many implications are more meaningful to Joab than to David. We might say that Joab is obsessed with this early incident.

One of the reasons Joab repeats the tale of "Abimelech killed by a woman" (rather than just naming the precept against approaching too close to a city's wall) is his intuitive understanding that a woman is somehow involved in David's enigmatic instructions to eliminate Uriah, a fierce and loyal soldier.[18] The analogy between the Abimelech example and Joab's present situation might be doubly significant in Joab's eyes: he may see in a woman the cause of both David's potential downfall and Uriah's death.[19] Beyond that, Joab, as an astute and seasoned military commander, is bothered by the fact that he has acted against a well-known tactical rule. By imagining David's anger at the violation of this important principle, and instructing the messenger to answer

David by saying that "thy servant Uriah the Hittite died also" (11:17), Joab articulates an internal dialogue and reveals his own misgivings. We know from David and Joab's relationship that Joab does not hesitate to do things his own way when he believes that he knows better how to further David's interests. It is hard to imagine Joab is very concerned about David's fury; it is more likely that Joab is upset about other issues, such as having had to get rid of a good soldier, and, in the process, to act as an inexperienced commander, unschooled in military history and tactical thinking.[20] In the imagined dialogue between David and the messenger, Joab is actually talking to himself, rationalizing that he was forced to act as a careless, unprofessional general and order the soldiers to get too close to the city, because Uriah had to die in the least suspicious way.

We have three tales about women overpowering men, all linked together through Joab. The first is an event that happened generations before Joab's time. The second is the same historical event as evoked by Joab (who imagines David referring to it). The third is another historical event, narrated by the biblical storyteller, in which Joab and an unnamed woman figure prominently. All three narratives have structural similarities, as shown in the following table.

This table illustrates what Joab has learned from the history of Abimelech, and therefore it makes his actions during the siege of Abel even more surprising. The time is the aftermath of Absalom's rebellion, when Joab and his army are in hot pursuit of another rebel against David, who has found refuge in the city of Abel. The walled city seems doomed, with Joab and the army relentlessly battering its walls. The situation is similar to that of the cities of Shekhem and Tebets in Abimelech's times. The city's walls are about to fall when a "wise woman" cries from the city, taking a position on the wall and practically ordering Joab to approach so she can talk to him. Surprisingly, the ruthless and hardened man of war complies with the woman's wishes and approaches the wall, assuring the woman that he is listening. Joab's action is strange in two ways: first, he is making the error that he himself cited as the foolish act that cost Abimelech his life. Second, consulting with a woman on a military matter is not consistent with Joab's image as a hardened man of war.

The fact that the woman is named "a wise woman" is significant. Wisdom here is not only a description of the woman's intelligence, but a professional designation as well. The "wise woman" may be wearing a garment that would identify her as such, and therefore she is less afraid to expose herself to enemy archers, and Joab is more willing to listen. We know that on a previous occasion Joab hired a "wise woman" to make peace between David and Absalom. It is not strange for Joab to trust a wise woman in a case that has to do with a delicate family matter, but for him to listen to a woman in a military matter, and to allow himself to occupy the lower position strategically, appears at least initially to be a testimony to the wise woman's status in ancient Israel.

The Woman on the Wall and the Mighty Warrior

	Abimelech Killed by a Woman Judges 9:50–56 (a)	Joab Recalls the Tale of Abimelech 2 Samuel 11:20, 21 (a/b)	Joab and the Wise Woman 2 Samuel 20:13–22 (c)
Speaker	The biblical narrator	Joab (David) retelling (a)	The biblical narrator
Actors	Abimelech, an anonymous woman	Abimelech, an anonymous woman	Joab, an anonymous "wise woman"
Historical circumstances	Siege of the city of Tebets	Same	Siege of the city of Abel
Event	Woman drops a millstone on Abimelech and fatally wounds him	Woman drops a millstone on Abimelech and kills him	A wise woman starts a dialogue with Joab
Spatial positions	Woman is on a tower; Abimelech is at the bottom	Woman is on the wall; Abimelech is at the bottom	Woman is on the wall; Joab is on the ground
The man embodies	Cruelty, military power, imminent victory, folly	Same	Cruelty, power, imminent victory, good sense
The woman embodies	The city, powerlessness, resourcefulness	Same	Same
The strategic error	Abimelech comes close to the foot of the tower	Abimelech comes close to the wall	Joab comes close to the wall
Woman's tools	The millstone	The millstone	Verbal negotiations
Results	Abimelech is fatally wounded	Abimelech is killed	Sheba is killed
Lesson learned for future	Soldier should not approach the city wall	Same	
Fate of the city	Saved	Same	Same
Historical notoriety	A woman killed a man	A woman killed a man	Not cited
Function of tale	Historical narration	1) Joab's misgivings; 2) Joab sees an analogy with the David-Bathsheba event	Historical narration
Archetypal significance	Woman-on-the-wall is dangerous	Same	Same

In the earlier episode involving a wise woman, the woman indulges in a lengthy fable, since she has David's ear. In this case, the woman has no time for impersonation and storytelling. Thus, she quotes a short epigram that means, essentially, that before embarking on a military action Joab should have asked the city's residents if they were ready to hand over the fugitive (20:18). Having gained Joab's attention, the woman continues, not losing momentum: "Thou seeketh to destroy a city and a mother in Israel" (20:19). By using the Hebrew idiom to describe a metropolitan center, "a city and a mother in Israel," the wise woman achieves several ends: she emphasizes to David's advisor the importance of the city and the wisdom of leaving it intact, but she also points to the feminine nature of the city, thus shaming the fierce soldier into further realizing the absurdity of his actions. Joab would be destroying an important place, making a political mistake, and his victory over civilians, women and children, will prove hollow.

By alluding to the city's feminine nature, the woman also protects herself, justifying her interference in the male domain of politics and war by giving it a feminine dimension. She pleads on behalf of women, as well as of the woman that is the city. Her position on the wall of a city enhances her femininity as well as sexual vulnerability, thus disarming Joab. In other words, while the position of the "woman on the wall" is an image as frightening to men as that of the woman-at-her-doorstep, the wise woman is able to dilute that forceful image and persuade Joab of the wisdom of a peaceful solution.

This brief narrative is bifocal, centering equally on the woman and the man. The woman's wisdom lies in her ability to play different roles, all catering to the man's needs. She first presents herself and her people as peace-loving and faithful, and the city as "the inheritance of God" (20:19). Her plea is so passionate and feminine that the unemotional Joab must respond in kind and strongly deny that he has had any intentions of decimating the city, which of course is not the case. When Joab explains the reasons for his being here, the pleading, gentle woman changes her tone and becomes cold and businesslike. Her previous lexicon of piety and faith turns deadly when she tersely announces that Sheba's head will soon be thrown over the wall. This wise woman turns out to be as much of an actress as the one who was sent to David earlier. First, she plays the role of the beseeching, harmless female, but she knows that this image alone will not change Joab's resolve. The second role is that of the serious, no-nonsense negotiator who plays not only on the other party's sense of mercy, but who has something very substantial to offer. The woman's wisdom then lies in her ability to suppress her own personality and play the roles to which Joab will respond. These two roles are diametrically opposite, one necessitating the façade of innocence, vulnerability, and unworldiness, the other of pragmatism and cold-blooded determination.

From Joab's point of view, the woman appearing on the wall may seem a repetition of the old story about Abimelech, and as such she means danger, even if she is identifiable as a "wise woman." Given his preoccupation with the Abimelech example, Joab's coming close to the wall is a calculated risk. He may be taking a chance that the woman will turn out to be, indeed, dangerous, but not toward him. Joab's risk pays off; the woman who speaks tenderly on behalf of women and the cause of peace does not hesitate to betray the man who has found refuge in her city. Moreover, while Joab requests merely that the man be turned over to him, the woman promises to throw the man's "head" "over the wall" (20:21). For Joab, the image of the woman-on-the-wall held the promise that the solution would not necessarily have to be gentle and bloodless. Symbolically, the higher strategic position that the woman occupies indeed becomes dangerous to a man, though not to Joab but to Sheba.

That the woman is more inclined toward a solution that would result in the killing of Sheba than are her townspeople is clear from the fact that she still has to go to the city's people "in her wisdom" and persuade them that handing over Sheba's head is the right thing to do. As in the case of Yael, there is a duality to the image of the woman-on-the-wall. Within the historical narrative she is justified and viewed as peacemaker and savior. She is rewarded for her courage to appear on the wall unarmed and credited with teaching the experienced soldier the art of negotiations. But the woman's mobility, the suggestion of powerful sexuality implied in the spatial image, is at the same time menacing. The brutal ending of the story, indeed the gruesome nature of the act of beheading that is first suggested by the woman herself, confirms the darker side of this feminine image and the primal "fear of women" that it transmits. The representation of the woman-on-the-wall is thus a variation of the woman-at-her-doorstep, and Yael's duality parallels that of the anonymous wise woman.

The theme of feminine mobility is triple-edged. Some biblical tales, like those of Dinah and the concubine in Gibea, serve as cautionary reminders to women of the perils of the open road. Other tales seem to applaud the woman's daring and show how history rewards the enterprising female. The third kind consists of those tales about female mobility that are saturated with the "fear of women" message and serve as a warning to men. The "wise woman" on the wall is smart, peace-loving, and tender, but also a violator of the rules of hospitality and a traitor to men.

CHAPTER 4

WOMAN BEHIND THE SCENES

1. REBECCA EAVESDROPS

The Text
Genesis 27; 28:1–5

And Rebecca heard when Isaac spoke to Esau his son. . . . And Rebecca spoke to Jacob her son, saying: "Behold, I heard thy father speak to Esau thy brother, saying, bring me venison, and make me savory food, that I may eat, and bless thee before the Lord before I die. Now therefore my son, obey my voice. . . . Go now to the flock and fetch me from there two good kids of the goats, and I will make them into savory food for your father." . . . And Rebecca took the best clothes of her eldest son Esau . . . and put them upon Jacob her younger son; and she put the skins of the goats upon his hands, and upon the smooth of his neck. . . . And he came to his father . . . and Jacob said to his father: "I am Esau thy firstborn." (Gen. 27:5, 6, 7, 15, 16, 19)

The majority of biblical women do not come across as risk takers but rather as passive and acquiescent. If they step forward into the limelight, they endanger themselves; even if they are successful in accomplishing their mission openly, as is Abigail, they quickly recede into the background to assume the familiar stance of patience and reticence. Nevertheless, women have always had their own wishes and plans, which have not always coincided with those of men. Often, the most effective strategy of conduct used by women was to manipulate events from behind the scenes. They huddled indoors, ostensibly taking as little space as possible and leaving the open arena to the men, but they pulled the strings so that the men thought that they acted freely while at the same time they were unwittingly carrying out the women's wishes. The biblical text does not always reward the woman for acting behind the scenes. Two examples are presented here; in the first, the woman's triumph turns out to be defeat, while in the second, the woman succeeds in fooling not only the men around her, but perhaps also the chronicler of events himself.

We would like to believe that Rebecca's intervention in the selection of the third patriarch, by fooling her husband into giving the paternal blessing to her favorite son, was divinely inspired. We think that Rebecca had insight sharper than her husband's and that the underhanded means that she chose could be seen as a necessary evil: Isaac was going to make a colossal mistake by blessing Esau. Therefore, due to Rebecca the right person received the patriarchal blessing and mission and the course of Israelite history ran as it did.

There are, however, a number of problems with this scenario. First, in this episode the admirable Rebecca acts in a demeaning and humiliating way. She has to spy on her husband to learn that he intends to bless Esau, and does not hear it directly from him. Second, Rebecca does not feel free to discuss the matter with her husband and tell him her opinion, but instead, has to conspire with Jacob to perpetrate a hoax on the blind old man. Third, Rebecca's modus operandi in this episode marks a disturbing transformation from the personality of her youth.

As a young woman (Gen. 24) Rebecca seems independent and determined. The verbs that characterize her, "hasten" and "run," denote mobility and enterprise. She takes part in her own marriage negotiations and subtly but actively prompts Eliezer, Abraham's messenger, to make a marriage offer to her, on behalf of his master. When we meet her again as wife and mother, however, she has adopted the prototypical feminine pose: she is indoors and, like Sarah before her, stealthily listening behind the curtains to her husband's conversation. The aging Isaac, known to prefer his older son, asks Esau to prepare a feast for his father, after which the son will be blessed by the patriarch. Rebecca, younger and apparently more robust than her husband, feels that her husband has lost his good sense together with his sight. She will do everything in her power to put her son, Jacob, in his brother's place, so that the younger son will get the patriarch's blessing. She devises an elaborate scheme that calls for her to cook a lavish meal, as well as disguise her "plain" and "tent-dwelling" son so that his father will mistake him for Esau, the "cunning hunter" and "man of the field."

The dichotomy between the two sons is spatially forged. The mother loves the son who, like her, stays inside the tent. The father loves the son who roams the open fields, exuding masculinity and toughness. The sons' typical activities are also delineated along gender lines. Jacob cooks porridge while Esau hunts venison. In modern terms we might say that Jacob's closeness to his mother could be a problem, that a separation is in order so the son could break out of the enclosed "feminine" confines of the tent and join the "masculine" world of the open fields.

Rebecca proves capable of setting up a theatrical mask scene intended to benefit her son through a case of mistaken identity. In a frenzy of energetic activity, the mother cooks a meal, takes the clothes of her older son, and puts them on her younger son. She then puts goat skins on Jacob's smooth hands and neck, gives him the "savory food and bread" which she prepared, and sends him to his father. Rebecca's activities contrast with Jacob's passiveness; he seems reluctant, dragged along by his charismatic mother. By involving her son in this conspiracy and making him engage in pretense and duplicity early in life, Rebecca initiates Jacob into a twisted, tortuous, and complicated destiny. Henceforth, Jacob will either be outsmarted by others, or have to devise strategies to outwit his enemies and, in a sense, his own fate.

Furthermore, though the biblical narrator neither condones nor condemns Rebecca's and Jacob's actions, he makes clear that while Rebecca exhibited resourcefulness in her ability to fool her blind husband, she was far from instrumental in the selection of Jacob as the successor to Abraham's heritage. Rebecca was mistaken in doubting her husband's judgment. Isaac did understand the difference between his two sons and he therefore prepared a separate blessing for each of them, in accordance with their respective personalities and destinies.[1] Thus in the blessing that Isaac designed for Esau (though he unwittingly gave it to Jacob), he promised his son material things, abundance, fatness and dominion, but did not mention the Abrahamic mission, the blessing of seed and the promise of the land. Therefore, when the ruse is discovered, Isaac not only has to bless his son Esau, but he sees fit to bless his son Jacob again, this time giving him the promise of the land and charging him with upholding Abraham's covenant (Gen. 28:34). Although Isaac's sight was gone, his mental abilities were intact, and he knew very well which of his sons should be the next patriarch.

Rebecca's elaborate scheme is thus contrasted with her husband's judiciously crafted blessings. The sighted Rebecca, homebound and claustrophobic, turns out to be myopic and paranoid. The blind Isaac is seen as observant and discerning, with the ability to distinguish between his own emotional preferences for Esau and the needs of the clan and its heritage, which, he knew, would be better served by Jacob. Thus the biblical narrator lets us understand, subtly and indirectly, that the woman's elaborate scheme was completely unnecessary, and that her energy and talents were wasted on a ruse that only complicated her and her son's lives. Indeed, Rebecca is punished for acting behind the scenes and interfering in what was perceived as the patriarch's domain and his prerogative—mapping out the future of his sons. She now has to send her beloved son abroad, away from his brother's vengeful hand. When Jacob returns after many years in exile, his mother is dead.

Although Isaac loved his wife very much, as the Bible tells us, he did not share with her his plans for his sons. Ignorant of her husband's state of mind and not trusting his judgment, Rebecca decided to take matters in her own hands. Thus Rebecca the matriarch emerges as a woman discontent with her derivative status and confident of her wisdom, who feels that she has to resort to eavesdropping and manipulating behind the scenes. But her wiles and trickery lead only to disaster. At the same time, we are left to wonder about all those unused feminine talents that were laid to waste in Rebecca's adult life. Acting behind the scenes clearly did not produce beneficial results for Rebecca the matriarch.

2. BATHSHEBA ON THE ROOF

The Texts
2 Samuel 11
2 Samuel 12:1–15, 19, 24
1 Kings 1:11–31; 50–53; 2:13–25

And it came to pass one evening, that David arose from his bed, and from the roof he saw a woman bathing; and the woman was very fair to look upon. . . . And David sent messengers, and took her; and she came in to him, and he lay with her. . . . And the woman conceived, and sent and told David, saying: "I am pregnant." (1 Sam. 11:2, 4, 5)

And Bathsheba bowed, and prostrated herself before the king. And the king said: "What's with you?" And she said to him: "My lord, thou didst swear by the Lord thy God to thy handmaid, saying: 'Indeed Solomon thy son shall reign after me, and he shall sit upon my throne.' " . . . And the king swore, and said: "As the Lord lives, He who has redeemed my soul out of all distress, even as I swore to thee by the Lord God of Israel, saying, indeed Solomon thy son shall reign after me, and he shall sit upon my throne in my stead." (2 Kings 1:16, 17, 29, 30)

King David's Watergate

The story narrated in 2 Samuel 11 is so incongruous with the rest of the historical material regarding King David, and David's crime so heinous and out of character with the man depicted before and after the event, that a contribution by a writer who opposed the monarchy may be a possibility.[2] The tone of sarcasm and irony adopted by the storyteller toward David is also inconsistent with the deference usually accorded to David by the biblical narrator.[3] The complete absence of information regarding Uriah's motivation in refusing David's suggestion that he visit his home, as well as David's thoughts on it, teases the reader into conflicting hypotheses, adding depth and complexity to the characters and the drama that unfolds.

David's actions in this tale are surprising not only because of their immorality, but also because they cannot be the product of an intelligent mind. David behaves as a man in panic, adding mistake to mistake, until he has to resort to the killing of an innocent man. Even David's murderous plans are designed so clumsily and dangerously that only by sheer luck (Uriah does not open the letter spelling his doom which he is carrying to Joab) as well as Joab's shrewdness and ruthlessness, the plan is carried out in the least suspicious way. Even so, the horrible crime is brought to light and David is punished.

Commentators and scholars naturally gravitate to the major figure in the text—David—so that even the gaps are pointed out in relation to David's thoughts and his speculations. Indeed, while we know this as the David-and-Bathsheba affair, David, not the couple, is the focus in the tale; and the dominant theme of the narrative is not love, or adultery, but a man's panicked, unsuccessful attempts to rid himself of a grave mistake. We meet David in a state of mind that modern readers would identify as a "burnout," or a mid-life crisis, a mental and physical fatigue that incapacitates an otherwise energetic, capable person. After a lifetime of battles and campaigns David allows Joab to lead the army to the siege of Rabbah while he stays home in Jerusalem. The portrait that we get in the opening verses is that of a lonely man who has no close companion or intimate friend, restlessly pacing the roof of his palace at the end of the day. We know that David was very attractive to women, that he had several wives, and at least one of them, Abigail, was very beautiful. Yet there is no indication that David was in love with any of them.

The narrative gaps have been identified as the dominant technique in the tale. Another way of defining the narrative strategy in the tale is to recognize the system of evasions, the purposeful defeating of the reader's expectations and the aborting of the natural climax of events. The one-time love-making with Bathsheba never materializes into a great love affair. Uriah's arrival in Jerusalem never turns into a confrontation either with David or with his wife, nor does it provide an occasion for Uriah to learn the truth (even though Uriah surely met and talked with some people in town). Joab's anticipation of David's anger never comes true. (Or was David angry but avoided showing it to the messenger?) A face-to-face confrontation between Joab and David is never presented, though it must have happened later. (Was Joab not curious why David instructed him to do away with a good soldier?) The text builds up expectations of dramatic encounters and the unfolding of events in a certain way, only to leave those elements as blank spots. Just as David is time and again frustrated in his attempts to send Uriah home and solve the problem of Bathsheba's pregnancy, so the storyteller frustrates the reader's curiosity to learn important details and to witness key scenes. Furthermore, contrary to several contemporary readers of the text, I see in the narrative tone not only sarcasm but a mixture of pity and irony in the portrayal of David. The more he tries to untangle the web he has created, the more entrapped he becomes.

The tale has another historical purpose that, again, has nothing to do with the sexual affair: it adds a link in the chain of narratives regarding the complex relationship between David and Joab that underlies the David saga. By making Joab partner to the crime, David becomes more of a hostage in his hands. With Joab brazenly changing an important detail in David's plan, the tale explains further why David would instruct his son Solomon to get rid of Joab. Far from being a tale of love, or of "lethal love," to use Mieke Bal's phrase, the story is about David bringing about a major blemish in his thus-far untarnished reputation, falling out with God and with the people of Israel, and being gripped tighter in Joab's clutches.[4]

Thus, of all the enigmas in the tale, Bathsheba's role seems at first to be the least significant. Feminist critics may fault male critics for calling Bathsheba "an unfaithful woman" rather than regarding her as a victim of the man's lust, or may see her as another example of a female blamed for the downfall of man, but none makes Bathsheba the person the focus of an analytical reading. There are more fascinating aspects to the tale narrated.[5] By integrating this tale with later episodes where Bathsheba appears, and tying together all the Bathsheba narratives, as well as by backshadowing, that is, rereading the earlier text with the aid of information provided in the later text, Bathsheba moves from a background player to a major figure in the tale.

From the beginning the tale implies an existential divide between the male and female spheres. The men are involved in wars and the conquest of cities. The wars are seasonal, inevitable, part of the march of time and history "when the time of year came in which kings march out" (11:1). The conquest of cities is paralleled by the conquest of women: David takes the woman that he fancies, just as he tries to take a city that he wants. David's spying on the bathing woman and then "taking her" is also a form of a siege that ends with male victory. The two parallel lines of the opening verses, one revolving around an assault on a city and the other on a woman, are later united in Joab's evocation of the siege of Tebets that ended with a woman dropping a millstone on the commander and killing him.

The men in the tale seem to be free agents, acting in the arena of time and space. Their march over geographical space makes history. The woman's life is punctuated by the rhythm of her natural cycle: Bathsheba is first seen taking the ritual bath to purify herself from her menstrual "uncleanness." Then she is the passive female in the sexual act, after which she announces her pregnancy. She later gives birth, and when the child dies, David resumes relations with her, and she becomes pregnant again, this time giving birth to a healthy child. The only words that Bathsheba pronounces in the present episode are "I am pregnant" (11:5).

That the tale's true tyrant is not the king but the cycle of the woman's body is made even clearer when we understand that the biblical narrator makes a point of linking the act of purification with the pregnancy. It not only establishes that David is the undeniable father, but also brings to the fore the woman's biology, which David did not take into account and which would defeat him. For David, the woman's bathing is a chance to see her naked. For the logic of events that dominates the tale, Bathsheba's time in the month makes her ready for conceiving. The rabbis' interpretation that the Bible wants us to know that David did not sleep with an unclean woman diverts us from the true functions of this piece of information.[6]

Bathsheba's silence in the tale is somewhat reminiscent of Dinah's enigmatic presence/non-presence in the Genesis tale. While the men continue to plot and conspire, Bathsheba is absent from the scene, apparently immersed in her pregnancy, or trying to hide it from the public. Socially and spatially, she occupies the lower position to David's higher position as the king who is on the high roof. Whether Bathsheba takes a bath on her roof or in her house is not so clear, but David is certainly on a higher level to be able to see her bathing next door and notice that she is good-looking.[7] Bathsheba is further diminished in Nathan's parable of the poor man's ewe lamb, where she is metaphorically reduced to a lamb, while the two men, unlike the woman, are not dehumanized for the purpose of the parable, but become two neighbors, David the rich man and Uriah the poor. Yet the freedom and mobility of the men become illusive when the powerful king, his ruthless commander-in-chief, and the brave Uriah become puppets whose fates are determined by a woman's pregnancy.

Bathsheba: First Impressions

Our first impression of Bathsheba is that of a passive female, surrendering easily to the king, subject to the laws of her feminine cycle, and having no control whatsoever over either. She appears lacking any volition or emotion, though when her husband dies she does mourn for him. Did she fall in love with David, or was she reluctant about the whole affair but powerless to resist the king's messengers when they came to take her to David? We should be somewhat surprised that such a timid female was not afraid to confront the king with the consequences of his deed. Letting the powerful ruler know that she was in trouble was not without its dangers. Another despot could have had her killed, or tainted her reputation, and thus solve the problem. Was she so confident that David would do the honorable thing and try to help her? After all, an unwanted pregnancy was always a woman's problem. To her neighbors and family she would be an adulteress no matter what. Was she, then, in such panic that she was not thinking clearly? Or was she naïve and unacquainted with the ways of the world? Or was she simply courageous enough to confront David in spite of all the pitfalls involved? The last possibility would seem out of character for the diffident, passive image Bathsheba has cut so far.

When we next meet Bathsheba she is still the same placid person, this time manipulated by the prophet Natan, who prefers to see Bathsheba's young son Solomon, rather than the ambitious Adonijah, succeed David (1 Kings 1–2). We are not informed whether the relationship between David and Bathsheba evolved into a bond of love, but as we meet David in his old age, he is again lonely, and there seems to have been no communication between him and Bathsheba for a long time. David's curt address to the woman when he sees her in his bedroom, "what is with you" (1 Kings 1:16), which in Hebrew consists of two monosyllabic words, sounds distant and impatient.

The idea to approach David about Solomon's fate is completely that of the prophet. He initiates the interview between Bathsheba and David, putting in Bathsheba's mouth the exact words she should say to the old king. Natan has to scare Bathsheba into cooperating with him, implying that if Adonijah becomes king, he will get rid of her and Solomon. Natan therefore instructs Bathsheba to go to David and remind him of the pledge that he had given her, that her son would inherit the throne. The narrative gap regarding the veracity of this piece of information makes the scene unusually suspenseful, offering a multitude of possibilities. One option is that the king did indeed give such a promise to Bathsheba, either in front of the prophet, or repeating it to the prophet on a different occasion, or that Bathsheba told the prophet of the king's promise. Nevertheless, when the prophet talks to Bathsheba he does not remind her of any promise but only warns her that she has to save herself and her son. The king's promise is never referred to as something that happened; rather it is mentioned for the first time in Natan's instructions to Bathsheba. Bathsheba does not protest, which may mean that there was such a promise. Nevertheless we understand that she is reluctant to go to the king, since the prophet quickly adds that he will come in while she would be talking and "confirm thy words" (1:14). If there was such a promise, why does the prophet have to confirm it? Furthermore, before scaring Bathsheba, should not the prophet first announce that the famous promise is about to be violated? Bathsheba's primary reason for going to the king should be the vow made to her, but the prophet does not raise the promise as the reason for the need to approach the king. Instead, he tells Bathsheba that she and her son are in danger.

Again, a number of options come to mind: either the king is known to be frail and quite forgetful, and therefore Bathsheba would have to remind him of a vow he took some time ago, and would need the prophet's reinforcement. But would David forget such a momentous promise? Although physically frail he still understands that Adonijah is not the proper heir to the throne and therefore refuses to support him. David's mind is certainly not as weak as his body. Or, the idea that Bathsheba is going to plant in the king's mind, that Solomon should succeed him, is not foreign to the king. His preference of Solomon may have been known to those around him, but he never gave Bathsheba a firm commitment. The promise may thus be a hoax concocted by the prophet in order to force the king to do the right thing immediately, and therefore Bathsheba is uncomfortable with the idea and needs the prophet's backing. This explains why David himself would need the prophet's words to translate his intentions into an actual promise.

Although the possibilities are many, it seems Bathsheba has to be prodded into going to the king, and that she has to be given the whole script and rehearsed by the prophet. Thus far, Bathsheba is the same passive woman who has always been manipulated and acted upon by men. She is the "helpless" female, almost ruined by the king in the past, but later pitied and comforted by him when her first child dies. Although she may not have had the best reputation, Natan, the prophet and religious authority, tries to protect and save her. Natan's reasons, however, flow from his own agenda, or from his knowledge of God's wishes. When Bathsheba sees the king, she faithfully repeats the script. She first states that David made a vow to her that her son would inherit his throne; she then reports to him that it seems that Adonijah has declared himself heir to the throne; and then she adds that the situation is dangerous for her and her son.

Natan's words to the king add to our suspicion that there was never a clearly defined promise made by the king to Bathsheba, since the prophet is careful not to mention a promise. The prophet may have created in Bathsheba the feeling that he would support her on the issue of the promise to encourage her, but when he actually talks to the king he merely asks him whether it was the king's decision to crown Adonijah. Natan appears upset with the king for not sharing his decision regarding a successor, but he does not intimate that a decision was indeed made by the king and made known to Natan and Bathsheba—a long time ago. Further, he does not challenge the king on the nature of the decision itself.

Bathsheba, surprisingly, disappears from the scene, for when Natan is done talking, the king asks that Bathsheba be brought in. That Bathsheba is hesitant, uncomfortable, and not confident in the world of palace intrigue is thus further established. When she delivered her first lengthy monologue, she acted as Natan's puppet. She is happy to absent herself from David's presence as soon as Natan is announced, and she has to be called back by David. This time, it is David who mentions a promise made in the past, vowing to fulfill it immediately. Whether he is indeed reminded of the promise, or just thinks that he ever gave it is immaterial. Bathsheba and Natan have succeeded in their plan, which certainly coincided with David's own intentions.

Bathsheba reappears as the queen-mother in Solomon's court, seen from the unlikely perspective of Adonijah. Solomon's brother has been pardoned by the young king and sent home with the warning that if he does not stir trouble the king will not touch him (1:51–53). Then we have the puzzling scene in which Adonijah pleads with Bathsheba to intervene on his behalf and ask the king to grant him permission to marry Abishag, David's concubine. It is hard to imagine that Adonijah's motives are innocent. He has been presented as ambitious and wily, though vain and not very smart. Solomon's interpretation of Adonijah's request, that his ambitious brother wants to possess the former king's concubine as a symbolic gesture and a prelude to another attempt to claim the throne, is probably right.

Why does Adonijah approach Bathsheba? We are not given Adonijah's inner thoughts, but it seems that he knows Bathsheba somewhat, at least from the reputation that she has, and he figures that she would be the right messenger. Bathsheba must be viewed as a kindly woman, easily manipulated, who was once involved in a romantic story and might sympathize with star-crossed lovers. The scene between Adonijah and Bathsheba parallels the earlier one between Natan and Bathsheba. In both cases, the man has an agenda and is sending the woman to the king with a prepared script. That Adonijah thinks that Bathsheba is a woman with a sentimental heart and little sense is clear from his plea to her. He first reminds her that the throne was already his, and that the people wanted him, but it was taken away from him by the wish of God. If the first part of the sentence might be offensive, that "all of Israel" wanted him, than the second part defuses the offense: God's will is more important than that of the people, and it makes Solomon's kingship irrevocable.

Again we have to retrace Adonijah's reasoning. Why risk Bathsheba's wrath by reminding her that the people wanted him and not her son? He may want to emphasize to her his sense of loss, or even make her feel somewhat guilty, since she was the one who went to the king and asked for his intervention. "I lost the kingdom, but at least do not let me lose the woman," he seems to be saying to her. He flatters her by expressing his confidence that her son the king will surely not turn her down. What makes Adonijah take such a risk with Solomon? Again we have to consider Solomon's public image and his reputation. It seems that Solomon and his mother are not really known to the people. Adonijah may think of Solomon as the pampered son of a loving, if foolish, woman. If Solomon grew up under the tutelage of this woman, as seems to be the case, then he must not be so smart or cunning himself. Casting his request in a romantic halo would induce Bathsheba to help, and the devoted mother's intervention would guarantee the inexperienced king's positive response. Interestingly, Bathsheba does not ask Adonijah for further information, such as whether Abishag loves him, how long this affair has been going on, or whether they loved each other while David was still alive. Adonijah seems to count on Bathsheba's sympathetic response to anything that is flavored with romance and intrigue, since she herself was not unacquainted with these in her youth.

The scene of Bathsheba's appearance before Solomon is in some ways a reversal of her earlier appearance in David's bedroom. Not only is Solomon young and vigorous, he refuses his mother's petition almost rudely. Whereas David passionately vowed to accede with Bathsheba's request, Solomon reprimands his mother for making the request. He angrily and sarcastically tells her that she might as well have asked him to surrender the throne to his older brother, for this is the true meaning of Adonijah's "innocent" plan. He implies that his mother is gullible. Bathsheba seems stunned and speechless, while Solomon goes on to pronounce Adonijah's death sentence as a rebel to the throne. Thus the story ends happily for Solomon, who is smart enough to have seen through Adonijah's scheme and avert the danger that he posed to him, through Solomon's unsuspecting mother.

Bathsheba Masterminds Her Fate

Too many elements are wrong with the portrayal of Bathsheba in the previous chapter. Our last impression is created through a reconstruction of Adonijah's thinking, which may be based both on his private assessment as well as on Bathsheba's public reputation. We should not accept Adonijah's view of Bathsheba as a naïve and foolish woman. Although Adonijah seems to be successful with Bathsheba, he has made a fatal mistake with regard to Solomon's response as well as Bathsheba's control of her son. The many similarities between Adonijah and Absalom—the good looks and charisma, the ability to attract the people, the murderously fierce ambition—draw our attention to both men's Achilles' heel. Absalom made the wrong decision at a crucial moment, preferring Hushai's bad plan to Ahitofel's excellent plan because the former appealed to his vanity. Adonijah, too, may be cunning, but his vanity leads him to believe that he can outsmart Solomon and his mother. We might go a step further and say that not only is Adonijah completely in the dark with regard to Solomon, he is also very mistaken in his view of Solomon's mother. Bathsheba's eagerness to help a man who was perceived by many to be a mortal enemy a short while ago should have seemed strange to Adonijah.

There is something suspiciously theatrical and artificial about the last scene in which Bathsheba plays a major role, her plea to her son. The formality that dominates the scene shows that it takes place in public, when Solomon is holding court surrounded by his advisors, courtiers, guards, and other attendants. He may be trying a case in public, as we find him doing when the two prostitutes appear before him with a baby, each claiming to be the mother of the baby. Surely Solomon does not get up whenever he speaks to his mother and ceremoniously offer her a chair to his right, unless it is a public occasion. The scene is filtered through the eyes of a spectator who is not an intimate of the two main protagonists. Therefore, Bathsheba is referred to by her formal title as "the king's mother." After the commotion that arises from the queen-mother's appearance, the king's getting up to bow down to her and offering her a seat next to him, everyone would be looking at them and listening attentively to their dialogue. Bathsheba prefaces her request by telling the king that she is asking a "small," insignificant favor and that he surely will not turn her down. The king then answers, again in a grand, theatrical gesture, that he will not turn his mother down. When Bathsheba makes her plea, she sounds surprisingly brief, dispassionate, even cold: "Let Abishag the Shunamite be given to your brother Adonijah for wife" (2:21). There is no appeal to Solomon's feelings, and no mention of Adonijah's loss and present misery and loneliness, or of the unhappy lovers. Solomon's reply to his mother is angry, rhetorical, and sarcastic.

The unavoidable impression is that this scene is a set up between Solomon and his mother. There was no need for the mother to have made this request in public. If Bathsheba truly thought that it was a family issue involving only matters of the heart she would have approached her son in private. Unless, of course, Bathsheba has understood from the beginning the Machiavellian meaning of Adonijah's request, and concluded that the only forum appropriate for it would be in public. Bathsheba must have known that Adonijah is a thorn in her son's side, and that a way must be found to get rid of him that would not offend the people and be deemed justified by them.

Solomon and his mother may have rehearsed this scene and then acted it out for the benefit of the public, with Bathsheba acting innocent, and Solomon angry at his mother's gullibility and his brother's audacity. Or, there may have been no need for a rehearsal or a prior understanding between Solomon and his mother, for the clever Solomon, who will soon emerge as the wisest man in the ancient world, knows what nobody else does, that his mother is smart and politically astute. If his mother really wants a favor she would find a more appropriate, private occasion to approach her son. There is an implicit understanding between Solomon and his mother that when the mother appears before her son in public, she has an important agenda—to strengthen her son's throne. When she "innocently" asks her son for something so outrageous as giving the former king's concubine to the man who was still harboring ambitions for the throne, Solomon takes the cue and acts accordingly. Thus Solomon's anger with his mother is feigned; it is a strategy to arouse the public's anger at Adonijah for stirring trouble and exploiting a well-meaning if naïve queen-mother. Solomon will now have no problem with public opinion when he executes his brother. There is no doubt that the court scene helped recruit to his side even those who had borne no ill feelings toward Adonijah before.

Most of the scenes involving Bathsheba as a minor player may be reread with Bathsheba as the main player. With the aid of backshadowing, applying what we have learned from the last episode to the previous ones, a different person emerges. Is Bathsheba Natan's puppet? After all, Natan serves her interest, which happens to coincide with the prophet's and with God's. Perhaps Bathsheba told Natan about a supposed royal vow before, and Natan is only reiterating what Bathsheba told him. Although Natan and the uninitiated reader may think that the prophet is manipulating her, perhaps the opposite is right. By playing the helpless mother, Bathsheba empowers Natan to take a bolder, more decisive action in her favor and force the issue on David.

In the scene with Natan, Bathsheba is the helpless female and the prophet the wise advisor, the man of God who is also politically active. Natan appeals to her as "Solomon's mother" (1 Kings 1:11). Bathsheba may be playing the role of the confused mother who needs help and direction. She needs the support of the prophet in appealing to the king not because she is timid and afraid, but because the king would be more inclined to listen to Natan. The question of the sacred vow, David swearing in the name of God that Solomon would succeed him, can also be looked at from the flip side. The idea came from Bathsheba, and through the years she repeated it so many times to Natan that he had no doubt about its veracity. It seems that Bathsheba has made Natan her advisor and confidant, and that her past as an adulteress did not prevent the prophet from associating with her.

In every scene where she appears, Bathsheba is at first blush the guileless and naïve female, but it seems that her dangerous and ill-advised acts turn out to be beneficial to her. A reading that assumes that Bathsheba aspired to be the king's wife and to bear the heir to the Davidic throne may also shed a new light on the opening verses. Since we have already learned that nothing about Bathsheba is accidental or casual, why should the first scene in which we see her be a mere accident? It is true that the storyteller never accuses the woman of putting herself in a position where she could be seen by David, on the roof of her home which happened to be right below David's roof, or in a room at her home where the open window was right under David's roof.

The nuances of Bathsheba's actions may be only partially recognized by the chronicler.

By suggesting that it is possible to read the Bathsheba narratives with the woman as the prime mover of events, it is not necessary to subscribe to Bal's theory of "lethal love," namely that the storyteller wished to present the woman as setting a deadly trap for the man and causing his downfall. The men in this tale, except perhaps for Uriah, are far from idealized, and Bathsheba lacks the malice and deadliness of other "lethal" women. Furthermore, it is Joab, a man whose actions and point of view we have learned to suspect, who introduces the theme of the killer woman into the story by evoking the image of the woman of Tebets. Joab may be revealing his suspicion that a woman was involved in David's wish to get rid of Uriah, and he may be blaming her for threatening to ruin David as well as causing the death of Uriah. Nevertheless, we never identify with Joab's point of view, and the fact that he casts the shadow of the "killer woman" on Bathsheba would not necessarily make the reader identify with his view. The storyteller himself may not have viewed Bathsheba as a pivotal figure in the narratives discussed, but he (or she) has given us enough material to read into these lines a tale that he was not interested in pursuing.

A slightly different conclusion would be that the young and passive woman of the first episode, whom some rabbis excused by implying that she was forced by David, evolved into the shrewd manipulator of the 1 Kings episodes. From the very beginning, however, Bathsheba appears to be in need of fulfilling the natural rhythm of her feminine body. The wish to bear a son, and a special son at that, is a familiar biblical motif and may safely be construed to be shared by Bathsheba as well. Uriah the warrior was always away, and even when he came back to Jerusalem, his soldierly code prevented him from visiting his wife. At least this is what he claims in our tale, though, of course, his reasons for refusing to go home this time may have been different. Bathsheba is mentally and biologically ready to have a son when we first see her. The biblical storyteller has left so many gaps in the tale precisely because he wanted us to consider all possibilities. In this case, the reader's midway realization of the possibility that Bathsheba may have planned her fate does not serve to highlight the danger of the woman, but to enrich this complex and multi-layered tale. We can add Bathsheba to those biblical women whose existence is first anchored completely in their natural cycles, whose only verbal expression is limited to the lexicon of pregnancy, but who emerge out of this state to take part in history and in "male" politics. As Bathsheba exits the scene she is the queen mother of a glorious king whose enemies have been disposed of and whose throne has been secured, due largely to her efforts.

The following table follows Bathsheba's career in reverse chronology, from end to beginning; it starts with the last scene through all major scenes in which she appears to the first scene when she is seen by David. In the last episode she makes a voluntary appearance that has a great impact on the observers in King Solomon's court: the king rises up to welcome her and seats her at his right. By contrast, in the first episode she is beyond the canvas of the scene itself, spotted by David as a distant figure while the king occupies the center of the canvas. The following table, however, highlights the similar patterns underlying all these scenes: Bathsheba's "right" to participate in each of these scenes is always due to her feminine nature; this results in an action that might seem naïve, lacking in complete understanding of the given situation. Her naïveté, however, has a flip side of cunning and calculation, reinforced by the outcome: each case concludes with the enhancement of Bathsheba's status and power.

Bathsheba: A Backward Glance

The scene	Bathsheba's Femininity	Bathsehba's Naïveté	Bathsheba's Cunning	Results: Beneficial to Bathsheba
Bathsheba-Solomon	She pleads for lovers	Might put Solomon in jeopardy	Public forum to guarantee public outrage	Solomon's throne is safe
Bathsheba-Adonijah	He appeals to her "romantic" nature	Agrees to help her son's enemy	Hands Solomon an opportunity to get rid of his enemy	Adonijah can be executed without public wrath
Bathsheba-David (1 Kings 1)	She pleads as a mother	Asks for safety	Evokes (invents?) a past promise	David declares Solomon his heir
Bathsheba-Natan	"Solomon's mother"	Unaware of danger	Natan reiterates royal promise	Recruits the prophet's support
Bathsheba-David "I am pregnant"	Sex, pregnancy	Puts herself at risk	Puts pressure on David	Marries the king
Bathsheba Bathing	Menstruation, beauty, nakedness	Unaware that she is being spied on	Entraps the king?	Pregnant by the king

CHAPTER 5

IN THE PALACE
OF WORDS

1. WOMEN AND LANGUAGE

Language in biblical literature is much more than a medium of communication, or a necessary vehicle of social interaction. It is more than a means for men and women to converse with God and express their spirituality. The function and status of language within biblical thinking are reflected in the very opening of the Pentateuch, in the story of creation, when God creates the world with His word. The act of creation is not transmitted via movements in space, which characterize human action, but rather through the medium of verbal utterance. God states the coming into being of the world in words, and the divine statements are then animated into life and concrete existence.

Furthermore, within the biblical lexicon the law is God's "word," and violation of it is expressed in terms of defying God's word, or voice. God's command, as well as a divine mission given to a person such as the prophet, is always expressed as the word of God coming to humanity: "Now the word of the Lord came to me, saying" (Jer. 1:4) is how the prophet Jeremiah marks the beginning of his mission. Through the divine word, His commandments and laws, God's presence in the world is incarnated, in contrast with the graven images of the pagan world.

Countering the notion that language was created by people to facilitate and expand human interaction, the Bible offers the idea of language as preceding human life and utilized by God in the unparalleled and never-to-be-repeated act of creation. Human language is thus an imitation of the divine word, and as such it is anchored in holiness. Abuse of language is as much a sin as abuse of anything else created by God. For the human tongue to bear false witness, to pronounce God's name in vain, or to utter blasphemy is defiance of God and desecration of His word. The loss of God has been expressed as an inability to hear the word of God. Spiritual alienation is estrangement from language. The prophet has his lips touched with burning coals by the angel of fire (Isa. 6:6,7) and only then does he qualify to spread God's word. The reluctant prophet Jonah's flight from God proves futile as a means of escaping God's "word" (Jon. 1:1–3).

It goes without saying that language also functions as a stylistic tool in biblical narrative. The tales are distinguished from the prophetic utterances as well as from the style of the wisdom sayings. Biblical poetry has its own unique characteristics that differentiate it from the historical narration. The biblical narrators were indisputably excellent storytellers, but it is hard to say that the biblical actors are assigned speech that is specific to each as an individual—a style, choice of words, and distinct metaphors—that would differentiate them from each other and make each of them recognizable and singular.

We know that certain words, idioms, and syntactic configurations are sometimes helpful in determining the date of a biblical text. In a few of the Bible's dramatic, human-centered narratives, there is an attempt to characterize personalities through the style of their verbal intercourse. The difference between Jacob and Esau is made clear especially in the dialogue that accompanies the selling of the birthright. Esau's words sound uncouth and vulgar, a comic linguistic foil to Jacob's legalistic style. Esau's choice of words is body-centered, earthy, showing his concern with the *physis* aspect of life. Jacob's lexicon is directed by *nomus;* it is coldly formal, precise, and detailed. Samson has a predilection for riddles and pithy sayings, which consistently follows his career from his days as a young groom done in by his bride, to his last scene as the blind prisoner planning revenge on his enemies. David is recognized by his lofty, religious rhetoric. His public speeches are always effusive in their praise of God and thus pleasing to God as well as the crowds. Saul's inner thoughts, on the other hand, are so obvious that they are immediately translated into spoken language, whether Saul indeed articulates his hidden designs (mainly his intentions to do away with David) through explicit verbal communication or through the transparency of his conduct.

Nevertheless, the reader's ability to discriminate between different personalities in the Bible is limited to the more prominent biblical figures, and only in a number of key dramatic situations. It is hard to claim that biblical language aims at capturing the everyday vernacular of the speakers, or that it consistently attempts to portray its characters through their use of language.

From our perspective, the rhythmic cadence and elegance of discourse are stylistic features common to all biblical speakers. Within this larger framework some figures sound more colloquial, some more lofty and sublime than others, and some more flamboyantly rhetorical than others. It is, of course, possible to identify several sets of techniques and rules that underlie the biblical art of storytelling, and some outstanding studies have been done in the past two decades or so in this direction.[1]

The biblical style is male-intoned, written by men and addressing the community through its males. If it is not always possible to tell the biblical protagonists from each other through their linguistic style, then the question of whether women have a voice that is uniquely theirs is rife with problems. Do women's dialogues transmit an attempt on the part of the storytellers to capture individual women, or even that which is typically "feminine" in their colloquy? Does the biblical narrator try to emulate the feminine cadence and nuances of speech to distinguish them from men? These are questions that cannot be easily answered.

Nevertheless, two factors regarding female language in biblical literature are undeniable. The majority of women in the Bible are not only nameless and faceless, but also voiceless, and silence and anonymity sum up the existence of the multitudes of mothers, wives, and concubines of the men whose deeds are chronicled in the Bible. It is assumed either that women are represented through male discourse, or that the concerns particular to women, that could be expressed in a typical female language, are not important enough to be recorded.

The women's mute universe bothers us because language is what characterizes us as free, intelligent, and rational beings. The human language is more than a tool of communication, it articulates mental and intellectual processes. If women were discouraged from expressing themselves, or if their voice was deemed unimportant, then by necessity their language skills did not develop and mature as well as the men's did. As Derek Bickerton explains, "only language could have broken through the prison of immediate experience in which every other creature is locked, releasing us into infinite freedom of space and time."[2] By being denied growth in their linguistic abilities women were locked in a mental and intellectual prison that kept them from conceiving of ideas or envisioning a reality that was not in their immediate physical surroundings.

Furthermore, as George Steiner suggests, "Eros and language mesh at every point." Both "arise from the life-need of the ego to reach out and comprehend, in the two vital senses of 'understanding' and 'containment,' another human being," and both are subject to the "shaping force of social convention."[3] The muffling of the female voice also meant the erotic subjection of women, making the sexual experience the man's domain—he "knows" her—and thus another form of stunting the mental and social growth of women.

The second feature pertaining to female language in the Bible is therefore more significant. Biblical women who do come to the fore and periodically take center stage to capture briefly the reader's attention often exhibit great linguistic talents, using rhetoric as a means of establishing their names within the recorded history of their people. Although only a few biblical women actively participate in a dramatic tale, when they do they exhibit the whole spectrum of communication: from the silence of Dinah, Jacob's daughter, that screams more than words, through a great variety of verbal expressions culminating in the majestic psalm of praise recited by Hannah, the prophet Samuel's mother. To study how biblical women express themselves when they are given the opportunity, as well as the cases where their voices are blatantly muffled, is to juxtapose a culture where women have a resounding presence with one where the female voice is only seldom heard and verbal directness on the part of a disenfranchised group not easily tolerated.

When female protagonists in the Bible step out of the anonymous masses of mothers and wives, they speak in a clear and steady voice, usually with great and decisive impact on men and their course of action. Verbal dexterity and linguistic creativity characterize many female protagonists in the Bible. The ability to articulate and communicate often becomes a source of female power that counteracts and even outweighs women's legal and economic powerlessness within biblical civilization. Furthermore, when compared with the male protagonists in the same episodes, it seems that women's oratory is often more inventive, elegant, metaphorical, and loftier in style than that of the male protagonists. Women's countercultural attitudes are reflected mainly in their language. Their pose, demeanor, and way of life may be viewed according to patriarchal standards; they may appear to subscribe to their roles as the contributors of the next patriarchs, but their language often betrays a distant echo, a nuance that allows them to challenge their fate and create new possibilities while at the same time articulate nothing that is truly dangerous.

I have chosen four examples where women's ability to lift themselves out of their designated procreative role in biblical society is accomplished by the language of vision, opening broad vistas of destiny otherwise closed to them. Interestingly, the very opening of the biblical text contains quite a bit of female language; the primordial woman, Eve, is given a clear and personal voice that becomes even more distinct once compared with that of the primordial man. Zelofhad's daughters render the lawgiver Moses speechless. Hannah's language, which imitates that of God Himself by creating reality, first has to overcome the practical, no-nonsense lexicon of the men around her: Eli the priest adopts the disparaging language of sarcasm and condemnation when he addresses the woman as she is praying; and Hannah's husband is kind, but somewhat patronizing. Naomi and Ruth catapult themselves from their economic and social misery as well as alienation from God through the language of redemption, employed by the male protagonist as empty rhetoric, but by the women as a destiny-altering mechanism. Thus these four examples reflect female language that is elegant and sophisticated (Eve), diplomatic and cunning (the five daughters of Zelofhad), spiritual and creative (Hannah), and redemptive (Naomi and Ruth).

2. EVE IS "BEGUILED"

The Text
Genesis 1–3

So God created mankind in His own image; in the image of God created He him, male and female created He them. (Gen. 1:27)

And when the woman saw that the tree was good for food, and that it was a delight to the eye, and a tree to be desired to make one wise, she took of its fruit, and did eat, and gave also to her husband with her; and he did eat. (Gen. 2:6)

And the man said: "The woman whom thou gavest to be with me, she gave me of the fruit and I did eat." . . . And the woman said: "The serpent beguiled me and I ate." (Gen. 2:12, 13)

The Primordial Woman and Her Language

This discussion of the primordial woman begins with two premises regarding the tale of creation narrated in Genesis 1–3. One is the unity of the text despite the dual versions it contains, and the other is the need to read this text independently of the myths, interpretations, and commentaries that have accompanied it from the first exegetical efforts to this day.

The narrative material within this section contains two tales that recount the same event, but several scholars have made persuasive arguments for reading the two versions of creation, the P and the J, as one literary entity. Robert Alter, for example, compares the biblical tale to modern works that narrate the same event from different perspectives, and suggests an analogy with film montage.[4] Joseph B. Soloveitchik, studying the duality of the creation tale from a theological and philosophical perspective, has also arrived at the conclusion that the two narratives are complementary, that one could not exist without the other, as each version presents only a partial perspective of the nature of humanity and its relationship with God.[5] Phyllis Trible has proven the integrity of the two tales structurally as well as in terms of its view of gender. By presenting humanity as one creature (1:27) which then is divided into two (2:22) only to be reunited and made "one flesh" again (2:24), the text creates an envelope structure that is in line with biblical stylistic practices; it also makes a statement regarding sexual life as a means of returning to the primordial oneness.[6]

If these two narratives came down from two different schools, the Priestly tradition and the Jahwist narrator, originating from different periods, they nonetheless have existed as one single literary tale since the Hebrew Bible became canonized.[7] As a written text, the two versions are one tale, in spite of their different styles and contradictory and even antithetical outlooks on the nature of humanity and its creator. Whatever the reasons may have been for the redactors to leave the two versions side by side, one of which was undoubtedly their great respect for the sacred texts, the result is a literary bonus to the reader, a tapestry that enriches the narrative. For a reader not searching for the historical evolution and the various peregrinations of the text, but rather interested in preserving the integrity of a narrative that has been available in its present format for almost two millennia, the opening of Genesis is a single tale recounting a momentous event in two versions. Each version highlights distinct aspects of the event, offering another dimension, and approaching it from a different perspective. Together, both versions forge a complete, integrated tale that makes sense as literature, theology, and in its view of the origins of the sexes. The narrative as a whole is an independent tale that can stand by itself, with the unifying element being God with whom the narrative starts and ends. Genesis 4, on the other hand, shifts the narrative from God to Adam and Eve, thus setting the previous tale of the creation of the world and the drama of the Garden of Eden apart from the following stories.

The second thesis that informs the present discussion is that the literary text of Genesis 1–3, pried loose from both traditional and modern myths and misconceptions, yields a portrait of the primeval female that is different from the debased seductress of tradition. Contemporary scholars mostly agree that the primeval story is not the product of a sexist or misogynist mind, though it contains elements that, taken out of literary and linguistic context of the original text, fueled misogynist sentiments in later theological commentaries as well as in fictional recreations.[8]

There is no denying that the woman's defiance of God's command and the subsequent expulsion of the primeval couple from the Garden of Eden has had a great influence on the Judeo-Christian perception of women. The tale has become the justification for the narrowing of women's space as well as the silencing of women. The first female became the prototype of all women and her story a paradigm of female existence. If the woman put to evil use the freedom of mobility and of linguistic expression that she seems to have enjoyed in the Garden of Eden, then women's sphere had to be constricted and their ability to use language stifled.[9] God's reprimand to the woman, which describes her future as bound to her female-biological functions, "in sorrow thou shalt bring forth children" (1:16), may be read as the divine mandate of the Eriksonian theory of the woman's "biological destiny." The modern paradigm suggests that the female's physiological "inner space" determines the woman's spatial preferences of enclosed, sheltered structures and dooms the female to a circumscribed life, immersed in familial and biological functions.[10]

After the expulsion from Eden, Eve becomes the prototypical female: the bearer of children who suffers the agony of childbirth and is ruled by her husband. The tale leading to this, however, makes it clear that this familiar female state is a transformation, a radical change rather than a natural evolution. The Genesis tale of the Garden of Eden has become the justification for constricting women's space and depriving them of language precisely because spatial and linguistic freedom defines the woman's existence in Eden. The transformation that the woman will experience, once she is expelled into the geographical space that humanity occupies, is signaled through the reversal of the spatial mobility and linguistic versatility that characterize the existence of the first female.

In Eden, which is beyond space and time, the woman creates a distinct "space" for herself and further distinguishes herself through the lexicon she uses to depict her experience. Although we know the first woman as the one who defied God's law and brought death to the world, she is more memorable for her inventive language.

The myth of a female coming to the world after the male and cut out from his rib, narrated in Genesis 2:21–22, has been the most popular and deeply embedded creation myth. Nevertheless, the biblical sequence of narratives opens with the tale of a primal human that is both male and female: "In the image of God created He him, male and female created He them" (1:27). The Talmudic sages, interpreting this verse, suggested a double-faced original human: "*Du partsuf panim haya lo le'adam harishon*" (the first human had two faces).[11] This ancient legend was repeated by the medieval commentator Rashi (in his commentary on Genesis 1:27), as well as by The Zohar, the primary source of Jewish mysticism. Post-biblical commentators differed as to whether the first creature was an androgyne, a bi-sexed creature, or an ungendered, spiritual being. They further differed as to whether the tale in Genesis 2 describes the female being made out of the male's rib, or the sexually undifferentiated creature being separated into male and female.[12] The Priestly version suggests that the primal human, be it an androgyne with a corporeal body or a sexless, spiritual being, enfolded the potential of both sexes, and was not decidedly male. Since the bi-sexual or sexless human was created "in the image of God," there is no explicit assumption of male supremacy in the opening of Genesis.

Although the first version of creation in Genesis introduces an idealized version of humanity—male and female both created in the image of God, sharing together in that image, and having complete dominion and supremacy over nature—it is mainly focused on the majesty of the creator. Human language is not heard, and instead we have the divine word repeated several times and manifesting its awesome power. God's word creates the world. There is no dialogue, only God talking to Himself, proclaiming commands and blessing His handiwork. Each day is sealed with a blessing and is seen as a one-time, unique, never-to-be-repeated event. The divine word has put everything in place and whatever will come into being now will be a replication, a derivation, of God's primal creations. Human time and experience will now repeatedly emulate these six days, but there will never be another six days like these, nor another speech like this.

The second version of the creation narrative, beginning in Genesis 2:4, disrupts the grand symmetry of the previous tale, with the concepts of time, language, and space taking on different characteristics, or, we may say, becoming more humanized. Eden is framed within geographical parameters of the more familiar grounds of a garden that needs watering and tending, trees that bear tasty fruit, animals that roam the grounds, and rivers that flow through. Death is mentioned by God as a consequence of disobedience, so that the possibility of time limited and curtailed is established. Only here is human speech introduced. The conversations include human participants, and even God's language is more humanlike, tentative, less majestic than in the first version. Actions move chronologically and sequentially and are causally connected; there is a before and after.

The human faculty of speech is first implied when the primordial human names the animals. Significantly, it is the human before it is split into two different sexes who names the animals, thus demonstrating its ability to classify its environment, an ability that is not gender-differentiated. Yet, the first time that we actually hear the human voice is when the male is confronted with the female. The male uses precise, intelligent language to identify her and therefore, himself: "This is now bone of my bones, and flesh of my flesh, she shall be called woman because she was taken out of man" (Gen. 2:23). The man does not here name the female creature separated from him; rather, he defines her as a being different from him, and thereby discovers his own sexual identity. He recognizes his maleness only when confronted with her femaleness.

Nevertheless, it soon becomes clear that the female that sprang out of the primordial being is endowed with outstanding verbal gifts that go far beyond the ability to classify and name the physical environment, for she manifests the powers to articulate motivation and internal processes. In the famous seduction scene (3:1–6), the biblical narrator pauses his terse, fast-paced storytelling to delve into the woman's mind, giving us a glimpse into her reasoning and internal discourse. Although the third-person narrative voice is employed, the detailed statement proves the narrator's intention to transmit the woman's verbal articulation of her internal reflections as closely as possible, and not just summarize them for us. The woman eats from the fruit of the tree because she has discerned in it three distinct attributes: "that the tree was good for food, and that it was pleasant to the eyes, and a tree to be desired to make one wise" (3:6). In one brief moment, the primordial female has a keen vision of the totality of the human experience as complex and multi-layered, and is able to differentiate lucidly and distinctly between three areas of human experience, the physical, the aesthetic, and the intellectual.[13]

Bickerton's theory of the development of human language and its emergence from protolanguage is helpful in illuminating the significance of the woman's insight into the tree's qualities. If the primordial couple represents humanity in its infancy, in a pre-civilized and pre-technological environment, then the woman has already reached a high level of linguistic ability. Mature human language goes beyond representation of what is visible and perceptible through the senses.[14] The woman's account of the tree reaches beyond the utilitarian representation of reality typical of early hunters and gatherers. She does not just report about the tree's size or color, but analyzes it and defines the precise gifts with which it can endow her. The woman's language formulates thought: surmising that the tree will give her aesthetic pleasure as well as intellectual capacity is not a function of observing the tree. Furthermore, her language is conceptual; only after the articulation of the concepts of the aesthetic and the intellectual can she transpose these qualities onto the tree. Thus the woman's language creates internal states that are not dependent on raw data. Noting the tree's attributes on the basis of her sensory perception would be protolanguage, used by some animals, pygmies, and very young children, but the woman's language is not learned by the environment, as protolanguage is, but rather is based on intellectual reflection and conceptualization. Bickerton writes: "Thus language . . . is not a system that passively mirrors what it represents, but rather one that creates a new and parallel world constrained by the laws of its own nature just as much as by the nature of the phenomena that it represents."[15]

The woman's sophistication is also suggested by the hierarchical order with which she presents the tree's qualities: she starts with physical gratification which has to do with sensory perceptions, smell and appearance, as well with the sensation of hunger and its appeasement. As living beings, both she and her mate must be acquainted with these sensations, and thus the woman is relying on experience when she remarks that the fruit will satisfy her palate. The second category, evoking the aesthetic sense, includes both the physical—seeing—and the mental response to it—the intangible pleasure that we derive from observing a beautiful object. The third category, wisdom, represents the woman's intellectual hunger, her desire to augment her mind. Her ability to articulate the concepts of the aesthetic and the intellectual must precede the craving for them and the hope to find them in the fruit of the forbidden tree. It is her level of linguistic aptness that is responsible for this sophistication; to quote Bickerton: "Only language could have refined the primitive categories of other creatures and built them into complex systems that could describe and even seek to explain the world" as well as design "futures different from our past and then seeking to make those imagined futures real."[16]

The woman's obvious ability to verbalize internal processes, as well as concepts as yet untested by her, becomes more manifest when juxtaposed with Adam's tendency to report only the observable and the known. Although both the man and the woman try to shake off their personal responsibility by blaming another party (he blames the woman and she the serpent) the difference between the two is dramatized by how each explains the act of disobedience and its causes. Adam uses the simplest possible verb "give," twice: "The woman whom thou gavest to be with me, she gave me of the tree, and I did eat" (3:12). The woman, by contrast, uses the complex, richly connotative, and rarely used verb "beguile": "The serpent beguiled me, and I did eat" (3:13). The poetic quality and the suggestiveness of the verb "beguile," compared with the rudimentary quality of the verb "to give," point to the fact that these two protagonists describe two very different experiences. He describes an automatic act of putting in his mouth something that was given to him, an infantile act, and a daily experience for Adam as a living being. The woman moves beyond the mechanical and the external to describe an internal process. Before she put the fruit in her mouth something happened to her internally, in her mind, or her psyche. Thus, she first creates the concept of seduction before she reports on the physical act of eating. Although both the man and the woman have had ample occasions to observe and experience the act of giving, as well as putting food in one's mouth, they have not seen or experienced the act of beguilement. The woman introduces a new concept to the human experience and a new term to the human lexicon, thus adding mental and psychic depth to the human existence, which, for Adam, is still physical and mechanical. Adam describes an act that is reflexive and automatic, while Eve describes an event that started as an internal discourse, a mental perception and the verbal articulation of it, and then culminated in a physical act. The man's language represents reality in a way that does not stray far from the reality represented, which Bickerton would characterize as closer to protolanguage. His vocabulary is still rudimentary, analogous to that of a child just beginning to talk. The woman, on the other hand, constructs what Bickerton says is a prerequisite for human language, which is "mental representations of the external world in terms of concepts rather than percepts."[17]

Although the woman ostensibly blames the serpent as the seducer, by admitting that she was "beguiled," she implies that it was an inner conviction that led her to the act of disobedience. The woman may be lying about the moment in which the seduction started, for when the serpent initiates the dialogue of temptation, the woman is already in the throes of it. Her curiosity about and fear of the tree are indicated by the fact that the serpent finds her already by the tree and that she immediately adds the prohibition not to touch it, which is not part of God's instructions. By placing the tree "in the midst of the garden," the woman reveals how intrigued she is by it; she discloses that the tree is at the center of her being at this moment, rather than trying to locate it geographically. Thus the serpent is not the agent that plants the idea in the woman's mind. Temptation comes from within her mind, and the talking serpent serves merely as a catalyst, an enabler.[18] Putting the blame on the serpent is a tactic that emulates the man's. Nevertheless, by acknowledging that the act was triggered by an internal conviction as well, the woman, in effect, does take some responsibility for her act, while the man takes none.

Furthermore, the woman's vocabulary of seduction is also remarkable in that she has chosen a verb that has retained an extraordinary flavor in Hebrew and is only used on rare and unusual occasions. Translations that opt for "deceive" or "trick" (instead of "beguile") lose the wealth and innovation of the woman's lexicon. By using "beguile" she says not only that the act of eating was triggered by an inner state, but also that this inner state was so puzzling, that only a rare and suggestive verb could fully capture its significance. Through her elegant wording, the woman has lifted her disobedience to the level of a momentous event of great mental and existential significance, while Adam has degraded his to a mere mechanical, unthinking act.

Although in terms of the wealth and sophistication of vocabulary the woman is the man's superior, it might seem initially that they are equal in the syntactic make-up of their respective responses. Abstract thinking, explains Bickerton, is possible only if the ability to construct sentences exists. A deep thought exists only in a complex sentence. Syntax is the hallmark of language, and the casting of events into a cause-and-effect framework is the main difference between humans and other species. Both the man and the woman use paratactic conjunction, the prevalent biblical pattern. Adam's sentence is compound-complex "the woman (whom thou gavest unto me), she gave me / and I ate." The woman's is compound: "The serpent beguiled me / and I ate." The word "and," representing the *waw* conversive in Hebrew, is usually multifunctional; it changes the tense, and may mean not only "and" but also "and therefore." A closer look, however, would indicate that Adam's sentence is no more than the representation of a series of actions that are connected chronologically—one came after the other—but not causally. Adam does not clarify why he ate, only how it happened. He does not explain but complain. He narrates a sequence of three events: God gave him a woman, she gave him the fruit, and he put it in his mouth. His "and" is not meant as "therefore." The fact that he was given the fruit would not logically and inevitably lead to eating.

The woman, on the other hand, narrates two events that are causally connected. Her "and" means "therefore": I was tempted and therefore I ate. The beguilement not only preceded the eating chronologically, but also directly caused it. Adam talks only about "observables in the external world," while Eve's language communicates "the contents of one's mind," to use Bickerton's words.[19] Her reasoning is complex and multi-tiered, casting the events in a cause-and-effect framework; his is simplistic, telling how rather than why. It is not that the man's statement does not qualify as language. In embedding the fact that God gave him the woman in the first clause, the man cunningly uses syntax to insinuate God's part in the blame. Yet the information he delivers in this sentence is sequential, linear, and single-tiered, placing him at the level of immature humans.

Furthermore, the dichotomy between the male as "logic-speech" and the female as "body-place," identified by Julia Kristeva as underlying the biblical dietary and purity laws, is significantly absent from this narrative.[20] Unlike in later texts, woman is not nature, and man is not mind and law. Adam comes from *adama,* earth; thus the generic creature Adam and the male Adam are both nature-bound. Eve speaks, reflects, and surmises, while he appears to be more body-centered and reflexive: he takes the food and puts in his mouth. Significantly, the division of "logic-speech" and "body-place" along gender lines is established only after the expulsion from Eden, when the man "names" the now-silent woman, implying in her name the designation of fertility and procreation: she is named Eve because she is the mother of all living (3:21).[21]

In sum, the primeval woman's language exhibits more of the characteristics that separate mature human language from the mere information-bearing function of protolanguage. These include the representation of reality that implies causality, offers reasoning, refers to internal states, and creates new concepts that name new experiences. Moreover, through the use of the inventive verb "beguile," as well as betraying intellectual cravings in her internal discourse, the woman has cast her predicament in near-heroic, Faustian terms. These linguistic features endow the woman's voice with a sober, serious, even tragic cadence, by far more dignified than the plaintive, infantile sound that reverberates in the man's words.

3. THE LANGUAGE OF DIPLOMACY

The Text
Numbers 27:1–11

And the Lord spoke to Moses, saying: "The daughters of Zelofhad speak right; thou shalt surely give them a possession of inheritance among their father's brethren; and thou shalt cause the inheritance of their father to pass to them. And thou shalt speak to the children of Israel, saying: 'If a man die, and have no son, you shall cause his inheritance to pass to his daughter.'" (Num. 27:6, 7)

The Five Daughters of Zelofhad

The most eloquent women in the Bible use their vocabulary with caution, aware that the pronunciation of the woman's opinion may be too audacious. It seems that a combination of powerful language that proposes daring ideas cleverly clothed in humbleness very often produces results that advance the woman's agenda. An early example is the case of the daughters of Zelofhad who successfully challenge the Mosaic law of inheritance and bring about an amendment in that law. Significantly, instead of just stating the amendment that gives certain privileges to women, the Bible tells the origins of this legal addition, and how women had a role in initiating it.

The Bible narrates that by special legislation, daughters were permitted to inherit their father's estate when there were no male heirs. When the children of Israel were divided into tribes and families for the purpose of distributing the land, the daughters of Zelofhad petitioned Moses saying: "Our father died in the wilderness . . . and had no sons. Why should the name of our father be done away from his family, because he has no sons? Give us a possession among the brethren of our father" (Num. 27:3–5).

The drama of the five sisters is framed in the most patriarchal setting, following a patrilineal list of the Israelite tribes and subtribes. Although the multitude of women in the background remains faceless and anonymous, the text inexplicably provides the names of five women. Soon after, these five women separate themselves from the rest and become individuals, with their names listed again. To dramatize how daunting it should be for five women to approach the male lawmakers, the text lists all the awesome male authority figures whom the sisters have to confront—Moses, the High Priest, and the heads of the tribes. Although the women implicitly challenge the law, their tone is subdued, self-effacing, and not provocative. They speak of their father, not of themselves, reminding Moses that he was a meritorious person who did not take part in the rebellion against Moses. The women make sure that their claim stays within the patriarchal legal system, so they ask that their father's name be not removed from the annals of history. Only after they establish that their intent is to preserve the patriarch's memory and name do they proceed to make the bold demand: "Give us a possession among the brethren of our father." Instead of openly challenging the patriarchal legal system, the daughters couch their request in the language of patriarchy, emphasizing that they want land for their father's sake and "among the brethren of our father."

The sisters' careful and shrewd speech is calculated not to antagonize the patriarchal authorities. While their request does question the status quo, they do not openly dispute the logic behind the law that bans daughters from sharing in their father's inheritance. The sisters understand implicitly that if they appear to wish to change the system and the philosophy behind it, they would fail. Yet at the same time they insist on the justice and logic of their demand. The women's overwhelming rhetoric renders Moses speechless and in immediate need of consultation with God. God, too, seems to be impressed not only with the women's argument, but with their carefully worded address: "The daughters of Zelofhad speak right."

The women successfully bring about an amendment to the divinely or-dained Mosaic law of inheritance that initially ruled that only male heirs could acquire their father's estate. Moses and the elders of Israel may have believed that the women meant to reinforce patriarchy by securing the perpetuation of their father's name, but the words that ring loud in our modern ears are: "Give us a possession among the brethren of our father." In fact, the ancient sages did sense the hidden argumentation in the women's language and brought it to light by paraphrasing the women's speech: "They said: The compassion of men extends to men more than to women, but not so is the compassion of God; His compassion extends equally to men and women and all."[22] In this Midrashic recreation of the biblical story, the women imply that in the present social structure there is solidarity among men against women, and a tacit agreement to protect men's rights at women's expense. In other words, the rabbis saw the antipatriarchal impulse in the women's seemingly innocuous speech. According to the rabbis the women exonerated God from the evil of patriarchy and put the blame on the male-made system, rather than on Him. The rabbis thus help us uncover the rather revolutionary aspect of this early tale, which rewards women handsomely for speaking their mind in a circuitous, clever way.

The ancient tale of the five daughters who are cut off from their father's estate by law brings to mind a modern analogy: the five Bennett girls in Jane Austen's classic novel *Pride and Prejudice*. The link between the predicament of Austen's female protagonists and the daughters of Zelofhad has not been made before, but Austen's clerical family and upbringing would indicate that she was acquainted with this biblical episode, and that she chose not three or four daughters, but rather five, as a parallel to the biblical tale. The British law of entail is basically the same as the ancient biblical law that bequeaths a man's estate to the nearest male relative. The Bennett girls' lives are clouded by the knowledge that should their father die before they are married, they would lose their home and face destitution. Neither the early nineteenth-century writer, nor any of the Bennett girls, challenges the absurdity of the law of entail directly. Of course the novel as a whole may seem an implicit condemnation of the system. It gives ample evidence of the harmful psychological effects— self-debasement in front of men and lack of self-esteem—that this kind of insecurity breeds in the young women as well as their mother. Nevertheless, unlike the Bennett sisters, who seem to accept the inevitability of the transfer of the father's estate to a distant relative, the daughters of Zelofhad face the patriarchal authorities and make a bold request. The ancient sisters, who would be expected to be more docile and accepting of the cruel patriarchal code, actually turn out to be more enterprising in their resolution to position women as the legitimate heirs to the patriarch's legacy.

4. HANNAH WILLS A SON

The Text
1 Samuel 1–2:1–10

But to Hannah he gave a double portion, for he loved Hannah. And her rival [co-wife] also provoked her sore. . . . Then said Elkanah to Hannah: "Why dost thou weep, and why dost thou not eat, and why is thy heart grieved? Am I not better to thee than ten sons?" . . . And Hannah rose up [and] . . . Prayed to the Lord and wept bitterly. And she vowed a vow, and said: "Oh Lord of hosts, if thou wilt indeed look on the affliction of thy handmaid . . . and give to thy handmaid a man child, then I will give him to the Lord all the days of his life, and no razor shall come upon his head." (1 Sam. 1:5–11)

And she said: "Oh my lord . . . I am the woman that stood by thee here, praying to the Lord. For this child I prayed; and the Lord has granted me my request that I asked of Him. Therefore also I have lent him to the Lord; and as long as he lives, he will be a loan to [or: borrowed by] the Lord." (1 Sam. 1:27, 28)

The tale of Hannah, the charismatic mother of Samuel the prophet (1 Sam. 1–2), illustrates how language, treated as a sacred medium, can deliver a woman from her physiologically bound existence and place her in an honorable spot in the memory and recorded history of her people. There is an almost deceptive quality to the tale's opening, which suggests motherhood as the woman's sole redemption and defines the feminine existence as anchored in procreation and fertility. As we watch Hannah evolve from a linguistically restrained, almost mute presence to a shrewd manipulator of words as well as a sublime psalmist, the tale reveals a purpose and a message that sharply depart from its opening verses.

The tale combines two important themes: that of language and its variety of functions, and that of empowering women through a sparing but creative use of language. The narrative covers the whole gamut of roles that language plays in human life, with its two female protagonists displaying the diametrically opposite uses of language. Peninah, by humiliating and taunting Hannah for her infertility, employs words as a deadly mental weapon, and therefore she exhibits the abuse of language. Hannah, by launching a daring dialogue with God that culminates in an impressive psalm of praise, illustrates the majesty and magic of language. Prayer is thus represented as the most sublime use of language.[23] The dramatic heart of the tale manifests the power of petitionary prayer, but the narrative exhibits the broad spectrum of the prayer modality: from the simple, perhaps even primitive, request for a favor from God, to the more sophisticated philosophical meditation on the glory of divine providence, crafted in brilliant verse.

The contours of the tale's plot-line are familiar within the biblical tradition, following a woman's journey from the heartbreak of childlessness to the glory of motherhood. The position of the tale within the biblical canon as an introduction to the Book of Samuel and to Samuel the man is also in tune with narrative practices in patriarchy. The woman serves history by contributing a great leader to the people of God, but it is the male son, in this case Samuel, whose deeds the tale follows. At its core, this tale seems to be a classic example of the biblical attitude toward women: the woman's story is quickly abandoned and the text resumes its "male" concerns regarding proper leadership, the laws of the cult, acquisition of land and territory, and the history of the people.

Although the initial recounting of events confirms the familiar precepts of the culture, some of the rhetoric reveals an attempt to reach out to a different, distant vision, one that introduces a set of values generally alien to biblical people. This is accomplished by verbal statements made by some of the main players as well as by the shifting of narrative focus from the desired son and the miracle of his conception to the linguistically talented woman and the power of her speech.

In terms of both language and spatial imagery, the tale at its outset reinforces the patriarchal view of the woman's role and functions. We encounter Hannah in the polygynous household, one of two wives of the wealthy, God-fearing patriarch Elkanah. Hannah's anguish in her childless state is not only a typical biblical situation, it also reinforces some modern theories about women's biological destiny. Hannah seems to illustrate perfectly Erik

Erikson's theory of the tyranny of the woman's inner "empty space."[24] Over-whelmed by her biological "inner space," and controlled by her powerful physiological needs, to use Erikson's terms, Hannah can appease her sense of emptiness and deprivation only by pregnancy and motherhood. Not even her husband's love can compensate for the vacuum stemming from the roots of her femininity, which can be filled only in the most literal and physical sense, when the woman's painfully "empty" inner space, her womb, finally hosts an embryo. Hannah's lonely, unfulfilled state at the opening of the tale seems to confirm Erikson's theory that the very existence of the inner reproductive space exposes women early to a specific sense of loneliness, to a fear of being left empty or deprived of treasures, and of remaining unfulfilled. This, then, is an ancient legend whose underlying presumptions would appear much later in the form of a psychiatric paradigm of women that locates the core of feminine existence in the woman's internal feminine organ, and narrows the parameters of the female experience to a response to a mere physical urge.

The initial thrust of the story accords with the code of a male-dominant society by offering a glimpse of the vast expanses of space and time that are part of the male existence and are closed to women. If women are defined by their "natural" functions, men are seen as occupying a niche in history. Elkanah's family tree, recorded through the male line in the tale's very first verse, places him within a long, respectable continuum of time and history. Elkanah is further introduced in terms of his place in the territory, "of Ramatayim-Zofim, in Mount Efrayim," as well as in history ("son of . . . son of" and so on). The man's life is defined as a presence in a geographical territory allocated to the family by God Himself and as a link in a historical chain, while the women are removed from the sacred geography as well as divinely controlled history. They move only within the four walls of the polygynous home, their lives defined as looking inward, immersed in their biological cycle and the call of their empty inner space.

The man's mobility in space is further illustrated in the pilgrimage that Elkanah undertakes every year, when he leaves his home in Mount Efrayim and travels to Shiloh to worship God. Here mobility in space is tied to the sanctification of time. The territory within which the patriarch journeys to the holy site and the historically significant holidays coalesce to reflect his essence. True, it is implied that Elkanah's wives and children also accompany him on his journey to Shiloh, yet this is his religious experience: "And this man went up out of his city year by year to worship and to sacrifice to the Lord" (1:3).

The patriarch is seen in the glory of his religious and familial authority: he leads the family on the pilgrimage, offers the sacrifice to God, and then divides portions of it for his wives and children. The women, on the other hand, are introduced in terms of their reproductive abilities: Peninah has been blessed with many children, while Hannah is childless. Within the confines of the women's environment, we find the co-wives engaged in rivalry, with the fecund Peninah taunting Hannah for her barrenness or, rather, for having been singled out by God for misery "because the Lord had shut up her womb" (1:6). Twice in rapid succession Hannah's childlessness is attributed to divine intervention: once in the context of Elkanah's love for his wife and his attempts to compensate her for her barrenness (1:5), and then as a means for Peninah to taunt Hannah (1:6). The Hebrew term for a co-wife, "adversary," implies that an antagonistic relationship between the wives in the polygynous family is inherent in the structure, and thus it contributes to the reader's awareness of the evils of polygyny, though the text does not condemn the practice directly.

Hannah slowly emerges from her position as the passive object of her husband's love and her rival's torment to become the tale's axis. In verse 5 the narrator suddenly shifts gears. Having bowed to patriarchal tradition in his introductory statements, the storyteller feels more at ease pursuing a different narrative. The opening lines, weighted with patriarchal premises and vocabulary, recede to the marginal status of a perfunctory concession to the conventions of historical recording in a patrilineal society. They may be an integral part of the story-as-history, but they are outside the domain of the dramatic yarn. Hannah the individual becomes the pivot of the plot. The narrator has seen in Hannah the person a legitimate subject of his story. He intends to immortalize her not through her mere eponymic function as the progenitor of the prophet Samuel, but through the character traits that she manifests as a person. The beauty of her character is accentuated in her name (in Hebrew related to the noun "grace") and is dramatically displayed in her dignified conduct throughout her ordeal. Her noble bearing in the face of her adversary's constant teasing is the first expression of the dignity and grace she exemplifies. The Bible does not provide the exact words that Peninah uses to hurt Hannah, but it makes clear that Peninah torments Hannah with the latter's childlessness. Within the context of the biblical text it is not Peninah's lexicon of teasing, but Hannah's noble mien, her unwillingness to stoop to Peninah's level and respond to her badgering, that is important.[25]

Elkanah's household represents a divided female community. We know that biblical society was gender-segregated, so that women associated with women only, and men with men only. In wealthy households, women had their own quarters and even their own entrance and staircase. Hannah and Peninah find themselves unwillingly and reluctantly under one roof, vying for the attention of the same man. They enact, or rather foreshadow, the stereotypical female community in literature, which is characterized by mutual betrayal and intrigue.[26] Although Peninah conforms to the stereotype and views this "community" as a battleground for winning the man's favors, Hannah transcends it. She does not stoop to fight for her man, and male approval alone does not satisfy her. Her lack of response to her adversary's provocation ultimately points to a personality whose sights rise above the petty domesticity that is Peninah's boundary. Given Hannah's later eloquence, it seems that in her silence she communicates her respect for language. She does not lack for words, but her verbal restraint shows concern for the right and dignified use of words.

Elkanah's love for his wife functions as character testimony about Hannah and is amply illustrated, surprisingly so against the Bible's usual stylistic rule of economy and terseness. It is first displayed through action: Elkanah gives his wife a "worthy" (or a "double") portion (1:5) in the sacrificial festival in Shiloh. This act is doubly significant: since the childless woman's economic position was precarious, Elkanah indicates that Hannah should not worry on that account, that she will always be amply provided for. The vital need for children as the future economic security for the parents, coupled with the high rate of infant mortality, was a factor that determined much of the ancient family's culture. The preference for male children was probably based on the simple reality that women left the family to contribute children, and thus manpower, to another family, while male children were seen as workers within the family and therefore as custodians of the family's wealth and security. The custom of polygyny was undoubtedly fueled by the family's need for male children as an assurance that if one wife were barren, then another wife would most likely be fertile. A childless woman like Hannah might have been concerned about her future survival, but the husband's double portion was a symbolic act of promise that she would never suffer deprivation. Hannah's wish for a child, then, is not to be taken simply as a tactic for survival, but as stemming from needs that have to do with her personality and her special talents that unfold later.

Elkanah's love for his wife is both symbolically enacted and explicitly stated by the narrator: "for he loved Hannah" (1:5). His love is further confirmed by his words: "Am I not better to thee than ten sons?" (1:8). His words are exceptional not only in their comforting tone, but in their rejection of sexist norms. In ancient Israel the wife's primary contribution to the family was her sexuality, both her ability to please her husband as a woman and to present him with children. In such a climate Hannah undoubtedly felt that she had disappointed her husband. One could expect a loving husband to solace his barren wife by assuring her that she satisfied him in other ways. If Hannah worries that she did not provide her share to her husband's well-being, then the loving husband could reply by listing all those aspects of her presence that did contribute to his contentment and happiness. Elkanah could have said: "Do not worry, Hannah, you are as good to me as ten sons." In other words, starting with the premise of the woman's role as the provider of sons to the male, he could have juxtaposed the ten sons, the contribution that Hannah has failed to make, with Hannah's many gifts of which she has given to her husband during their marriage. Instead, Elkanah's attitude is surprisingly modern; he views himself not as the patriarch who has magnanimously forgiven his wife for not having done her duty to his family, but as the loving partner whose duty it is to make his wife happy. "Love is primarily giving, not receiving," says Erich Fromm, and in his relationship with Hannah Elkanah, indeed, seeks to give, not receive.[27] He does not define his relationship with his wife in terms of her familial or sexual duties, in terms of what she has or has not given him, but in terms of his contribution to her contentment: "am I not better to thee than ten sons" (1:8).

In several ways, through action and language, Elkanah indicates that while in his matrimonial practices he conforms to the polygynous culture, in his attitude to Hannah he has been able to rise above the familiar and accepted norms. Fromm's description of love as an active practice rather than a passive experience applies to Elkanah in a deeper sense, for he must actively overcome the prejudices of his culture to be able to address his wife in this manner.[28] The giving of the double portion is an act intended to comfort, but the words come from a consciousness that has transcended the mind-set of Elkanah's generation.

Elkanah's extraordinary character introduces an egalitarian, nonpatriarchal tone to the story, yet it is significant that after his initial intrusion, Elkanah recedes to the background, reappearing only later, in his capacity as the impregnator of Hannah: Elkanah "had intimacy with his wife" (1:19). Although it was Abraham who first received the good news of Sarah's pregnancy, and Isaac who prayed for his barren wife, Elkanah is not the one who turns to God. Rather, Hannah is the sole architect of her redemption. From the start, she seems determined not to involve her husband in her misery; this may be contrasted with Rachel's petulant outburst to Jacob: "Give me children or else I die" (Gen. 29:1).

But Hannah's silence, while adding nobility and dignity to her person, may also indicate a certain emotional numbness. Her muteness and failure to respond to either her husband's kind words or her adversary's taunts may bespeak quiet desperation, even depression. In her speechlessness early in the tale, Hannah cuts the figure of an introverted, preoccupied person, oblivious to her surroundings.

Looking inward, however, is the ideal state of mind for praying. That prayer begins with introspection is suggested by the Hebrew verb to pray which conjugates the root *pll* in the reflexive form. Philosophers and scholars of prayer have always emphasized the introspective nature of prayer, its origins in a person's turning inward.[29] It might appear that by excluding herself from the sacrificial family meal Hannah closes one avenue of communication with God, yet when Hannah finally expresses herself, she addresses God Himself.

Creating a bond with God through gifts and sacrifices was certainly a way for biblical people to reach God. As a residue of pagan practices, however, sacrifices would later be considered by the prophets a more primitive, less desirable way of reaching God.[30] Indeed, Samuel, Hannah's son, started the prophetic tradition of belittling the value of burnt offerings (1 Sam. 15:22–23). The ancient rabbis, too, emphasized the supremacy of prayer over sacrifices.[31] By not participating in the ritual of sacrifices Hannah may be groping toward a more sophisticated way of conversing with God.

Until she finds her voice, Hannah's presence in the tale is inscrutable and impenetrable to us. Only when she finds the courage to address God directly does her vocal dam finally break and her words, though soundless, flow freely and eloquently. Although humiliated and embittered, Hannah feels confident enough to approach God without an intermediary. She finds the appropriate address and the right addressee at one and the same time, so that the first sentence that comes out of her mouth is a prayer to God.

Hannah's prayer first takes the form of wordless cries (1:10), with the Hebrew text offering two variations of the verb "to cry," thus implying the large volume of sobs and tears that flows out of Hannah. This cry is different from the previous cries, which were a reaction to Peninah's taunting (1:7). This time the cry is already part of the act of prayer: "And she was in bitterness of soul, and prayed to the Lord, and wept bitterly" (1:10).[32] Nevertheless, she does not remain in the self-absorbed act of weeping; behind the grieving exterior there is a determined woman able to verbalize her request to God and enter the realm of hope and expectations for the future. When Hannah finally talks, she does not wallow in her sorrow, nor does she elaborate on her grief, but states her request clearly and effectively. The heretofore voiceless Hannah turns out to be a master of language and a shrewd negotiator.

Hannah's negotiating tactics are cleverly made up of several clearly defined steps. First, her address to God is couched in the language of an oath, thus endowing it with the sanctity of a promise made to God. Instead of asking, Hannah frames her request within a sacred vow. She displays humble deference to God that is nevertheless combined with great tenacity. Although prefacing her entreaty to God with the conditional, tentative "if," and modestly referring to herself as God's "handmaid," Hannah seems to be resolved not to leave God empty-handed. She actually wills Samuel into being by proceeding to describe the kind of life that she maps out for him before God has agreed to His end of the bargain. Hannah moves from the lexicon of the tentative to the vision of a certain future. Once she has verbalized her request for a male child, that child, at least in Hannah's mind, has already come into being: "I will give him to the Lord all the days of his life" (1:11). Hannah's word has created a world, and the certainty of a male child born to her is so undeniable that she can already describe the kind of life that he will have as a man of

God. She can even visualize him physically "and no razor shall come upon his head" (1:11).

If the son is now a reality for Hannah, then the lengthy prayer that follows (1:12) is no longer within the realm of a plea to God. Rather, it is an expression of a heart overflowing with emotions, of a soul that has suddenly found a way to talk to God freely and openly and thus already feels gratified. The mere spiritual experience of praying is for Hannah the beginning of her reward, for, as the philosopher Judah Halevi suggested, prayer is a form of nourishment for the soul.[33] Furthermore, the mere attempt to communicate with God involves daring and, as such, is in itself an act of self-empowerment leading to spiritual growth.[34]

Hannah's tactics are to use the larger framework of a vow within which she petitions God, negotiates with Him, proceeds to make Him a promise, and then goes on to delineate the details of her "contract" with God. Hannah's address to God thus covers the whole gamut of the prayer modality; it consists of the pouring out of the soul, followed by a petition, a pledge, and thanksgiving, which culminates in a hymn of praise to God. No wonder the ancient rabbis saw in Hannah's prayer a paradigm and a prototype of the prayer activity.[35]

Hannah's initial prayer is petitionary in nature. This type of prayer, though the most fundamental and universal form of religious expression, has always posed a difficulty to Jewish commentators, from the ancient Talmudic sages to modern theologians.[36] It seems an act of ultimate selfishness and perhaps hypocrisy for people to praise God only so their prayer may be answered. It might also seem that the petitioners make the assumption that God is changeable, and that He can be swayed by people to change His plans.[37] The most prevalent attitude to any prayer, whether consisting of petition or praise, has been that it is a form of the cleansing of the soul, and as such the experience of prayer changes the person, not God.[38]

Yet Hannah's prayer is different. It not only comforts her, but its petitionary aspect, Hannah's intention to persuade God to change her lot, is explicitly and unabashedly pronounced. If, as the biblical narrator assumes and explains, God has "closed Hannah's womb" so that Hannah's infertility is divinely mandated, then Hannah indeed sets out to change God's decree. God is viewed as a protagonist who, though invisible and uncommunicative, is made to enter into some kind of discourse with the woman and become a party to the negotiations. Hannah's faith in the power of her prayer is so strong that it seems that God has no choice but to follow suit and comply with her request. She has made a one-sided bargain with God, but she has cleverly involved God in such a way that it seems that she has imposed her will on Him and made Him an active partner in bringing her wish to fruition.

Furthermore, Hannah's petition to God involves pleading for a change not in the past, but in the future. This proves Hannah's optimism, her faith that no matter what the past has been, the future is always open to change and progress. She views time as a redemptive mechanism and human existence as a journey within changing history, rather than as an entrapment within the cycle of nature. This attitude ties Hannah to the very core of biblical thinking and may explain her sense of freedom and independence not only as a character trait, but as a philosophical attitude toward life and its immense possibilities and choices.

Hannah's communication with God is an inner experience; therefore her monologue is soundless. When Eli the priest confronts her, however, the tongue-tied Hannah proves that she possesses passionate eloquence. The experience of prayer has unlocked Hannah's tongue and she can reply to the priest's harsh reprimand whereas before she was unable to respond either to kind words or taunts. Eli is so impressed with her delivery that he changes his initial impression of her as a drunk and sends her away with a blessing. Eli's blessing only supports what Hannah's own language has achieved. Once she has made the bargain with God and created a destiny and a way of life for her son, Hannah achieves an inner peace, born of a certainty that she never possessed before. After she has turned the forbidding priest into an ally, Hannah is able to rejoin the family at the celebratory meal and appear calm and undisturbed (1:18).

Hannah's powerful command of language is demonstrated again when her son is born. Her manipulation of the verb "to ask" (*s'l*), exploring all of the verb's possible conjugations, illuminates the tragedy of the woman who "asked" or "borrowed" a child from God but will have to make good on her promise to let God "borrow" the child from her. She calls her son Samuel, "because I have asked [or "borrowed"] him of the Lord," implying his temporary stay with her as a "borrowed" gift. Hannah thus concedes the child's unique origins as part of a bargain made between herself and God, implying that she will not renege on her part of the agreement. Yet her actions belie her words; Hannah is a normal mother who clings to her long-awaited son, and delays going on a pilgrimage to Shiloh to postpone the fulfillment of her promise to God. In one brief statement to Elkanah, Hannah encapsulates her painful predicament: she explains to her husband that when she goes to Shiloh with Samuel, it will be only for the purpose of leaving him there forever (1:22).

When Hannah finally brings her child to Shiloh, her gratitude is tinged with regret, reflected in a small speech in which she again utilizes the various possibilities of the verb "to ask." "For this child I prayed; and the Lord has granted me my request [the noun is of the root *s'l*] that I have asked [the root *s'l*] of Him. Therefore also I have lent [the root *s'l*] him to the Lord, for all his life he will be borrowed [*s'l*] by the Lord" (1:27). When the child was born and the process of bonding was just beginning, it may have been easier for her to admit that the boy was, in a sense, a "loan" from God. Yet, after a few years of nursing and rearing the child, Hannah will concede only that she is "lending" the child to God (1:28). The changes in Hannah's moods and the journey she makes from the heartbreak of barrenness to the joys of motherhood to the sorrow of parting from her young child are thus transmitted to us through her ingenious play on the verb "to ask," which she uses for praying, asking, borrowing, and loaning.

Hannah's spiritual journey and her walk through the whole range of prayer modalities culminates with the psalm attributed to her (2:1–10), the Song of Hannah.[39] As a hymn of praise to God, this psalm is the ultimate, most sublime form of prayer. The psalm cautions people against excessive pride (the sin of hubris) and celebrates God's benevolence and redeeming powers, His ability to bring about change in human fortunes and lift people out of misery and suffering. This hymn is not a paean to motherhood, nor does it focus exclusively on Hannah's salvation, nor on the salvation of barren women in general. Hannah starts with an expression of her jubilant spirits, rejoicing in her triumph over her unnamed "enemies" and attributing it to divine munificence. Even in the first verse, where Hannah exults in her personal victory, she does not specify the feminine nature of this victory, her triumphant journey from barrenness to motherhood. Rather, she revels in her good fortune and the elevated status that her experience has conferred on her as a person remembered and therefore exalted by God. As the psalm unfolds, Hannah offers a catalog of reversals of fortunes that covers a wide range of human experiences; the barren woman who gives birth to seven children and the "mother-of-many-sons" who ends up in misery (2:5) embody just one example, out of many, by which God's "actions are weighed" (2:3). Hannah demonstrates a far-reaching vision that transcends the parameters of her own particular situation and goes beyond the stereotype of the barren woman. Her song shifts her predicament from the traditional feminine orbit to that of a dialogue between humanity and God, and places her particular situation within the larger pattern of justice with which God rules the human world.

Abraham Heschel's description of prayer applies perfectly to Hannah's psalm. Heschel explains that prayer, as an act of worship, lifts people out of the triviality of existence, giving them a sense of living "in ultimate relationships."[40] In her psalm, as in her conduct throughout the tale, Hannah rises above circumscribed female boundaries. It is a measure of Hannah's delicate personality, as well as her great respect for language, that she does not confront Peninah directly and flaunt her own victory and Peninah's defeat. The domestic situation is an occasion for Hannah to make a general philosophical observation on the nature of life and its changing fortunes, but she does not use the opportunity of her victory for the articulation of feelings of revenge and the denigration of the loser. The verse "while the barren woman has born seven / and she that has many children has become wretched" (2:5) might be seen as an oblique reference to Peninah's status at home as the fertile wife who nevertheless is not loved by her husband.

The breadth of Hannah's vision is made clear, too, by the future she paints for her child. She anticipates God in her determination that her son will dedicate his life to God. In a telling revision of the story of Samson's origins (Judg. 13), wherein the angel of God defines the future son's role to a barren woman, Hannah carves out for her son a role in the religious and cultic history of the Israelite people and their continuous covenantal dialogue with God. Hannah uses the prospect of her son as dedicated to God's work as a bait for God, but her tragedy is that she begets a son only after she offers to lose him. She could have made a satisfactory bargain with God that would not involve losing the desired child. The terms of her bargain in fact express her ambition, her craving to cross over from the constricted existence of the woman in polygyny to the exciting life of history-making and dedication to God.

Our storyteller has indeed endowed Hannah the individual with diversified talents: verbal dexterity and poetic gifts, a powerful influence on men (her husband and the high priest Eli), strong determination, and an ability to bargain and negotiate. He has also attributed to her views that differ from accepted norms. Hannah interprets the successful outcome of her struggle to become a mother as a victory that is social and moral rather than feminine and biological. Therefore, within the context of the tale, Hannah's son is not seen as an instrument to appease and fill her inner "empty space," a means to satisfy a raging biological need. Hannah has created around her an ambiance that departs from the prevalent sexist and patriarchal attitudes. We might say that Elkanah's unusual view of his relationship with his wife has empowered Hannah and increased her self-esteem and ability to perceive of herself as an individual rather than an instrument of procreation. Or we may conclude that it is Hannah's unusual presence that has bred in the polygynist Elkanah ideas and attitudes not shared by most men and the general culture of his time. Indeed, Elkanah and Hannah emerge as a couple whose unorthodox voices stand out in the Bible's predominantly patriarchal cadence.[41]

If Hannah's presence radiates an understanding of women's existence that is different from that of Peninah, or the rest of the culture, then it is also incongruous with the heart of the tale, which is a woman's monolithic pursuit of motherhood. Perhaps it is anachronistic to apply modern attitudes to a woman who, albeit charismatic, is still steeped in patriarchal traditions. Nevertheless, the question is one of narrative choice: if Hannah functions only as Samuel's mother, why did the storyteller digress from the course of his tale to build up a personality of dignity and memorable talents, a woman who is the sole architect of her son's glorious career? Why does Elkanah reveal a consciousness that is ahead of his time in a remark that is jolting in its implications?

That a woman like Hannah would center her total being on producing an offspring indicates the paucity of opportunities that existed in ancient times for creative expression. Only very few people, men or women, could aspire to become prophets, teachers, and leaders in the community. One is reminded of George Eliot's complaint, in the "Prelude" to her novel *Middlemarch,* regarding the circumscribed options for the unique woman and the fate that usually awaits her: "Many Theresas have been born who found for themselves no epic life wherein there was a constant unfolding of far-resonant action; perhaps a life of mistakes, the offspring of a certain spiritual grandeur with the meanness of opportunity."[42]

In contrast to Eliot's explicitness the biblical narrator shows reticence and perhaps only partial awareness of the limited opportunities open to a gifted woman. Hannah is another illustration of Eliot's woman of "spiritual grandeur," but her choice of motherhood is not viewed by the biblical narrator as a "mistake." Yet the creation of a remarkable woman who seems to identify totally with what Eliot calls "the common yearning of womanhood" adds a disturbing note, however muted, to our story. Why Hannah chooses motherhood as the supreme expression of her talent and creativity may be due precisely to her unique gifts. For Hannah, the only opportunity to exercise her creative talents and eloquence within the tight social system could have been by educating her son, directing his life and instilling in him the "spiritual grandeur" she possesses. In a system where the burden of educating the children often fell on mothers, Hannah could have channeled her frustrated, unused gifts into the intellectual and spiritual nurturing of a son.

The vision of her son's future as the leader of the people as well as of his glorious place in the history of Israel is a source of great satisfaction for Hannah. With the force of her will she carved out for her son a place in the history of the Hebrew nation and in their sacred text. In turn, Hannah takes an important spot in that historical and textual space by occupying the center of a story that launches an important biblical narrative, the Book of Samuel.

In the performance of the ritual of pilgrimage, Hannah's status is radically altered. The pilgrimage, tied to the three main biblical holidays that celebrate critical historical events in the life of the people of Israel, serves in the opening verses (1:3, 4) as the utmost symbol of a man's existence. At the end of chapter 1, however, Hannah-as-pilgrim becomes the narrative and grammatic subject: "And she took him up with her after she had weaned him . . . and brought him to the house of the Lord in Shiloh" (1:24). She would later go on a pilgrimage regularly. Our heroine is no longer an accessory in the religious journey, but initiates it and goes on pilgrimages on her own.

Thus the narrow domestic parameters in which the tale and its heroine are anchored in the opening verses are transmuted to envelop the expansive arena of time, the epic history of the Israelites, and of the eternal script, the biblical text. It is the charismatic woman who drives events and moves from one mode to the other. What seems at first sight to be the prototypical story of maternal yearnings and their ultimate gratification turns out differently. Its crux lies in the universally recognized human aspiration to make a mark that will live forever and in a person's iron-willed ambition to go beyond the temporal, to make an impact on history, if not for herself then for her son. That this individual's particular aspirations take the form of maternal longings is culturally, not biologically determined. Like all people past and present, the heroine is subjugated by powers beyond her control; but she is under the tyranny of historical and social circumstances, not of her biological fate.

The tension between Hannah's great potential and the narrow path she pursues rings loud in the modern ear but may not be an integral part of the text itself. It seems appropriate, at this point, to study the reading given to the tale by the ancient sages, the creators of the Midrash. The Talmud names Hannah as a prophet, thus acknowledging her portrayal in this tale as a woman of eloquence and vision.[43] Nevertheless, the sages' sensitive reading of the biblical text and the additional tales that they have created to fill its narrative lacunae prove that they, too, recognized the alien, nonpatriarchal aspects of the tale; they tried to whip it back into the patriarchal mold. In the Midrash's appraisal of the characters of the female prophets Deborah and Huldah, the sages responded negatively to even the smallest spark of feminine assertiveness and challenge to male authority.[44] The early commentators could not overlook the unusually large portion dedicated to the female character in the tale of the birth of Samuel. Therefore, they offer a number of midrashim which elaborate on Elkanah's meritorious qualities, one of which centers on his ability to persuade people to join him on his pilgrimage to Shiloh.[45] This particular legend not only corrects the narrative imbalance in the biblical text by shifting the focus from our heroine to Elkanah, but also seems to imply that Elkanah had already manifested the leadership qualities that would later appear in his son. The biblical text, however, by building up the mother's and not the father's character, undoubtedly directs us to see in the talented mother the source of Samuel's leadership qualities.

The Midrash goes even further in its attempts to bring the biblical text into conformity with then-prevalent sexist standards. This alerts us again to the unusual perspective from which the biblical narrator sees Hannah. The following midrash is illuminating: "She [Hannah] spoke right up to the Holy One: Master of the universe, of all that you created in woman, there is not one part without its purpose—eyes to see, ears to hear, nose to smell, a mouth to speak, hands to work with, legs to walk with, breasts to give suck. The breasts You placed over my heart—what are they for? Are they not to give suck? Give me a son, that I may give him suck with them."[46]

By attributing to Hannah the complaint that her breasts have not been put to use, the Midrash steers her predicament to the orbit of exclusive feminine fate and anchors her need for a child in her uncontrollable biological drives. The biblical text, on the other hand, attributes to Hannah words that take her away from the feminine ordeal as such. The incongruity between Hannah's diversified talents and her monolithic pursuit of motherhood is not to be understood as a reductive attitude to women, a way for the Bible to instruct us that even the brightest of women is ultimately enslaved to her procreative needs. Rather, it is a way to illuminate to us that Hannah's request for a son is part of her ongoing dialogue with God, a means to fulfill her spiritual needs, and to come in contact vicariously with God on an almost daily basis.

The tale of Hannah may be viewed as a dramatic treatise on language and its full range of possibilities. At its lowest, language is the abuse of the defenseless and the deprived; at its highest form, prayer, language is a means for a person to transcend the frivolous, base nature of the human existence and reach great heights. That a woman is made to epitomize the grandeur of language and chart out the model for all prayers to come is a unique feature of this tale. Through a creative use of language and an awareness of its sacred possibilities, Hannah catapults herself from the immediate prison of her biological role, from becoming forever frozen in the position of the "woman at the window," into the eternal memory of her people. She has directed the course of Israelite history and therefore has been given a place of honor within that history and the sacred text that chronicles it.

5. LANGUAGE IS POWER

The Text
The Book of Ruth

"Turn back, my daughters, go your way, for I am too old to have a husband. If I should say, I have hope, even if I have a husband tonight, and should bear sons, would you tarry for them till they were grown? Would you, for them, refrain from having husbands? No, my daughters, for it grieves me much for your sakes that the hand of the Lord is gone out against me." . . . And Orpah kissed her mother-in-law, but Ruth held fast to her. And she said: "Behold, thy levirate-sister has gone back to her people and to her gods, go after your levirate-sister."

And Ruth said:
"Entreat me not to leave thee / or to return from following after thee,
For wherever thou goest, I will go / and where thou lodgest I will
lodge;

Thy people shall be my people / and thy God, my God;
Where thou diest, I will die / and there will I be buried.
The Lord do so to me, and more also / if aught but death part me
and thee."
(Ruth 1:12–17)

And she said to them:
"Call me not Naomi, call me Mara [Bitter] / for Shaddai has dealt
bitterly with me
I went out full / and the Lord has brought me back empty
Why do you call me Naomi / seeing that the Lord has testified against
me / and Shaddai has afflicted me."
(Ruth 1:20–21)

And it came to pass at midnight, that the man was startled and
turned over; and, behold, a woman was lying at his feet. And he
said: "Who art thou?" And she answered: "I am Ruth thy handmaid;
spread therefore thy skirt [wing] over thy handmaid, for thou art a
redeemer."
(Ruth 3:8–9)

Language Is Power

In the previous examples we have seen three techniques manifest in
women's rhetoric in the Bible. Eve's language consists of declamation that
endows the woman's experience with distinction and grandeur; the daughters
of Zelofhad exhibit the cunning use of language to challenge and modify
patriarchal rules while ostensibly submitting to them; Hannah exemplifies the
creation of a seemingly unattainable reality through the power of the word.
In the addresses and discourses of the female protagonists in Ruth, it seems
that these linguistic strategies are practiced to perfection.[47]

Unlike the typical biblical episode in which women appear and speak
briefly in a narrative focusing on men, the tale of Ruth provides numerous
examples of female speech. It is structured as a series of dramatic scenes
revolving around two women, animated by spirited and dynamic dialogue.
Except for Boaz's exchange at the gate with the older, unnamed kinsman,
each dialogue takes place either between Naomi and Ruth or between one of
them and others.

Naomi and Ruth first appear together, with Naomi's other daughter-in-
law, Orpah, in the memorable scene in which the older woman pleads with
her daughters-in-law to return to their mothers' homes, and Ruth remains
determined to accompany Naomi to her homeland. The three women have
reached the nadir of existence within their world; they are destitute, homeless,

and deprived of male protection, the only guarantee of women's survival in a male-dominant economy. Yet while the women cry profusely, dwelling on those who have died and on their own misery, neither woman strikes the reader as weak, helpless, or lost. In two quite elaborate speeches (1:8–9, 10–13) Naomi thanks her daughters-in-law for their past kindness, urges them to turn back and leave her, and wishes them well. Her explicit argument is that she is past her childbearing years, that therefore the young women cannot expect to be "redeemed" by a brother-in-law. Naomi's language, describing hypothetically the improbable event of her marrying a man that very night and eventually bearing sons, however, is so outrageously exaggerated that it points to a subtext different from the point that is ostensibly being made. Naomi describes at length what cannot happen, but merely elaborating on the impossible—that she will remarry and give birth to sons, that her daughters-in-law will wait for those sons to redeem them—points to hidden desires and hopes. Although on the face of it Naomi rules out any possibility of her daughters-in-law remarrying within her family, her protestations create an imaginary world in which the unlikely might indeed come true; behind the language of seeming desperation lurks the vision of a potential miracle. Naomi's absurd scenario plants the idea and the hope of its being realized.

Although seeming to dismiss the possibility of a levirate marriage for the two young women, Naomi introduces the concept into the tale and the reader's consciousness. Moreover, to build up further her vision of the possible, to enhance her subliminal message, and to create a world out of the word, Naomi names the relationship between the two women using a term that technically does not denote the link between women whose husbands are brothers. Naomi tells Ruth to follow her sister-in-law, Orpah, who has finally taken Naomi's advice and is headed back to Moab. In Hebrew, Naomi does not use the term sister or sister-in-law; rather, she calls Orpah *yebimtekh,* using the term *yebamah* to describe the familial relationship between the two women. In biblical Hebrew the noun *yebamah* designates the childless widow in relation to her dead husband's brother. He is the *yabam,* or "redeemer" as it is usually translated, and she is the *yebamah,* the feminine form of the same noun. Nowhere else in the Bible is it suggested that sisters-in-law are each other's *yebamah.* This should not be taken as a slip of the tongue, a careless mistake on the part of a wretched woman. Naomi takes a liberty with the language, but in the process creates a new frame of reference within the tale by filling the dialogue with intimations of *yibbum,* levirate marriage, thus mitigating the language of the unattainable. Like the desperate Hannah, Naomi creates a world with the force of her tongue, and the reader is left to wonder how the misnomer will force itself on reality and whether a time will come when either of these two young women will indeed be rightfully called *yebamah.*

Furthermore, even as she pronounces her wretchedness, Naomi proclaims her self-worth by framing her present misery as part of an ongoing dialogue between herself and God: "The hand of the Lord is gone out against me" (1:13). At first we might consider these words a common utterance in a God-fearing culture, a cliché probably used universally by Naomi's contemporaries to describe their misery, but this is not just a case of resorting to popular language. Rather, it is a well-thought-out argument on the part of Naomi, who repeats and elaborates on the same idea later: "The Lord has testified against me, and the Almighty has afflicted me" (1:21). Naomi's rhythmic lament reverberates with Job-like echoes, endowing her plight with a colossal significance. Her polemical, philosophical language evokes the vision of a divine court, where God is both witness for the prosecution and the judge determining the verdict. In this heavenly courtroom, Naomi sees herself playing a major role, that of the accused.

Naomi's personal complaint against a wrathful God places her in the biblical tradition of men challenging God for great, undeserved suffering. By couching her grievances in the language of a Job-like predicament, Naomi suggests that she calls God to task, that she sees herself as having been singled out by God for persecution. Behind the image of the woman punished by God is the image of the woman recognized by God, not of a woman swept away by accidental, meaningless catastrophe. What is more, the dialogue of retribution and suffering also implies deliverance and salvation. Job suffers by the hand of God but is ultimately rewarded by Him. Thus, Naomi's vision of the heavenly court both asserts her importance within the divine scheme of things and suggests the possibility of a reversal of her divinely ordained fortune.

The dialectic of powerlessness suggesting hidden power is reinforced by Naomi's creation of a "community of women" characterized by solidarity and affirmation of life. Naomi is not a modern feminist. She realizes that a woman's economic survival hinges on her ability to find a husband and protector. She therefore suggests that each of her daughters-in-law return first to her "mother's house," and from there eventually to the security of a husband's home. The widowed Tamar, another enterprising woman related to this tale as an ancestress of Boaz, returns to her father's house after losing her second husband (Gen. 38:11). In our present tale, the image of the "mother's home" as a refuge for the grown daughter, together with the actual scene of three women, fiercely loyal to one another, huddled to discuss plans for the future, creates a vision of strong, independent women who unite to protect themselves and who believe in their ability to rise out of misery and devastation. This community of women exists only temporarily, until each woman departs to her husband's home, but it is a haven and an option, reaffirming the women's self-reliance and sense of hidden power.

Naomi's faith in the power of the word as mirror as well as creator of reality is further expressed in the small speech that she gives to the women of Bethlehem: "Call me not Naomi, call me Mara: for the Lord has dealt bitterly with me. I went out full, and the Lord brought me back empty, why then do you call me Naomi?" (1:2–21). The lamenting tenor of these words does not conceal the strength of their message: a person's name conveys their essence and fortune. Naomi claims that her name, which means pleasure, contrasts with her sorry reality, and that therefore it should be changed to express the bitterness of her lot. She is in line with biblical tradition, which attributes great importance to names; children, cities, and memorial sites are given meaningful names that denote the emotions and often the hopes of the name givers. However, Naomi does not mean that her name should be changed, but that her reality should be altered to conform to her original name. Her elaborate polemics about her name are meant as a challenge to her own fate, a call to God to adjust her life so that it will again reflect the true meaning of her name.

On the two occasions when Naomi laments her misery she is in an open area. When she complains to her daughters-in-law, she is somewhere between the plains of Moab and the Israelite city of Bethlehem. The second scene takes place in the streets of Bethlehem, where the local women gather around the newly arrived Naomi. Yet both times Naomi succeeds in raising the geographical location to a philosophical plane; she makes us forget the setting and opens before us the vision of the heavenly court.

Ruth's rhetoric in chapter 1 is as overwhelming as that of her mother-in-law. We can understand the special relationship between these two strong, articulate women, for the dialogue between them seems as much a clarification of positions as a hidden contest of the power of the tongue. To match Naomi's persuasive plea that she and Orpah return home, Ruth comes up with an even more effective pronouncement that seems to leave Naomi speechless. Ruth's famous oath of loyalty to Naomi herself, as well as to Naomi's people and God, has become in the Western tradition the ultimate declaration of devotion, effective in its simplicity and in the sense of determination that it transmits:

> "For wherever thou goest, I will go / and where thou lodgest, I will lodge;
> Thy people shall be my people / and thy God my God;
> Where thou diest, I will die / and there will I be buried;
> The Lord do so to me, and more also / if aught but death part thee and me." (1:16–17)

Only death will separate her from her mother-in-law, she claims. The finality of death gives Ruth's speech the stamp of finality, too, convincing Naomi that any more words would be wasted: "Then she [Naomi] left off speaking to her"(1:18).

149

What is quite surprising is that, while in Naomi's language God is a stern judge who pronounces harsh verdict, Ruth nevertheless includes God in her proclamation of loyalty, "Your God is my God" (1:16). Ruth seems to understand that the implication of Naomi's words goes beyond the explicit meaning of her complaint. Although God is the one who punishes, He can also be addressed with one's grievances, complained to, and beseeched. The same God who sits in judgment also metes out reward and redemption. Moreover, in choosing to return with Naomi, Ruth has not only made a decision about the person she wants to stay with but also about the faith and people that she wishes to adopt. In her conversation with Naomi, Ruth also starts a dialogue with Naomi's God and His people. Both women are daring in their religiosity, since matters of faith and intimations of the divine are seen in the Bible as mostly within the male domain. God reveals Himself to Abraham, and it is with Abraham that He makes the covenant.

Thus, Naomi's thinking can be defined as theological, Ruth's as historical. Naomi perceives herself as expelled from the orbit of divine mercy, and her mission is to be embraced again by God's bounty and kindness. Ruth the foreigner is outside the trajectory of Israelite destiny, and she wishes to put herself on this people's historical track.

The scene of the women's arrival in Bethlehem is a dialogue between Naomi and the women of Bethlehem, who play the part of the chorus, spectators who participate actively in the dramatic events. The two words (in Hebrew) that they speak—"Is this Naomi?"—convey a wide spectrum of responses: initial surprise at seeing their old townswoman, shock at the obvious change in Naomi's appearance, and the wish to know much more. The women also set up a little ceremony of welcome that allows Naomi to release her anger. They provide the audience for Naomi's grievance against God and serve a therapeutic purpose by allowing Naomi to express herself and vent her emotions of sorrow and bereavement.

Naomi's language in chapter 1 sets the tone for the whole tale and establishes the leitmotif of fullness and emptiness. Again, Naomi, in her use of language, bows to the standards of a patriarchal society. She claims that she was "full" when she left Bethlehem but that she is "empty" now. In a male-dominant socioeconomic order, a woman bereft of husband and sons is indeed "empty," but Naomi does not consider herself insignificant, small, or unimportant. Moreover, her present emptiness is set against her former "fullness," thus implying anticipation of a return to the earlier state. It also reverberates loudly against the scene of seasonal abundance the women encounter on their return.

The close and intimate understanding that exists between Naomi and Ruth is fully displayed in Ruth's quick adoption of Naomi's linguistic imagery of emptiness and fullness. Later, when Boaz promises to help Ruth after discovering that she has slept at his feet all night, he ceremoniously measures out a significant portion of barley and tells Ruth to hold up her apron so that he can fill it (3:15). Ruth returns "full," both symbolically and physically: she has received a definite pledge of redemption, and her bulging apron serves as evidence and promise of things to come. When Ruth comes home she quotes Boaz, but also adds words that he did not say to her, which would comfort a woman who had complained about her "emptiness": "For he said, 'You shall not go empty / To your mother-in-law' " (3:17). Since we witnessed the actual dialogue between Ruth and Boaz, in which Boaz did not address the question of Naomi's emptiness, we can conclude that Ruth has put these words in Boaz's mouth. We see here another linguistic tactic used by women: Ruth does not exactly lie, but while ostensibly quoting Boaz, she attributes to him the use of an image, especially meaningful to Naomi, that he probably never used.

In spite of the great emotional and spiritual bonds that exist between Naomi and Ruth, the two women come from different backgrounds, and Ruth has to become acquainted not only with the religious laws and social customs, but also with the prevailing code of conduct in this society. Naomi must have explained to Ruth the meaning of the levirate custom, as well as the tradition of kin responsibility that prevails among the Israelites. She also directs Ruth toward a conduct more in line with a society bound by the laws and customs prescribed by their God. The differences in culture and class between these two women are displayed in the nuances of language. Ruth the Moabite comes from a morally loose, corrupt society, and in order to learn the customs of her adopted people, she has to shed many of her old ways. For example, when Boaz meets Ruth for the first time, he requests that she cling to his girls, or "maidens" (2:8). Yet when Ruth repeats his words to her mother-in-law, she says that Boaz instructed her to stay close to his "young men" (2:21). Ruth may still be struggling with the language, making the mistake of using the masculine plural instead of the feminine plural, but it is more likely that she uses the masculine plural to mean "young people," namely, all the hired hands who are working in the field. She may not have understood that Boaz was making the specific point that she should stay with the women, and may have thought he was telling her to stay close to his workers, male or female. Naomi redirects the young Moabite by suggesting that she go out to the field with Boaz's "young women." Naomi thus teaches Ruth not only what proper conduct is, but also that language should not be used loosely and freely, since it is a mirror of culture, signifying the ethics of the speaker and of the civilization in which it arose.

In Bethlehem, Ruth's language is markedly different from Naomi's in other ways, too. Ruth uses the vocabulary of deference and humility, which is nevertheless invigorated by a youthful spirit of adventure, curiosity, and questioning. Naomi seems to have exhausted her own storehouse of words after arguing with God, and it is Ruth who, respectfully but also somewhat impatiently, suggests to her mother-in-law that she, Ruth, venture out to the fields to glean after the reapers. Ruth's vigorous words are contrasted with Naomi's terse, perhaps tired "Go, my daughter" (2:2). In her dialogue with Boaz, Ruth adopts the language and posture of respect and self-effacement, calling herself a "stranger" and his "handmaid" and bowing down before him, a gesture of subservience.

At the same time, Ruth elicits from Boaz perhaps more than he initially meant to say: she asks him why he has singled her out for special treatment by his servants in the field, and he has to admit that he has heard about her meritorious qualities and actions. It even seems that Boaz gets carried away when describing Ruth's kindness toward her mother-in-law, and he invokes God's name in wishing that Ruth be rewarded by Him under whose "wings" she has come to take refuge.

Ruth has thus achieved two purposes: she has established herself as a relative of Boaz, one who deserves preferential treatment in the field, and she has made Boaz acknowledge the fact that he knows much more about Naomi and Ruth than his actions so far have shown. After all, if Boaz has indeed heard about the women's tragedies and their present destitution, why hasn't he approached them and offered his help before? Why is it that Naomi and Ruth have to sit home, desolate and hungry, until Ruth, the foreigner, decides to set out to the field and test the kindness of the townspeople? Ruth's question to Boaz, while seemingly rhetorical and meant to emphasize her great surprise at his unusual magnanimity, achieves almost the opposite effect: perhaps by having to articulate Ruth's admirable actions and needy situation, Boaz is led to ask himself if he has done enough for his female relatives. Both the women's actions and their language are meant to stir in Boaz, their distant kin, a sense of responsibility, and perhaps even guilt, that would drive him to do more for them than he has so far or than he ever meant to do.

The geography of the tale moves on the axis home—the open fields. The women's indoor accommodations are not described, but we get the sense of a desolate, empty, and lonely place. The field is a crowded, busy environment, but for Ruth it is equally lonely and alien. The dynamics of the tale are anchored not in the sites where the scenes take place, however, but in the patterns of linguistic activities. Within the structure of this tale, silences are as meaningful as the dialogues themselves, and the movement of a set of dialogues punctuated by speechless intervals invigorates the dramatic tension and reflects transitions in moods and states of mind. Chapter 1, containing the most provocative and memorable dialogues in the tale, ends with silence: the women's stunned, hushed reaction to the abundance that they encounter in Bethlehem, which contrasts sharply with their own destitution. Chapter 2 starts with the statement that Naomi has a relative in town, a man of position and capacities, but the text does not disclose why this information is given at this point, and the women make no comment concerning Boaz. The opening to this chapter chronicles a painful period in which the women expect help from neighbors and relatives (such as Boaz) but are offered nothing. Naomi's uncharacteristic reticence regarding her situation signifies a dispirited, disappointed state of mind, revitalized only when Ruth takes the initiative and in impatient but animated language suggests that she go out to glean in the fields. This triggers the set of events narrated in chapter 2, including an unexpected encounter with Boaz and a lively series of dialogues. Yet this chapter, too, ends with silence; the season of harvest is over, nothing came of Boaz's kindness and interest in Ruth, and the women find themselves alone at home, probably too discouraged to talk: "And [Ruth] dwelt [stayed at home] with her mother-in-law" (2:23).

It is Ruth's turn to feel dejected and wordless, and therefore it is Naomi who starts the dialogue in chapter 3. Naomi describes an elaborate and cunning scheme to which Ruth responds tersely, and perhaps also somewhat mechanically and unenthusiastically, "All that thou sayest to me I will do" (3:12–15). Soon Ruth's buoyant and daring spirits as well as her eloquence are revived, and she expands on her mother-in-law's initial plan. Naomi had instructed Ruth to wait for the man to speak when he discovers her, but Ruth says more than the man's question warrants. When Boaz, startled, asks who she is, Ruth not only identifies herself but makes a courageous, almost audacious suggestion: "I am Ruth thy handmaid: spread therefore thy skirt [or wing] over thy handmaid; for thou art a near kinsman [or, a redeemer]" (3:9).

Naomi's intention is probably to arouse sexual feelings and fantasies in Boaz, and thus instill in him a sense of sexual guilt that will lead him to solve Ruth's problem. Naomi, however, had not specifically indicated that she meant for Boaz himself to redeem Ruth. We know that in the technical sense, Boaz is not a redeemer, since he is not Ruth's brother-in-law. For Ruth to suggest, openly and unequivocally, that Boaz marry her is a bold move, in which her ability to combine the language of deference with that of implied challenge is illustrated once more. While again describing herself as Boaz's "handmaid," Ruth does not refrain from using the imperative "spread," in effect commanding the man to redeem her. She also gives him a clear reason why the responsibility falls on him: "You are a redeemer."

In this nocturnal encounter, the tale's climax, Ruth reveals in both her words and the manner in which she delivers them that she has completed her education in Israelite customs and traditions, that she is spiritually ready to become one of them, and therefore worthy of being assimilated and accepted by them. Not only is she acquainted with the law of *yibbum,* the redemption of the childless widow by her brother-in-law, but she uses the appropriate language when offering herself to Boaz. She designates him as a "redeemer," not simply as a potential husband. Ruth thus proves to Boaz that she now moves within the patriarchal legal system. At the same time, Ruth, like the daughters of Zelofhad before her, succeeds in shaping this system to her advantage. By calling Boaz a "redeemer," whose responsibility it would be to marry her, Ruth is technically wrong. But she makes Boaz understand the spirit of the law, rather than simply its narrow meaning, for the law itself does not always cover all the cases confronted in real life. With Ruth's subtle help, Boaz broadens his conception of the levirate custom to include not only the widow's brother-in-law but also her more distant relatives. Ruth teaches Boaz a lesson in the humanitarian interpretation of the law, which he readily accepts. She also creates a new reality with the aid of language: by naming Boaz a "redeemer," Ruth makes him one. Ruth's linguistic wisdom is further manifested in that she refrains from pleading with Boaz to "marry" her and thus rescue her from destitution. Instead, she uses the ceremonious phrase that Boaz himself employed in 2:12, "under [God's] wings," thus playfully linking God's wings and the corners of Boaz's garment. The play on words carries a serious message: by marrying her Boaz will be fulfilling his God's law, as well as his own earlier good wishes.

Elsewhere I have discussed the link between the Ruth tale and two previous biblical tales that also revolve around the seduction of a man by a woman who finds herself in a hopeless situation: the Genesis episodes of Lot and his daughters (Gen. 19) and of Judah and Tamar (Gen. 38).[48] The tales are linked not only stylistically, through the motif of the seduction of a man, but genealogically. The product of the incestuous relationship between Lot and his daughter is Moab, Ruth's ancestor, and the product of the sexual encounter between Judah and his daughter-in-law is Perez, Boaz's ancestor. The three tales can be viewed as a chain of narratives that exemplify stages in the evolution of attitudes toward sexual taboos and mores. It starts with the barbaric, cave-people tale in which Lot's daughters get their father drunk and then lie with him, moves to the somewhat more civilized ambiance of the tale in which Judah's widowed daughter-in-law uses guile in order to conceive from Judah, and climaxes in the cleaned-up tale of Ruth's successful efforts to make Boaz recognize his familial responsibilities and "redeem" her.

The tale of Ruth is purged of the many unseemly elements of the two previous tales. It offers no graphic description of the sexual act during Boaz's encounter with Ruth on the threshing floor. The narrator uses the euphemistic, suggestive phrase, the uncovering of the man's "feet" (or legs) (3:7), which is laden with sexual connotations, but does not explicitly indicate that Boaz was seduced by Ruth. More importantly, Ruth herself, in her use of language, "redeems" her female precursors by converting the crass, vulgar, and unabashedly explicit vocabulary that prevails in their tales to the dignified language of redemption and moral responsibility. Lot's daughters are very blunt when they connive to "lie" with their own father, and Tamar, dressed as a harlot, is forced also to talk like one. She is, therefore, no less graphic when she asks Judah, "What wilt thou give me, that thou mayest come in to me" (Gen. 38:16). By contrast, the nocturnal dialogue between Ruth and Boaz is laced with the honorable concepts of covenantal law, familial obligations, and divine blessing and approval.

Although both Ruth and Boaz resort to the same lofty rhetoric, it seems that Ruth is the one who sets the tone. Instead of dwelling on the sexual indiscretion, feigning innocence and demanding restitution, or hinting at the potential embarrassment for the old man, the quick-witted Ruth repeats the image that Boaz himself used earlier, the spreading of the wings. By naming him a "redeemer," she places him within the respectable tradition of a man who fulfills his familial obligations as prescribed by Mosaic law. Ruth's precursor, Tamar, consumed with the problem of immediate survival and not possessing a historical awareness, reminds Judah of the recent past when she asks him, sarcastically, to recognize the pledges, evidence of the sexual encounter between them several months before. Ruth, on the other hand, speaks in the name of time-honored social and religious laws that alert Boaz's historical memory and sense of responsibility. She reminds him of a tradition that underlies his own culture, and that was founded at the inception of his own civilization. Boaz, who at first sounds alarmed and angry, calms down and picks up the tone and meaning of Ruth's speech. He continues in the same vein by repeating the verb "to redeem" a number of times. Being an old man who, as we have seen before, can become emotional and effusive, he proceeds to bless Ruth and commend her profusely.

A cynical view of Ruth might regard her grand, metaphoric language as a strategy to win Boaz, a respectable elder and pillar of the Israelite community who is himself given to flowery speech. In this interpretation, Ruth's cunning rhetoric complements her ruse of surprising Boaz in the middle of the night after he has eaten and drunk perhaps more than usual. Boaz himself, however, discards this notion when he reminds us that some of the young men, both poor and rich, have shown an interest in Ruth which she did not reciprocate.

Boaz understands that Ruth has not been waiting merely for material salvation, ample food and comfortable shelter, nor for the appeasement of her maternal yearnings. She could have satisfied these needs by marrying one of the younger men in town. Ruth is looking to find a niche for herself within the Israelites' religious and ethical structure and therefore wishes to enter the Israelite family through the institution of the levirate marriage. This custom, intended to perpetuate a dead man's name and at the same time rescue his widow from poverty, is a new framework within which Ruth finds fulfillment and a sense of completeness. The earlier women, Lot's daughters and Tamar, are seen as terrorized by their fear of remaining "empty" in the biological sense. Driven by material concerns as well as their feminine instincts to become mothers, they act in a manner that recognizes no morality or civilized custom. In the Ruth tale, the theme of emptiness and fullness is first related to nature and to women's physical needs, but is then converted into a spiritual, religious, and historical concept. Ruth's reward is that she becomes an important link in the Israelites' historic journey toward redemption, by becoming the ancestress of the glorious David, and thus she "fills" and completes the generational chain.

Through the language of honor and respectability, Ruth converts her tale from the familiar pattern of a poor woman's rise to riches and prominence through a man to a religious *bildungsroman* in which a foreign woman espouses a people and a faith, learns their legal code and customs (anchored in patriarchy), and proceeds to educate the patriarch and direct him toward a more humane interpretation of his God's law.

Significantly, the last episodes of the tale, narrated in chapter 4, are characterized by Naomi's and Ruth's untypical silence. There are no exclamations of joy on the part of either woman, and, surprisingly, the women of the town, rather than the mother herself, name Ruth's newborn. Again playing the role of the chorus, they sum up the protagonists' miraculous journey from bereavement to redemption. Naomi and Ruth's great respect for language and their faith in its power is revealed precisely in their reticence. They have exercised their linguistic ingenuity with the best possible results, but they are not wasteful of their eloquence. Their initial harsh fate has yielded to the power of their language. Naomi's lexicon of the unattainable—*yibbum,* redemption, matrimony—has forced itself on reality and materialized, and the nonexistent "redeemer" has come to life on Ruth's tongue, with Boaz persuaded to play the role. Naomi's grand vision of herself being tried by a heavenly court and her discourse with God, and Ruth's lofty style of sacred responsibility and covenantal redemption, have proven to be more than shallow ornamentation or calculated tactics. The women's colloquy of grandeur and religious ardor is genuine, corresponding to the greatness of their minds and hearts. Their verbal ability is testimony to their inner powers and indestructible nature. It empowers them to continue their struggle for status and recognition and to carve out a magnificent destiny in a community, a system, and, indeed, a divinely mandated order that were not ready to yield easily to them.

Skeptics might argue that Ruth's story ends on a disappointing note: another woman has become pregnant and given birth to a male child who would grow up to be a patriarch. By bearing a child who would carry her dead husband's name, however, Ruth has secured not only her own private survival but the future of a family. Ruth's descendant would become the king of Israel and the carrier of its Messianic dreams, and so Ruth has put herself at a juncture where the historical memory of past traditions and cultural values converges with an eschatological vision of a destiny the horizons of which transcend time and place.[49]

EPILOGUE

The theory of the woman-at-the-window is set forth in the first chapter of this book, underlying all ensuing discussions. Biblical women were not, however, fully cognizant of the theological and historiosophic repercussions of this ancient image. Nevertheless, a scrutiny of women's actions and reactions amply proves that some women were fully aware of being demoted from history to nature in the culture's mind, while some grasped it emotionally, if not intellectually. The last chapter in this study illustrates that women countered being relegated to an inferior state of being through creative and inventive language. They attempted to imitate God Himself by making the word a means of creating a world. At times, male authors chronicled women's actions with unsuspecting accuracy, while in other instances they infused their narratives with agendas of their own. In a number of tales, however, the male writers were fully aware of the purpose pervading their protagonists' actions, reporting their enterprising doings with delight and even relish, and their sorrows in darkly nuanced, even sympathetic tones. If we acknowledge that biblical authorship was varied and multiple we cannot insist that when it came to the representation of women all male writers were united by a single, monolithic intent.

Although a spatial image associated with a particular female protagonist drives each discussion, the narrow boundaries of a single theory never subsumes the entire study. The method of analytic, dramatic retelling of the female protagonists' stories unravels the intricate tapestry of the action and the differing, often conflicting purposes of the protagonists. Reading the ancient tales is an act of dramatic participation and reciprocal understanding. We bring to them our own perspectives, decoding and illuminating in their narrative fabric those areas that may have gone unnoticed by ancient readers. By luring us to their cultural and psychological ambiance, the ancient tales reveal universal structures and help us understand contemporary attitudes and behaviors that have deep roots in our collective memories.

By following the intrigue and suspense in these tales, I have tried to impart the sense of joy that comes with studying them. The predicament of ancient women may often be abhorrent to us, but dissecting the complex narrative texture is always a delight. To illustrate a truism known to readers and lovers of mimetic art: revisiting the suicide scene in Tolstoy's *Anna Karenina* is always a riveting and moving experience, though witnessing a woman hurling herself in front of a speeding train is not a sight most of us would welcome.

NOTES

INTRODUCTION

1. See Carla Gottlieb, *The Window in Art: From the Window of God to the Vanity of Man* (New York: Abaris Books, 1981), 34.
2. Ibid., 35.
3. Ibid., 419n. 36.
4. Ibid., 36–37.
5. Ibid., 32.
6. On the archetype of the Great Mother and her association with the earth and natural forces, see Erich Neumann, *The Great Mother: An Analysis of an Archetype,* trans. Ralph Manheim (Princeton: Princeton University Press, 1970).
7. Johannes Vermeer's windows "often furnish the only means of escape from his dense, potentially claustrophobic spaces. Were it not for these windows, the very life would drain from many of these severe, domestic habitats, for their light is sometimes the only active force." See Suzanne Delehenty, ed., *The Window in Twentieth-Century Art* (Purchase, N.Y.: Neuberger Museum, State University of New York, Purchase, 1986), 12.
8. Ibid., 13.
9. The woman-at-her-doorway as a universal motif implying the female's sexual powers as menacing and dangerous has been utilized by James Joyce in *A Portrait of the Artist as a Young Man.* See Nehama Aschkenasy, "Biblical Females in a Joycean Episode," *Modern Language Studies* 15, no. 5 (1985): 28–39.
10. Tom Driver, *The Sense of History in Greek and Shakespearean Drama* (New York: Columbia University Press, 1959), 17.
11. Ibid., 28.

12. See ibid., 27–30.
13. Ibid., 27.
14. Erich Auerbach, *Mimesis: The Representation of Reality in Western Literature,* trans. Willard Trask (Garden City, N.Y.: Doubleday, 1957), 14, 15.
15. *Ruth,* trans. and intro. Edward F. Campbell (Garden City, N.Y.: Doubleday-Anchor 1975), 21.
16. For the methodology of the Bible's early interpreters, see James L. Kugel, *The Bible as It Was* (Cambridge, Mass.: Harvard University Press, 1997).

CHAPTER 1

1. Simone de Beauvoir, *The Second Sex* (New York: Knopf, 1953).
2. The text may also be suggesting that Sisera intended to ask for Yael's husband's protection, since there was peace between their tribes.
3. This image was not lost on James Joyce either, who made it central in an episode that revolves around a woman-at-her-doorstep. See Aschkenasy, "Biblical Females in a Joycean Episode."
4. See Wolfgang Lederer, *The Fear of Women* (New York: Harcourt, 1968), 126. For the same symbols in Hebraic tradition, see Jacob Nacht, *Simlei Isha* (Feminine symbolism) (Tel Aviv, 1959), passim.
5. The ancient sages were attuned to the erotic subtext in the tale. The Jewish commentator Radak, in his discussion of Judges 5:27, cites an ancient midrash (although he dismisses it) that Sisera had intercourse with Yael.
6. Mieke Bal sees this scene differently. She claims that by taking the milk from the woman, Sisera has put himself in the position of the baby, and therefore he tries to reestablish his authority as well as his previous status in the world as commander of men by ordering the woman, as well as by using the masculine imperative, *amod.* See Bal, *Murder and Difference* (Bloomington: Indiana University Press, 1988), 121. A comparison of Sisera's initial polite address to the woman with his commanding tone points to his self delusion: yes, he has lost his power and is on the run, but he deludes himself that he is the master of this woman by virtue of the sexual encounter.
7. The theme of a man erroneously supposing that the sexual act has endowed him with mastery and knowledge, while in reality it put him in the woman's hands, is universal. Zvi Jagendorf discusses this pattern in the Bible as well as in several Shakespearean plays, in "Genesis and the Reversal of Sexual Knowledge," in *Biblical Patterns in Modern Literature,* ed. David Hirsch and Nehama Aschkenasy (Chico, Calif.: Scholars Press, 1984), 51–60.
8. The same image can transmit opposite messages to different generations. Although to the modern reader Deborah's sitting under the palm tree

indicates freedom contrasting with the restrictive lives of her female contemporaries, the commentary of Metsudat David explains that Deborah had to conduct her court in the open because the principle of female modesty dictated that she not receive men in the privacy of her home.

9. Ralbag gives both interpretations, while Radak mentions the possibility that Deborah is alluding not to herself but to Yael, and rejects it.

10. On biblical parallelism see James L. Kugel, *The Idea of Biblical Poetry: Parallelism and Its History* (New Haven: Yale University Press, 1981).

11. The traditional commentators Radak and Ralbag both comment on the peculiar use of the verb in Judges 5:1. Radak says that the verb appears in the third person feminine singular because Deborah is the pivot of the tale. Ralbag believes that Deborah herself composed the ode, but that it is a common biblical practice to include the listeners, or those who join in the reciting of the poem, in the syntactical subject while the verb itself appears in the singular.

12. In folk tales and children's literature, contests testing physical prowess or intelligence often end with the winner getting the princess or the beautiful girl. Oedipus winning the widowed queen for solving the riddle of the Sphinx is an example. Bruno Bettelheim, in *The Uses of Enchantment* (New York: Knopf, 1976), says that the solving of riddles in folk tales is taken as proof of sexual maturity.

CHAPTER 2

1. Lynn A. Higgins and Brenda R. Silver, comment on the "simultaneous presence and disappearance of rape as constantly deferred origin of both plot and social relations" which is repeated in so many tales so as to suggest "a basic conceptual principle." See their *Rape and Representation* (New York: Columbia University Press, 1991), 5.

2. See Meir Sternberg, *The Poetics of Biblical Narrative* (Bloomington: Indiana University Press, 1985), 475–445; idem, "Delicate Balance in the Story of the Rape of Dinah: Biblical Narrative and the Rhetoric of the Narrative Text," *Hasifrut* 4 (1973): 193–231. See also Nahum Sarna, "The Ravishing of Dinah: A Commentary on Genesis, Chapter 34," in *Studies in Jewish Education,* ed. A. Shapiro and B. Cohen (New York: Ktav, 1984), 143–56.

3. Sternberg studies the syntactic and linguistic ambiguities that reveal the subtle condemnation of the father and the familial tension in the tale. His in-depth study of the text is still focused on the foreground of the tale, the father-vs.-sons and family-vs.-rapist dramas. Yet he is oblivious to the sexual discourse in the tale, to the brothers' sense of having been feminized through the rape of their sister, and their measure-for-measure

response which in essence is the emasculation of the rapist and his tribe. Furthermore, Dinah's disappearance from the text is viewed as a structural technique that aids in casting the brothers in a favorable light once we learn, late in the tale, that Dinah is still incarcerated in her rapist's home. Beyond this, Sternberg notes "Dinah's disappearance from the text" in a footnote. Sternberg's male-centered reading is oblivious to the connection between Dinah's silence and her spatial diminution, as well as to the reduction of the woman from a person to a cipher denoting an inferior state—femaleness— which functions in the context of male rivalry. See Sternberg, *The Poetics of Biblical Narrative,* 537n. 10.

4. Elision is not only the writer's strategy but the readers' as well. Readers responding to Sternberg's initial essay on this tale responded by calling the rape a seduction, thus erasing the event of rape. See Sternberg, *The Poetics of Biblical Narrative,* 536n. 1. Elsewhere, I have identified a "Dinah corpus" that runs through the Hebraic literary tradition, with prevalent cultural attitudes constantly giving new perspectives to the biblical tale, but all based on a component in the original tale itself. See Nehama Aschkenasy, *Eve's Journey: Feminine Images in Hebraic Literary* (Philadelphia: University of Pennsylvania Press, 1986; reprint, Detroit: Wayne State University Press, 1995), 124–38.

5. Adrienne Rich deplores the silence that has surrounded the mother-daughter relationship in culture and literature since early times: "We acknowledge Lear (father-daughter split), Hamlet (mother and son), and Oedipus (son and mother) as great embodiments of the human tragedy; but there is no presently enduring recognition of mother-daughter passion and rapport." Adrienne Rich, *Of Woman Born: Motherhood as Experience and Institution* (New York: W. W. Norton, 1976), 237.

6. For an analysis of the meaning of Leah's sons' names, and their link to the mother's matrimonial agonies and dwindling hopes regarding Jacob's love for her, see Aschkenasy, *Eve's Journey,* 84–85.

7. Feminist scholars have indicated the difficulty for women to mother daughters in a society in which women are deprived of a sense of self-worth and are therefore unable to transmit such a sense to their daughters, sometimes to the point of being unable to nurture them. See Judith Arcana, *Our Mother's Daughters* (Berkeley, Calif.: Shameless Hussey Press, 1979), 31 passim. For more on the intricacies of the mother-daughter relationship in the context of patriarchy, see Marianne Hirsch, "Mothers and Daughters," in *Ties That Bind: Essays on Mothering and Patriarchy,* ed. Jean F. O'Barr, Deborah Pope, and Mary Wyer (Chicago: University of Chicago Press, 1990), 177–99. For a popular view of this relationship in contemporary culture, see Nancy Friday, *My Mother, Myself: The Daughter's Search for Identity* (New York: Delacorte Press, 1977).

8. *Genesis Rabbah* states that the brothers had to force Dinah out of She-chem's home. *The Midrash: Genesis,* 2d ed., trans. H. Freedman and M. Simon (London: Soncino Press, 1961), 743.

9. Ibid., 738.

10. The rabbis call Dinah a "gadabout" and describe how she exposed her arms seductively. Ibid.

11. See Maya Angelou, *I Know Why the Caged Bird Sings* (New York, Bantam, 1971), 57–73.

12. In another memorable rape scene in the Bible, that of the rape of Tamar in 2 Samuel 13, the woman's verbal reaction is amply recorded. Yet her pleadings with her molester, first trying to reason with him, and then pretending to go along with him and appeasing him with the promise of a shared future, do not work and make her attacker angrier and more determined. Although the ancient Tamar uses the appeasement tactics suggested to modern women, namely attempting to communicate with the potential rapist, she fails miserably. For further discussion of the similarities and differences between the two tales, see Aschkenasy, *Eve's Journey,* 138–40.

13. That rape is not only a manifestation of individual psychopathology but a socially patterned phenomenon is a theory held by many modern students of rape. Of the four aspects of rape that explain state-to-state variation in rape, three are also applicable to the society reflected in our tale: sexual inequality, cultural support for violence, and the level of social disorganization. See Larry Baron and Murray A. Straus, *Rape in American Society: A State-Level Analysis* (New Haven: Yale University Press, 1989), 57, 174–89.

14. *The Elementary Structures of Kinship,* trans. James Harle Bell, John Richard Von Sturmer, and Rodney Needham, ed. Rodney Needham, rev. ed. (Boston: Beacon, 1969), 494.

15. E. M. Forster's novel *A Passage to India* provides an intriguing modern variation of the tale of Dinah, where cultural rivalries and questions of dispossession and occupation of foreign territory are enacted on the woman's body, while the woman herself is silenced and elided. Brenda R. Silver reads Adela's experience in the cave "not in terms of sexual desire or repression, but in terms of a deployment of sexuality within a system of power that posits a complex network of sameness and difference. . . . What is at stake is both gender difference and racial difference . . . to be *rapable* [is] a social position that cuts across biological and racial lines to inscribe culturally constructed definitions of sexuality within a sex/gender/power system." See "Periphrasis, Power, and Rape in *A Passage to India,*" in *Rape and Representation,* 115–37. A modern Hebrew story that reverberates with echoes from the tale of Dinah and also bears a resemblance to Forster's

novel is Amos Oz's "Nomad and Viper." For a study of the way Oz ties the ancient and the modern precursors to his tale of rape, or imagined rape, see Aschkenasy, *Eve's Journey,* 210–13.

16. By a "rape society" I do not mean to suggest that biblical society condoned rape. The term as used here denotes a culture where rape is a prevalent phenomenon. There are a number of biblical tales which revolve around rape, as well as many intimations of the prevalence of rape in war situations. Biblical legislation distinguishes between several types of rape, rape of a virgin, a married woman, a betrothed woman; rape in the city, outside a residential area, and so forth. Even the penalty for rape, which is the obligation on the rapist to marry the woman without ever being able to divorce her, also points to the prevalence of rape in biblical civilization (Deut. 22: 28–29). For a somewhat different use of the term and its applicability to contemporary society, see Emilie Buchwald, Pamela R. Fletcher, and Martha Roth, eds., *Transforming a Rape Culture* (Minneapolis: Milkweed, 1993).

17. A sexual offender suffers from a personality dysfunction and needs medical and therapeutic intervention in order to achieve successful rehabilitation. See Nicholas Groth, *Men Who Rape: The Psychology of the Offender* (New York: Plenum Press, 1984), 215–23.

18. See Susan Brownmiller, *Against Our Will: Men, Women and Rape* (New York: Simon and Schuster, 1975).

19. *The Midrash: Genesis,* 743.

20. Even the intelligent, feisty Tamar in the 2 Samuel tale, who is obviously upset and disgusted by her rapist, her half brother Amnon, still begs him to let her stay with him after the rape, thus indicating to us that in biblical society a woman would prefer to stay with her hated violator, rather than return home to a life of isolation as a "tainted" woman. See Aschkenasy, *Eve's Journey,* 138–40.

21. The 2 Samuel tale of the rape of Tamar seems much more realistic and aware of the psychology of the rapist than the present tale. First, Amnon, the rapist, is depicted as a crazed and obsessed man, not as a person who is genuinely in love. His irrational hatred of Tamar after the rape is borne out by modern studies that conclude that rape is usually not a sexually pleasurable experience for the offender and that it often is followed by greater fury and disgust. See Groth, *Men Who Rape,* 93–96.

22. Erich Fromm, *The Art of Loving* (New York: Harper and Row, 1974), 20–21.

23. See Auerbach, *Mimesis,* 1–20.

24. Mieke Bal offers a radical interpretation of the type of marriage implied here, which leads her to a reading that in many ways is diametrically opposed to the one offered here. Bal understands concubinage as patrilocal,

denoting (contrary to the accepted meaning of the term) the practice in which the woman continues to reside with her father, and thus the center of power remains the woman's father. In this reading, the woman betrays the father when she goes off to live with her husband. See Bal, *Death and Dissymmetry* (Chicago: University of Chicago Press, 1988), 84–86. I opt to follow the Jewish traditional commentators who understand the term "concubine" as a wife who enters her husband's home without *kiddushin,* a legal marriage ceremony, or *ketubah,* a document that protects her economically. See the group of commentators in the Hebrew text of *Shoftim/Miqraot Gedolot* (Israel: Pardes, 1954). See also Raphael Patai, *Sex and Family in the Bible and the Middle East* (Garden City, N.Y.: Doubleday, 1959), 41–43. Rachel Biale defines these terms as follows: "Ketubah: The Jewish marriage contract given by the groom to the bride specifying his obligations during the marriage and in the event of its dissolution." "Kiddushin: Betrothal: the actual legal act effecting marriage." See *Women and Jewish Law* (New York: Schocken, 1984), 287, 288.

25. Patai, *Sex and Family in the Bible and the Middle East,* 42.

26. Bal rejects commentators who maintain that a concubine is a legitimate wife, but of second rank, by claiming that if the concubine (according to common usage) is one who is not *legally* married, then the woman here engages either in "free love" or in living "in sin." See Bal, *Death and Dissymmetry,* 81. Both terms are anachronistic in the context of biblical civilization. According to the biblical, and later, Talmudic law, "legitimate" marriage necessitates merely cohabiting with a woman. Therefore, a concubine can be a wife who was not married by a legal ceremony but was still a "legitimate" wife.

27. Phyllis Trible's suggests that the Levite's intentions to "speak to her heart" throws a sympathetic light on the man. I prefer to read it as a sign of his guilt, especially since he is never seen speaking "to her heart." A chronological reading of this tale is simply impossible and the tool of "backshadowing" must be used. In light of what comes next, it is only possible to understand the Levite's intentions as insincere, as a plan to use guile and hypocrisy to get his abused slave back. See Phyllis Trible, *Texts of Terror* (Philadelphia: Fortress Press, 1984), 67.

28. It is possible to read the verb *vatizneh* in the Hebrew not at all as "and she played the harlot" but as "and she left" or "turned away from," or "was unfaithful to" him. Again I wish to consult the traditional Jewish commentators not only because they are very sensitive to the language, but also because they cannot be accused of employing a "woman-centered" method of reading the text. Nevertheless, those who comment on this verb suggest that the primary meaning of the verb is simply "to leave" or "to turn away." See Ralbag and Radak on this verse in *Shoftim/Miqraot Gedolot.*

Ralbag sees in the woman's daring act of leaving her husband, as well as in the husband's intentions to reconcile with her, an indication that the Levite had abused the woman. Robert G. Boling, in his commentary in the Anchor Bible edition of Judges also opts for a reading more favorable to the woman: "she became an adulteress by walking out on him," and "the Levite's concern to recover his concubine suggests that she, not he, is the offended party." Robert G. Boling, ed. and trans., *Judges* (Garden City, N.Y.: Doubleday, 1975), 274.

29. This recalls Adrienne Rich's comments about the lack of recognition, since early times, of the special dynamics and importance of mother-daughter relationships in culture and literature. See Rich, *Of Woman Born*, 237.

30. Contrary to Bal, who makes a reference to the Levite's "wealth," I sense a slightly ironic and comic tone in the description of the impoverished Levite, who resides in a desolate place and owns only a tent, attempting to appear prosperous when he goes to his father-in-law's house. See Bal, *Death and Disymmetry*, 90.

31. Bal reads the father's delaying tactics as attempts to keep the daughter, a "patrilocal wife" who lives in the father's house and whose primary loyalty is still to her father. If this is so, what power does the poor Levite have to insist on taking his wife and going home, other than the fact that she is his concubine in the traditional meaning of secondary wife? See ibid., 91.

32. For a study of the analogy between this tale and the Genesis tale of Lot and the wicked people of Sodom, see Trible, *Texts of Terror,* 74–76.

33. Boling comments that the verb "to know" is "never unambiguously used of homosexual coitus" Boling, *Judges,* 276; Trible, *Texts of Terror,* 73–74.

34. Nicholas Groth posits that the primary motive in gang rape is the search for peer sanction and support, resulting in camaraderie with the other members of the group. The sexual aspects of the crime are the means of such interaction. See *Men Who Rape,* 118.

35. These include Rashi (twelfth century), Ralbag (fourteenth century), and others. See *Shoftim/Miqraot Gedolot,* which offers a selection of the traditional commentators.

36. See Higgins and Silver, *Rape and Representation,* esp. "The Rhetoric of Elision," 67–137.

37. Sternberg views this gap as a literary technique that enriches the biblical text by creating ambiguity and pointing an accusing finger at both the thugs, in case the woman is indeed dead in the morning, and the Levite, in case the woman is not dead and the Levite later dismembers her while she is still alive. Sternberg argues as well that this ambiguity serves a historical purpose: blaming the two parties, the rapists and the husband, supports the storyteller's claims of the moral chaos in the country and the need for a king. This reading, however, ignores the text's specific narration of the

rapists sending the woman back after the rape and of the woman walking on her own to her host's home. As in the case of the absence of a reunion scene between husband and wife, I prefer to read this as a reflection of fact—namely that the Levite did not make sure that his wife was dead, and that she may have still been alive—rather than as a literary elision that creates ambiguity. The Levite's culpability is clearly established in the tale and is not a matter of ambiguity at all. See Sternberg, *The Poetics of Biblical Narrative,* 239

CHAPTER 3

1. On the role of the play element in the evolution of civilization as well as the growth of the individual, see Johan Huizinga, *Homo Ludens: A Study of the Play-Element in Culture,* trans. R. F. C. Hull (Boston: Beacon, 1955).
2. The position of Genesis 38, in the midst of the Joseph saga, has been considered problematic by both traditional and modern critics. Interestingly, however, rather than attribute the chapter's place to editorial failure to realize that the tale disrupts and breaks the flow of Joseph's adventures, critics have come up with interesting explanations, theological and literary, to justify the chapter's unusual placing. The Midrash sages pointed out linguistic patterns that are repeated in both tales and strung the tales together as pieces in a single eschatological, historical, and moral continuum. See *Genesis Rabbah* (London: The Soncino Press, 1961), 787, 788, 789. Bal sees the themes of deviation from the right path, deception and displacement as the links between, specifically, chapters 37, 38, and 39. See Bal, *Lethal Love* (Bloomington: Indiana University Press, 1987), 95–98. The literary integrity of the sequence of narratives ranging from chapter 37 to the end of the Joseph saga is discussed by Robert Alter, *The Art of Biblical Narrative* (New York: Basic Books, 1981), 5–12.
3. On archetypal themes such as the distance from the father as necessary for the hero's maturation, the rivalry between the father and the grown son, and the ogre father as inhibiting his sons' sexuality, see Joseph Campbell, *The Hero With a Thousand Faces* (1949; reprint Princeton: Princeton University Press, 1973), 49–58, 62, 129–171 passim.
4. The levirate custom is usually assumed to be an institution designed to perpetuate the dead man's memory and ensure his line. For a discussion of the levirate custom and its evolvement in post-biblical society, see Rachel Biale, *Women and Jewish Law* (New York, Schocken, 1984), 113–20. It is partly because of the predicament of childless widows who could not obtain a release from their brothers-in-law, in later times, that the economic benefits to the woman, which might have been part of the original intent of this custom in early society, have been overlooked.

5. For the father's aggression toward his sons and its resolution, see Phyllis Chesler, *About Men* (New York: Simon and Schuster, 1978), 204 passim.

6. The "killer wife" syndrome has occupied Hebraic literature since early times. In TB Yebamot, 65a the rabbis discuss the marriageability of women whose first two husbands have died. Some rabbis believe that a widow should not remarry for the third time if both former husbands have died; some believe that the widow can marry a third time but not a fourth time. On the "fear of women" see Wolfgang Lederer, *The Fear of Women* (New York: Harcourt, 1968) and Neumann, *The Great Mother.*

7. For more on the "mother's house" as the locus for matters pertaining to marriage, see Campbell, ed., *Ruth,* 64, 65.

8. On the fear of the father, and the "psychopolitical war" between fathers and sons, see Chesler, *About Men,* 193–210 passim.

9. *Genesis Rabbah,* 794.

10. In his discussion of the nature of mimetic behavior Bruce Wiltshire explains that our self-identity is tied to our experience as a body identifiable by others. See Wiltshire, *Role Playing and Identity* (Bloomington: Indiana University Press, 1982), 143–50, 166.

11. Bal, *Lethal Love,* 101–3.

12. For more on this series of tales see Aschkenasy, *Eve's Journey,* 85–88. For a discussion of the moral evolution in the "Ruth Corpus" see Harold Fisch, "Ruth and the Structure of Covenant History," *Vetus Testamentum* 32, no. 4 (1982): 425–37.

13. See P. Kyle McCarter, ed. and trans., *1 Samuel* (Garden City, N.Y.: Doubleday-Anchor, 1980), 392.

14. For this configuration in non-Jewish literature, see Harold Fisch, *The Dual Image: The Figure of the Jew in English and American Literature* (New York: Ktav, 1971).

15. For a discussion of these comic types, derived from Aristotle's *Ethics,* see Northrop Frye, *Anatomy of Criticism* (Princeton: Princeton University Press, 1957), 172–75.

16. P. Kyle McCarter sees the typological triangle here in a different way: David finds himself between the proverbial "fool," Nabal, and the proverbial "stalwart woman," who "opens her mouth in wisdom." See *1 Samuel,* 401.

17. For the comic extremes in Henry IV Part One, as well as the history and tradition of the fool, see Walter Kaiser in *Praisers of Folly* (Cambridge, Mass: Cambridge University Press, 1963).

18. See Bal, *Lethal Love,* 25, 33; Sternberg, *The Poetics of Biblical Narrative,* 219–22.

19. Bal takes issue with those who see an analogy between David and Abimelech, claiming that Abimelech was killed while David was the victimizer

of Uriah, and furthermore, that Bathsheba is also a victim in all this. The point is that Joab, as military man in a male-dominant culture, would sympathize with men who have been ruined by women. In his eyes, if David has been led by a liaison with a woman to commit this act, then both David and his victim are the woman's victims. Joab would certainly disagree with Bal's position that Bathsheba is a victim here. Bal, *Lethal Love*, 23–29.

20. Some of my conclusions here coincide with Fokkelman's analysis regarding Joab's state of mind and the general symmetry and asymmetry between the earlier tale and the present one. In general, I agree that Joab's imagined dialogue between David and the messenger reflects on Joab's own inner emotions rather than on David's actual reaction. See J. P. Fokkelman, *King David: Narrative Art and Poetry in the Book of Samuel* (Assen, Netherlands: Van Gorcum, 1981).

CHAPTER 4

1. For a similar interpretation of Isaac's position which does not, however, consider Rebecca's predicament, see Nehama Leibowitz, *Studies in the Weekly Sidra*, Series 4/5718 (Jerusalem: The Jewish Agency, 1957).

2. On the possible sources of this material, see P. Kyle McCarter's commentary in *2 Samuel*, 288–91.

3. For more on this as well as on the system of gaps in the narrative, see the landmark essay by M. Perry and M. Sternberg, "Hammelech bemabbat ironi" (The king through ironic eyes), *Hasifrut* 1 (1968): 262–91. See also Sternberg, *The Poetics of Biblical Narrative*, 186–229.

4. The problem with Bal's characterization is that this tale is very far removed from the genre of love stories. To talk about "David's love for Bathsheba" and suggest that "David killed Uriah for love" is to read into the text something that, to me, is not within the realm of possibilities. Bal, *Lethal Love*, 131.

5. See ibid., 27–29.

6. This rabbinic interpretation, repeated by Radak and other traditional sources, is part of the attempt to whitewash David's sin. According to this, Bathsheba was not a married woman because Uriah had given her a deed of divorce before leaving for the war, a custom that had been instituted by David. Other rabbinic commentaries, in attempting to legitimize Solomon, claimed that Bathsheba was forced by David, therefore she did not commit adultery, and therefore she was allowed to cohabit with both her husband and the man she slept with while she was married. Since she was never an adulteress, her son was not a bastard.

7. Most commentators, it seems, read 1 Samuel 11:2 to mean that David saw

her from the roof bathing in her house. Targum Jonathan, however, reads the verse to mean that David was on the roof of his house, and Bathsheba was taking a bath on her roof.

CHAPTER 5

1. For some of the key narrative techniques in the Bible, see Alter, *The Art of Biblical Narrative*, and Sternberg, *The Poetics of Biblical Narratives*.
2. Derek Bickerton, *Language and Species* (Chicago: University of Chicago Press, 1990), 255, 256.
3. George Steiner, *After Babel: Aspects of Language and Translation* (New York: Oxford University Press, 1975), 38.
4. Alter, *The Art of Biblical Narrative*, 140–46.
5. Joseph B. Soloveitchik, "The Lonely Man of Faith," *Tradition* (Summer 1965): 5–67.
6. See Phyllis Trible, *God and the Rhetoric of Sexuality* (Philadelphia: Fortress Press, 1978), 94–105.
7. On the various authorial sources in Genesis see E. A. Speiser, ed. and trans., *Genesis* (Garden City, N.Y.: Doubleday/Anchor, 1982), xx–xxxlv.
8. See Trible, *God and the Rhetoric of Sexuality;* Elaine Pagels, *Adam, Eve and the Serpent* (New York: Random House, 1988); and John Phillips, *Eve: The History of an Idea* (San Francisco: Harper and Row, 1985). Regarding Eve's desire to be wise, Bal writes: "We are far removed, here, from the belly oriented stupidity this woman is so often blamed for." See Bal, *Lethal Love*, 122. I have arrived at similar conclusions through a comparison of the biblical tale with its various recreations in Hebraic literary tradition. See Aschkenasy, *Eve's Journey*, 9–13, 39–76.
9. Judaic and Christian sources alike exhorted men not to engage in conversation with women: " 'And don't talk too much with women.' He spoke of a man's wife, all the more so is the rule applied to the wife of one's fellow. In this regard the sages said: 'So long as a man talks too much with a woman he brings trouble on himself, wastes time better spent on studying Torah, and ends up an heir of Gehenna.' " (Mishnah, Abot 1:15). For translation I consulted Jacob Neusner, ed., *The Mishnah: A New Translation* (New Haven: Yale University Press, 1988), 673. A letter to Timothy says: "But I suffer not the woman to teach . . . but to be in silence. For Adam was first formed, then Eve. And Adam was not deceived, but the woman being deceived was in transgression" (1 Tim. 2:11–14).
10. For more on this see Erik Erikson, "Womanhood and the Inner Space," in *Identity: Youth and Crisis* (New York: Norton, 1968), 261–94. Freud, too, viewed femininity as hostile to public affairs and the progress of civilization, which are the male domain.

11. Babylonian Talmud, Eruvin 18a.
12. For a comprehensive discussion of the two traditions of the sexual identity of the first human, see Daniel Boyarin, *Carnal Israel: Reading Sex in Talmudic Culture* (Berkeley: University of California Press, 1993), 31–46. See also Trible, *God and the Rhetoric,* 94–105. It this study Trible abandons her earlier interpretation of the primal human as bi-sexual in favor of the theory of the ungendered first human.
13. Eve thus defines the meaning of "wisdom" attached to the prohibited tree as its ability to enhance life's experiences in all of their dimensions and nuances. She does not limit the meaning of the tree to the moral capacity of distinguishing between "good and evil," nor to the sexual experience that might be implied by "knowledge." I believe that the strictly moral reading given to "good and evil" is wrong because it does not recognize the Hebrew which can be read as "good and bad," thus casting the tree's gifts in experiential (pleasant versus unpleasant, for example) rather than in strictly moral terms. Secondly, the verb "to know" becomes linked with the sexual element and with the physical differences between male and female only after the man and the woman have sinned, when they suddenly "knew that they were naked." The culmination of the sexual meaning of "to know" comes only when the narrator uses this verb to indicate the first sexual intercourse between Adam and Eve after their expulsion from the Garden of Eden. I therefore agree with E. S. Speiser who suggests that the phrase "knowledge of good and evil" denotes "full possession of mental and physical powers" (Gen. 26).
14. Bickerton, *Language and Species,* 294, 295.
15. Ibid., 46.
16. Ibid., 256.
17. Derek Bickerton, *Roots of Language* (Ann Arbor: Karoma, 1981), 295.
18. I disagree with Bal, who sees the serpent as the actual tempter who presents the tree's main charm as its ability to make humanity equal to God. See, Bal, *Lethal Love,* 125. When Eve considers, internally, the benefits of the tree, she leaves God out of the equation. Instead, she describes the human experience. The temptation came from within Eve's mind, and the serpent was only a catalyst. Dramatically as well, it is Eve's internal discourse, in its clarity and precision, that marks the climactic moment of her inner struggle, leading to the tasting of the fruit.
19. Ibid., 275.
20. Julia Kristeva sees in the laws of impurity as well as in the dietary laws in Leviticus "a separation between feminine and masculine," with the grouping of "*place-body* and the more elaborate one *speech-logic of differences*" as "an attempt to keep a being who speaks to his God separated from the fecund mother." Furthermore, only after the separation

of the nascent male body from the maternal body "comes speech, justice, honesty and truth. See Julia Kristeva, *The Powers of Horror* (New York: Columbia University Press, 1982), 100, 104.

21. The rabbinic sages offered a different etymology to Eve's Hebrew name, *Ḥawwah,* from the one given by the biblical text itself. They related Eve's name to the Aramaic noun *ḥiwwya,* which means serpent, implying that Adam saw her as his serpent, or seducer. See Umberto Cassuto, *A Commentary on the Book of Genesis* (Jerusalem: Magnes, 1972), 170–1.

22. From the commentary on this verse in Sifre, Numbers. For a slightly different translation, see Hayim Nahman Bialik and Yehoshua Hana Ravnitzky, eds., *The Book of Legends,* trans. William G. Braude (New York: Shocken), 97.

23. For a different version of this discussion, see Nehama Aschkenasy, "The Power of Prayer: Hannah's Tale," in Judith A. Kates and Gail Twersky Reimer, eds., *Beginning Anew: A Woman's Companion to the High Holy Days* (New York: Simon and Schuster, 1997), 124–42.

24. See Erikson, "Womanhood and the Inner Space," 261–94.

25. The Midrash, on the other hand, fleshes out Peninah's harangue of torment, which consists of taunting Hannah for her empty life and lack of maternal responsibilities. See *Pesikta Rabbati* 43:8, trans. in Bialik and Ravnitzky, eds., *The Book of Legends,* 113.

26. Nina Auerbach, *Communities of Women* (Cambridge, Mass.: Harvard University Press, 1978), 13 passim.

27. Fromm, *The Art of Loving,* 18.

28. Ibid., 17.

29. For a variety of commentaries that see prayer as self-scrutiny, see Earl Klein, *Jewish Prayer: Concepts and Customs* (Columbus, Ohio: Alpha, 1986), 1–5.

30. The view of sacrifices and offering of gifts as an important way of communicating with God had its roots in pagan practices, in which women had at least a limited role. The prophets later tried to restrict these practices. See Stefan R. Reif, *Judaism and Hebrew Prayer* (Cambridge: Cambridge University Press, 1993), 28.

31. R. Eleazar said: "prayer is more effective than offerings" (TB Berakhot, 32b).

32. Wordless crying has been always regarded by tradition as an integral part of praying. The Kabbalist work The Zohar maintains that crying is sometimes even more effective than actual verbal entreaty to God. See Robert Gordis, *A Faith for Moderns* (New York: Bloch, 1971), 271.

33. In Judah Halevy, *The Kuzari,* trans. H. Hirschfeld (New York: Schocken, 1978), 386.

34. Abraham Heschel writes: "Through prayer we sanctify ourselves, our

feelings, our ideas." See, Abraham Heschel, *Man's Quest for God* (New York: Crossroads, 1984), 18.

35. As suggested by Rabbi Hammuna in TB Brakhot 31a, in a discussion that starts with "How many important rulings may be derived from the verses about Hannah at prayer." Bialik and Ravnitzky, eds. *The Book of Legends,* 528.

36. For the theological issues concerning petitionary prayer, see Dan Cohn-Sherbok, *Jewish Petitionary Prayer: A Theological Exploration* (Lewiston, N.J.: Mellen Press, 1989).

37. The sages of the Mishnah warned against vain prayer: "If a man's wife is pregnant and he says [God] grant that my wife bear a male child, this is a vain prayer" (Mishnah Berakhot 9:3).

38. As summarized, for example, by Heschel: "Prayer . . . is an act of self-purification, a quarantine for the soul." See Heschel, *Man's Quest for Freedom,* 8.

39. P. Kyle McCarter contends that the concluding benediction of the psalm, "and he shall give strength to His king / and exalt the horn of His annointed" (1 Sam. 2:10), suggests that the psalm's original context is that of the birth of a royal heir, and therefore is anachronistic in the mouth of the pre-monarchic Hannah (*1 Samuel,* 73). Our view of Hannah as a female protagonist in a tale that manifests literary consistency and integrity, however, allows us to study the psalm as Hannah's composition and thus indicative of our heroine's state of mind.

40. Abraham J. Heschel, *The Insecurity of Freedom* (Philadelphia: Jewish Publication Society, 1966), 20.

41. I first studied Hannah and Elkanah as countercultural figures when we were only beginning to tune into the hidden voices that counter the patriarchal dominance in the Bible. See Nehama Aschkenasy, "A Non-Sexist Reading of the Bible," *Midstream* 27, no. 6 (1981): 51–55.

42. Geroge Eliot, *Middlemarch* (Cambridge, Mass.: Riverside, 1956), 3.

43. TB Megillah 14a.

44. TB Megillah 14b claims that Deborah and Huldah were named after hateful animals (hornet and weasel, respectively), because they displayed haughtiness and arrogance toward men. On the ancient rabbis' reading of the biblical texts involving women see Aschkenasy, *Eve's Journey,* 14, 42–5, 128–31 passim.

45. See *Legends,* 113.

46. Ibid.

47. For a different version of this essay, see N. Aschkenasy, "Language as Female Empowerment in Ruth," in Judith A. Kates and Gail Twersky Reimer, eds., *Reading Ruth: Contemporary Women Reclaim a Sacred Text* (New York: Ballantine, 1994), 111–24.

48. See Aschkenasy, *Eve's Journey,* 85–90, 251–2.
49. On the genealogical listing in Ruth 4:18–22 and its link to the rest of the literary material in Ruth, see Campbell, ed. *Ruth,* 172, 173.

SELECTED BIBLIOGRAPHY

Angelou, Maya. *I Know Why the Caged Bird Sings.* New York: Bantam, 1971.

Arcana, Judith. *Our Mothers' Daughters.* Berkeley, Calif.: Shameless Hussey Press, 1979.

Aschkenasy, Nehama. "Biblical Females in a Joycean Episode." *Modern Language Studies* 15, no. 5 (1985): 28–39.

———. *Eve's Journey: Feminine Images in Hebraic Literary.* Philadelphia: University of Pennsylvania Press, 1986; reprint: Detroit: Wayne State University Press, 1995.

———. "Language as Female Empowerment in Ruth." In *Reading Ruth: Contemporary Women Reclaim a Sacred Text,* 111–24. Ed. Judith A. Kates and Gail Twersky Reimer. New York: Ballantine, 1994.

———. "The Power of Prayer: Hannah's Tale." *Beginning Anew: A Woman's Companion to the High Holy Days,* 124–42. Ed. Judith A. Kates and Gail Twersky Reimer. New York: Simon and Schuster, 1997.

Auerbach, Erich. *Mimesis: The Representation of Reality in Western Literature.* Trans. Willard Trask. New York: Doubleday, 1957.

Auerbach, Nina. *Communities of Women.* Cambridge, Mass.: Harvard University Press, 1978.

Bal, Mieke. *Death and Dissymmetry.* Chicago: University of Chicago Press, 1988.

———. *Lethal Love.* Bloomington: Indiana University Press, 1987.

———. *Murder and Difference.* Bloomington: Indiana University Press, 1988.

Baron, Larry, and Murray A. Straus. *Rape in American Society: A State-level Analysis.* New Haven: Yale University Press, 1989.

Bettelheim, Bruno. *The Uses of Enchantment.* New York: Knopf, 1976.

Biale, Rachel. *Women and Jewish Law.* New York: Schocken, 1984.

Bialik, Hayim Nahman, and Yehoshua Hana Ravnitzky, eds. *The Book of Legends.* Trans. William G. Braude. New York: Schocken, 1992.

Bickerton, Derek. *Language and Species.* Chicago: University of Chicago Press, 1990.

———. *Roots of Language.* Ann Arbor: Karoma, 1981.

Boling, Robert G., ed. and trans. *Judges.* Garden City, N.Y.: Doubleday-Anchor, 1975.

Boyarin, Daniel. *Carnal Israel: Reading Sex in Talmudic Culture.* Berkeley: University of California Press, 1993.

Brownmiller, Susan. *Against Our Will: Men, Women and Rape.* New York: Simon and Schuster, 1975.

Buchwald, Emilie, Pamela R. Fletcher, and Martha Roth, eds. *Transforming a Rape Culture.* Minneapolis: Milkweed, 1993.

Campbell, Edward F., ed. and trans. *Ruth.* Garden City, N.Y.: Doubleday-Anchor, 1975.

Campbell, Joseph. *The Hero With a Thousand Faces.* 1949. Reprint, Princeton: Princeton University Press, 1973.

Cassuto, Umberto. *A Commentary on the Book of Genesis.* Jerusalem: Magnes, 1972.

Chesler, Phyllis. *About Men.* New York: Simon and Schuster, 1978.

Cohn-Sherbok, Dan. *Jewish Petitionary Prayer: A Theological Exploration.* Lewiston, N.J.: Mellen Press, 1989.

De Beauvoir, Simone. *The Second Sex.* New York: Knopf, 1953.

Delehenty, Suzanne, ed. *The Window in Twentieth-Century Art.* Purchase, N.Y.: Neuberger Museum, State University of New York, Purchase, 1986.

Driver, Tom. *The Sense of History in Greek and Shakespearean Drama.* New York: Columbia University Press, 1959.

Erikson, Erik. "Womanhood and the Inner Space." *Identity: Youth and Crisis.* New York: Norton, 1968. 261–94.

Fisch, Harold. "Ruth and the Structure of Covenant History." *Vetus Testamentum* 32, no. 4 (1982): 425–37.

———. *The Dual Image: The Figure of the Jew in English and American Literature.* New York: Ktav, 1971.

Freedman, H., and M. Simon, trans. *The Midrash: Genesis.* 2d ed. London: Soncino Press, 1961.

Friday, Nancy. *My Mother, Myself: The Daughter's Search for Identity.* New York: Delacorte Press, 1977.

Fromm, Erich. *The Art of Loving.* New York: Harper and Row, 1974.

Frye, Northrop. *Anatomy of Criticism.* Princeton: Princeton University Press, 1957.

Gordis, Robert. *A Faith for Moderns.* New York: Bloch, 1971.

Gottlieb, Carla. *The Window in Art: From the Window of God to the Vanity of Man.* New York: Arabis Books, 1981.

Groth, Nicholas. *Men Who Rape: The Psychology of the Offender.* New York: Plenum Press, 1984.

Halevy, Judah. *The Kuzari.* Trans. H. Hirschfeld. New York: Schocken, 1978.

Heschel, Abraham J. *The Insecurity of Freedom.* Philadelphia: Jewish Publication Society, 1966.

———. *Man's Quest for God.* New York: Crossroads, 1984.

Higgins, Lynn A., and Brenda R. Silver, eds. *Rape and Representation.* New York: Columbia University Press, 1991.

Hirsch, Marianne. "Mothers and Daughters." In *Ties That Bind: Essays on Mothering and Patriarchy.* Ed. Jean F. O'Barr, Deborah Pope, and Mary Wyer, 177–79. Chicago: University of Chicago Press, 1990.

Huizinga, Johan. *Homo Ludens: A Study of the Play-Element in Culture.* Trans. R. F. C. Hull. Boston: Beacon, 1955.

Jagendorf, Zvi. "Genesis and the Reversal of Sexual Knowledge." In *Biblical Patterns in Modern Literature.* Ed. David Hirsch and Nehama Aschkenasy, 51–60. Chico, Calif.: Scholars Press, 1984.

Kaiser, Walter. *Praisers of Folly.* Cambridge: Massachusetts, 1963.

Kates, Judith A., and Gail Twersky Reimer, eds. *Reading Ruth: Contemporary Women Reclaim a Sacred Text.* New York: Ballantine, 1994.

———. *Beginning Anew: A Woman's Companion to the High Holy Days.* New York: Simon and Schuster, 1997.

Klein, Earl. *Jewish Prayer: Concepts and Customs.* Columbus, Ohio: Alpha, 1986.

Kristeva, Julia. *The Powers of Horror.* Trans. Leon S. Roudiez. New York: Columbia University Press, 1982.

Kugel, James L. *The Bible as It Was.* Cambridge, Mass.: Harvard University Press, 1997.

———. *The Idea of Biblical Poetry: Parallelism and Its History.* New Haven: Yale University Press, 1981.

Lederer, Wolfgang. *The Fear of Women.* New York: Harcourt, 1968.

Leibowitz, Nehama. *Studies in the Weekly Sidra.* Series 4/5718. Jerusalem: The Jewish Agency, 1957.

Levi-Strauss, Claude. *The Elementary Structures of Kinship.* Trans. James Harle Bell, John Richard Von Sturmer, and Rodney Needham. Ed. Rodney Needham, rev. ed. Boston: Beacon, 1969.

McCarter, P. Kyle, ed. and trans. *1 Samuel.* Garden City, N.Y.: Doubleday-Anchor, 1980.

McCarter, P. Kyle, ed. and trans. *2 Samuel.* Garden City, N.Y.: Doubleday-Anchor, 1986.

Neumann, Erich. *The Great Mother: An Analysis of an Archetype.* Trans. Ralph Manheim. Princeton: Princeton University Press, 1970.

Neusner, Jacob, ed., *The Mishnah: A New Translation.* New Haven: Yale University Press, 1988.

Pagels, Elaine. *Adam, Eve and the Serpent.* New York: Random House, 1988.

Patai, Raphael. *Sex and Family in the Bible and the Middle East.* Garden City, N.Y.: Doubleday, 1959.

Phillips, John. *Eve: The History of an Idea.* San Francisco: Harper and Row, 1985.

Reif, Stefan R. *Judaism and Hebrew Prayer.* Cambridge: Cambridge University Press, 1993.

Rich, Adrienne. *Of Woman Born: Motherhood as Experience and Institution.* New York: W. W. Norton, 1976.

Ruethers, Rosemary, ed. *Religion and Sexism.* New York: Simon and Schuster, 1974.

Sarna, Nahum. "The Ravishing of Dinah: A Commentary on Genesis, Chapter 34." In *Studies in Jewish Education.* Ed. A. Shapiro and B. Cohen. New York: Ktav, 1984.

Silver, Brenda R. "Periphrasis, Power, and Rape in *A Passage to India.*" In *Rape and Representation.* Ed. Lynn A. Higgins and Brenda R. Silver, 115–37. New York: Columbia University Press, 1991.

Soloveitchik, Joseph B. "The Lonely Man of Faith." *Tradition* (Summer 1965): 5–67.

Speiser, E. A., ed. and trans. *Genesis.* Garden City, N.Y.: Doubleday-Anchor 1982.

Steiner, George. *After Babel: Aspects of Language and Translation.* New York: Oxford University Press, 1975.

Sternberg, Meir. "Delicate Balance in the Story of the Rape of Dinah: Biblical Narrative and the Rhetoric of the Narrative Text." *Hasifrut* 4 (1973): 193–231.

———. *The Poetics of Biblical Narrative.* Bloomington: Indiana University Press, 1985.

Trible, Phyllis. *God and the Rhetoric of Sexuality.* Philadelphia: Fortress, 1978.

———. *Texts of Terror: Literary Feminist Readings of Biblical Narratives.* Philadelphia: Fortress, 1984.

Visotzky, Burton I. *Reading the Book: Making the Bible a Timeless Text.* New York: Doubleday/Anchor, 1991.

———. *The Genesis of Ethics.* New York: Crown, 1996.

Wiltshire, Bruce. *Role Playing and Identity.* Bloomington: Indiana University Press, 1982.

INDEX